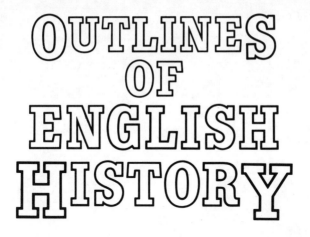

OUTLINES OF ENGLISH HISTORY

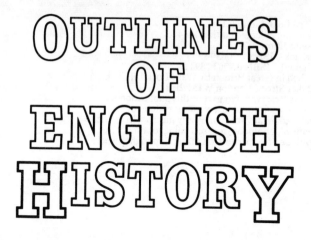

OUTLINES OF ENGLISH HISTORY

With Biographical Summaries and
Genealogical Tables

Originally compiled and arranged by
GEORGE CARTER MA
Late Headmaster of New College School, Oxford

Revised and extended to 1973

WARD LOCK LIMITED · LONDON

© Ward Lock Limited 1962
Revised and enlarged edition 1964
Revised edition 1974
Paperback   ISBN 0 7063 1895 1
Casebound   ISBN 0 7063 1894 3
Published in Great Britain by Ward Lock Limited,
116 Baker Street, London W1M 2BB.

Printed in Great Britain by
Fletcher & Son Ltd, Norwich and bound by
Richard Clay (The Chaucer Press) Ltd, Bungay, Suffolk

CONTENTS

OUTLINES OF
ENGLISH HISTORY

THE ROMAN OCCUPATION OF BRITAIN

55   The First Invasion of Julius Cæsar

The most powerful people in the world at this time were the **Romans.** They had conquered all the nations round the Mediterranean, and their greatest general, **Julius Cæsar,** having reduced the greater part of Gaul, wished to strike terror into the inhabitants of Britain, who were suspected of having sent assistance to their kinsmen on the other side of the Channel. Accordingly he crossed the Straits of Dover with two legions, but finding that the Britons had assembled to defend the coast, he sailed along to the site of the modern Deal. Here he landed, against opposition. His stay in Britain, however, was short, as the autumn was advancing, and all the tribes of the north were in arms against him, and so he returned to Gaul.

NOTE.—The Ancient Britons. About seven or eight centuries before Christ, swarms of Celts flooded Western Europe and the British Isles. They came in two great " waves "; the first called " Gael," who seized upon the north part of Scotland and Ireland, the second the " Britons," who occupied the greater part of England and Wales. The old savage race disappeared. Although the Britons were in some respects semi-barbarous, they had reached a certain stage of civilization. They tilled some portion of the ground and kept great herds of cattle. They knew how to make pottery for household use and large earthenware vessels in which they buried their dead. Before advancing to battle they painted their bodies with a bright blue colour to terrify their enemies. They fought with long swords, spears, and javelins, and had war chariots, in which they dashed into the ranks of the enemy, and then leaped down and fought on foot. They were divided into many tribes, each tribe having its own chief and following its own customs. When hard pressed by an enemy they took refuge in their strong stockaded villages.

The Religion of the Ancient Britons. The Britons worshipped many gods. Their priests, who were called Druids, " taught the doctrine of the immortality of the soul, which, they believed, had a tendency to inspire men with courage by making them indifferent to death." They practised human sacrifices.

54   The Second Invasion of Julius Cæsar

Cæsar landed with 25,000 infantry and 2,000 cavalry and pushed boldly into the interior, but the news that a storm had dashed to pieces many of his ships caused him to return to the coast. Meanwhile **Cassivellaunus,** the chief of the Catuvellauni, had roused the native tribes against the invader, but Cæsar forced the passage of the Thames, stormed and took the strong stockaded village of **Verulamium** (*St. Albans*). Many of the chiefs, including Cassivellaunus, did homage to Cæsar, who, on receiving hostages and a promise of tribute, returned to Gaul.

A.D.

43

The Invasion of Claudius

The Emperor Claudius sent his general, **Aulus Plautius,** to conquer the island. **Cunobelinus** (the *Cymbeline* of Shakespeare), the great chief of the Catuvellauni, had died and his two sons, **Togidumnus** and **Caractacus,** were ruling. Aulus Plautius overran the South-eastern part of the island and took **Camulodunum** (Colchester), the headquarters of the Catuvellauni. Subsequently Togidumnus was slain in battle, and Caractacus taken prisoner and sent to Rome.

Claudius visited Britain in person, and after remaining in the island sixteen days, returned to Rome.

NOTE.—Aulus Plautius completed the subjugation of the district lying between the Wash and Southampton Water.

The Government of Suetonius Paullinus

(1) The **Conquest of Mona** (*Anglesey*). To complete the conquest of the West, Suetonius Paullinus took the island of Mona, the sacred resort of the Druids.

(2) The **Rebellion of Boadicea.** While Suetonius was absent in Mona, Boadicea, Queen of the Iceni, rose against the Romans.

(*a*) **Cause:** Her husband, Prasutagus, chief of the Iceni, and a vassal of the Romans, had died sonless, and the Romans had seized upon his dominions. When Boadicea protested against this injustice, she was seized and publicly scourged. The Queen then called upon all the Britons to rise against their cruel oppressors. All the tribes of Eastern Britain obeyed her call. The towns of Londinium, Verulamium and Camulodunum were burnt, and 70,000 Romans massacred.

(*b*) The **Defeat and death of Boadicea.** Suetonius hastened from Wales, met Boadicea near Camulodunum, and won a hard-fought battle. Eighty thousand Britons were slain, and Boadicea herself, preferring death to slavery, put an end to her life by poison.

NOTE.—When the Emperor Nero heard of this revolt he recalled Suetonius Paullinus.

78

Julius Agricola completed the Conquest of Britain

His **Wars:** (1) He conquered Wales, and pushed the western frontier of the Roman territory to the sea. (2) He subdued the Lowlands of Scotland, and built a line of forts from the north estuary of the Forth to that of the Clyde. (3) He then marched against the savage tribes called Caledonians, who inhabited the Highlands of Scotland, and defeated them with great slaughter at a place called **Mons Graupius.**

A.D.

NOTE 1.—Agricola was afterwards recalled by the Emperor Domitian, who both envied and feared his military talents.

NOTE 2.—To keep the more restless tribes in order the Romans established three large military centres, **Eboracum** (York), **Deva** (Chester), **Isca Silurum** (Caerleon-on-Usk).

119 The **Emperor Hadrian** visited Britain.

121 The **Wall of Hadrian was built.** To keep back the Caledonians, who were continually making raids into Britain, Hadrian built a solid stone wall, eighty miles long from Carlisle to Newcastle, and garrisoned it by a number of " auxiliary cohorts," or regiments drawn from the various tribes which were subject to the Roman Empire.

139 The **Wall of Antonius was built.** The Caledonians still continuing their ravages, the governors of Britain connected Agricola's line of forts between the Forth and the Clyde by a continuous earthwork.

NOTE.—This structure is generally called the " Wall of Antonius," from the name of the Emperor who was reigning at the time it was built.

208 The **Emperor Severus arrived in Britain.** He strengthened the line of earthwork between the Forth and the Clyde, but failed in his attempt to reduce the Caledonians. He died at Eboracum in A.D. 211.

288 **Carausius,** the first " *Count of the Saxon Shore,*" threw off his allegiance to Rome, and proclaimed himself Emperor of Britain.

NOTE.—In the third century terrible disasters fell upon the Roman Empire. Hordes of barbarians invaded its northern limits, and the Empire had so sunk into decay that the Roman legions were unable to withstand them.

Even Britain did not escape them:

(1) The **Caledonians** or **Picts** (i.e., the " painted men "), as they were now called, crossed the Roman walls and ravaged the country.

(2) The **Scots** (i.e., the " tattooed men "), a tribe who occupied Northern Ireland, infested the shores of Britain from the Clyde to the Severn.

(3) The **Saxons,** a tribe of Germans who dwelt between the mouths of the Elbe and the Weser, harassed the east coast of Britain to such an extent that the Emperor appointed an officer called the " Count of the Saxon Shore," whose duty it was to defend the eastern coast.

305 **St. Alban** was martyred at **Verulamium,** now called St. Albans in honour of the martyr.

NOTE.—Christianity had been introduced previous to this event, by Roman soldiers and merchants from the Continent.

306 **Constantine** was proclaimed Emperor in Britain. *He was the first Christian Emperor.*

410 The **Emperor Honorius,** being hard pressed by the barbarians at home, told the Britons *that they must henceforth defend themselves against the Picts and Scots and Saxons.* From this time Britain ceased to be a Roman province.

NOTE 1.—In 446 the Britons in their extreme misery made a final appeal—" the groans of the Britons " they called it—to the Romans for help, but no help came.

NOTE 2.—**Results of the Roman Occupation of Britain.** The Romans had held occupation of Britain 360 years. During this period the country made great strides in civilization.

(1) Many fine roads were made, one of which, Watling Street, stretched from Dover to Chester, passing through London. These roads enabled soldiers to march rapidly from place to place, and at the same time helped to extend commerce.

(2) The Romans gave the Britons good laws and a strong government.

(3) Beautiful villas, public and private baths, temples, and amphitheatres were built, the remains of which are still to be seen and bear testimony to the advanced stage of civilization which the people had reached.

(4) Mines of iron, lead, and tin were extensively worked, the manufactures of pottery and glass established, the Roman customs and language introduced among the nobles. The land produced such great quantities of corn that Britain was called the " Granary of the North."

(5) Large and important " towns " sprang into existence, such as Eboracum (York), Verulamium (St. Albans), Aquæ Sulis (Bath), and Londinium (London), which had been used by the Romans as great military centres or for the purposes of trade.

(6) The Roman occupation of Britain was the indirect means of introducing Christianity.

THE ENGLISH SETTLEMENTS IN BRITAIN

The **English, or** " *Saxons* " as they are sometimes called, were a race of people who lived in the land bordering on the North Sea between what is now called Denmark and Holland. They belonged to the great **Teutonic race,** which inhabited the middle of Europe from the Baltic down to the Alps. Of the English who settled in Britain there were three tribes:

(1) The **Jutes,** who originally lived in the North of Jutland (Modern Jutland).

(2) The **Angles,** who lived in the South of Denmark.

(3) The **Saxons,** who inhabited the district now called Hanover.

449　　The **Beginning of the Kingdom of Kent**

Vortigern, a British chief, who ruled over Kent and the Southeast coast of England, was so harassed by the Picts and Scots that he sought the aid of the Jutes. The latter came to his assistance, but having driven back the Picts and Scots turned upon their employer, and after a series of battles overpowered him. The Jutes were the first of our ancestors who settled in this country, and established a line of Kentish kings.

477　　The **Beginning of the Kingdom of Sussex** (*i.e., South Saxons*). **Ella,** a great chief of the Saxons landed near the great Roman fortress of Anderida (Pevensey), took the fortress after a long blockade, and having put to death every Briton in it, reigned there as King.

495　　The **Beginning of the Kingdom of Wessex** (i.e., *West Saxons*). (1) Another band of Saxon adventurers under **Cerdic** landed on the shores of Southampton Water, took Winchester, and founded the Kingdom of Wessex.

520　　(2) **The Battle of Mount Badon**
While attempting to penetrate farther West the West Saxons were utterly routed by the Britons in a great battle at Mount Badon

A.D.

(probably Badbury in Dorsetshire), and their conquests held in check for many years.

527 The **Beginning of the Kingdom of Essex** (i.e., *East Saxons*). Another band of Saxon invaders landed on the northern shore of the Thames, and overran the low country between London and St. Albans. *They were the last of the Saxon race who formed a settlement on the British shores.*

547 The **Beginning of the Kingdom of Northumbria** (i.e., *North-of-the-Humber-land*).
This was founded by the **Angles** and comprised the two Kingdoms of **Bernicia** and **Deira**.

575 The **Beginning of the Kingdom of East Anglia.** This was founded by **two bands of Angles, called the** *North Folk* and the *South Folk*, and from them the counties of Norfolk and Suffolk have derived their names.

586 The **Beginning of the Kingdom of Mercia** (i.e., *March-land* or *land-of-the-Border*).

This Kingdom was also founded by the **Angles. It occupied** *Central England.*

NOTE 1.—These three races, the Jutes, Saxons, and Angles, were afterwards known among themselves as the " English." They held all the East, South-east, and central parts of the island from the Firth of Forth to the English Channel, and founded seven principal kingdoms to which the name of **Heptarchy** has been given. These kingdoms were:

(1)	The Kingdom of	Kent	founded by the **Jutes.**
(2)	,,	Sussex	⎫
(3)	,,	Wessex	⎬ founded by the **Saxons.**
(4)	,,	Essex	⎭
(5)	,,	Northumbria	⎫
(6)	,,	East Anglia	⎬ founded by the **Angles.**
(7)	,,	Mercia	⎭

The boundaries of these different kingdoms were not definitely fixed, as the boundaries of kingdoms are now. The Anglo-Saxon tribes were constantly at war with one another, each trying to get the upper hand, so that the kingdoms were often broken up and as often pieced together again. Sometimes the greater part of the country acknowledged the supremacy of one of these kingdoms, and sometimes that of another, and a very long period elapsed before the English were united into one nation. This want of unity weakened the English and made them an easy prey to invaders like the Northmen.

NOTE 2.—**Fate of the Ancient Britons.** The struggle between the Britons and English was long and deadly. As the land was gradually occupied by the new-comers the Britons were either put to death or driven out and compelled to take refuge in the fens, woods, and mountains of the unsubdued West. Those who survived were called Welsh (i.e., " foreigners," or " strangers ") by the English, but Kymry (i.e., " comrades ") by themselves.

597 The **Mission of St. Augustine**

Ethelbert, a King of Kent, was converted to Christianity by St. **Augustine,** a Roman monk. Augustine is said to have been sent to England by **Pope Gregory,** who had been attracted by the fair faces of some beautiful boys exposed for sale in the slave-market at Rome.

NOTE.—The " English " were heathen before their conversion to Christianity. They worshipped many gods, some of which were Woden, the wise father of heaven, Thor, the god of storm and strength, Freya, the goddess of peace and fruitfulness, Balder, the god of youth and spring.

SUPREMACY OF NORTHUMBRIA

607   **Ethelfrith,** a great King of Northumbria, defeated the Welsh in a great battle at **Chester.**

617   **Edwin,** King of Northumbria, subdued the whole of England except Kent, and was acknowledged as **Bretwalda,** i.e., " *Overlord.*"

NOTE.—Edwin married a Christian princess named **Ethelburga,** daughter of Ethelbert, King of Kent, and moved by the earnest entreaties of his wife and her chaplain Paulinus, who was one of the disciples of Augustine, he accepted Christianity.

633   **Edwin** was defeated and slain at **Heathfield,** near Doncaster, by Penda, the heathen King of Mercia.

NOTE.—After a long struggle between Northumbria and Mercia, Penda was slain in 655, and the Mercians gradually became Christians.

668   **Theodore of Tarsus,** a Greek monk, became Archbishop of Canterbury, and organized the Church of England into a united whole.

685   **Egfrith,** a powerful King of Northumbria, was defeated and slain in a battle at **Nectansmere,** with the Picts and Scots. *After his death the Kingdom of Northumbria began to decline and the supremacy of Northumbria passed into the hands of the Kings of Mercia.*

731   **The Venerable Bede,** a monk of Jarrow-on-the-Tyne, finished his " Ecclesiastical History of the Angles." He died in A.D. 735.

SUPREMACY OF MERCIA

757   **Offa, the Mighty,** became King of Mercia with the chiefs of East Anglia, Essex, and Kent as his vassals.

779   Offa constructed an immense dyke called " *Offa's dyke,*" from the Dee to the Wye to protect his dominions from the Welsh. *He was the greatest King that had ever reigned in England.*

787   **The Northmen or Danes began to ravage England.**

NOTE.—The Northmen were a branch of the great Teutonic race who settled in the countries now called Norway and Sweden and the islands of Denmark. At the end of the eighth century they took to sea-roving under their sea-kings. Sometimes they made raids on the coasts, at others they sailed up the mouths of broad navigable rivers, and leaving their ships under the protection of a strong guard scoured the interior of the country far and wide, and after plundering and burning towns and monasteries returned to their ships and sailed home laden with booty. The English had no war-vessels, and so were unable to ward off the attacks of these invaders.

796   **Death of Offa.** The supremacy of the English Kingdoms passed from Mercia to Wessex.

THE GREAT KINGS OF WESSEX AND THE DANISH INVASION

WESSEX GETS THE SUPREMACY AND KEEPS IT FOR 200 YEARS

802 **Egbert** became King of the West Saxons and reigned 37 years (802–839).

825 At **Ellandun (Wiltshire)** Egbert overthrew Beornwulf, King of the Mercians, and in 827 the whole of Mercia submitted to his rule.

826 The Kings of **Kent, Sussex, Essex,** and **East Anglia** all did homage to Egbert.

827 **Northumbria,** weakened by the frequent invasions of the Northmen, also submitted.

NOTE 1.—Egbert thus became " Overlord of Britain " as Edwin and Offa had been, but the supremacy of the Kings of Wessex was destined to be of a more lasting character than that of the Kings of Northumbria and Mercia.
The reasons of this were:

(1) The kingdom of Wessex had a strong central government, and consequently was better ruled than the other kingdoms.

(2) For six generations its sovereigns had been men of unusual strength of character.

(3) It was the only kingdom that stood out boldly against the Danes as the champion of the whole English nation, when Northumbria and Mercia, its great rivals, had both bowed down before their conquerors.

NOTE 2.—Egbert may be considered as the " First King of all the English." He is the ancestor of all the subsequent English Kings of England down to the present time, except Canute, the two Harolds, and William I.

836 Egbert defeated the combined forces of the Northmen and West Welsh in a great battle at **Hengists Down,** near Plymouth, and compelled the Welsh Prince of Cornwall to do him homage.

839 **Death of Egbert**

ETHELWULF, SON OF EGBERT, 839–858 (19 YEARS)

851 The Northmen continued their ravages, sacked **Canterbury** and London, but were defeated by Ethelwulf at **Ockley (Surrey).**

855 **The First Permanent Settlement of the Northmen.** The Northmen remained in the **Isle of Sheppey** the whole winter, and defied Ethelwulf to dislodge them. *This was the beginning of their attempts to settle in England.* Hitherto they had landed only to ravage and plunder.

856 Ethelwulf, in great distress of mind, made a pilgrimage to Rome to obtain the Pope's blessing on his efforts against the Danes. On his return he married Judith, daughter of Charles the Bold, King of the Franks.

858 **Death of Ethelwulf.** He was succeeded by his son Ethelbald.

ETHELBALD 858–860; ETHELBERT 860–866; ETHELRED I 866–871, SONS OF ETHELWULF (13 YEARS)

866   **The Conquest of Northumbria, Mercia, and East Anglia by the Northmen.** A vast confederacy of Northmen calling themselves the " *Great Army* " invaded England with the intention of conquering and occupying the whole country.

870   They landed in East Anglia, and, crossing the Humber, sacked York and overran Northumbria. They then pushed their way southward and captured Nottingham. One division of the invaders threw themselves upon East Anglia and, in a great battle, defeated and took prisoner **Edmund,** the king of that country; whom they put to a cruel death, because he refused to worship their gods.

871   **The " Great Army " of Northmen invaded Wessex.** The Northmen engaged with the West Saxons in nine pitched battles, in one of which, at **Ashdown** (*Berkshire*), Ethelred and his brother Alfred won a great victory. Ethelred died of the wounds he had received in battle and was succeeded by his brother Alfred.

ALFRED THE GREAT, SON OF ETHELWULF, 871–901 (30 YEARS)

871   **The " Great Army " of Northmen** forced its way up the Thames and defeated the men of Wessex, at **Wilton.** Alfred was compelled to make peace with them.
Finding the conquest of Wessex a somewhat difficult task the Northmen proceeded northwards, and subdued Mercia and *divided it out among themselves.*

878   **Part of the " Great Army,"** under their chief **Guthrum,** once more turned against their old foes the men of Wessex. Alfred was defeated in many battles and compelled to retreat to the **Isle of Athelney,** a stronghold among the marshes of the river Parret, and *all Wessex fell into the hands of the Danes.*
After seven weeks' stay in Athelney, Alfred issued from his hiding-place, and being joined by some of his faithful followers completely overthrew Guthrum at the battle of **Ethandun** (*Edington*, Wiltshire), and stormed the strong Danish stockade at Chippenham.

879   **The Treaty of Wedmore** (*Chippenham*) was made between Alfred and Guthrum, the terms of which were: (1) **Alfred** agreed to cede all England north of Watling Street (i.e., *the great Roman Road which runs from Dover to Chester*) to the Danes; (2) **Guthrum** promised that he and his followers would abandon Wessex, do homage to Alfred as overlord, and become Christians.
Guthrum was baptized under the name of Athelstan.

A.D.

NOTE.—The land thus ceded to the Danes by the Treaty of Wedmore was called **Danelaw**. That part of Mercia, which was ceded, was called the **Five Danish Boroughs**, and comprised the five great Danish towns of **Derby, Stamford, Leicester, Lincoln**, and **Nottingham**.

897   **Alfred built a fleet** and defeated the Danes at sea, thus putting an end to their invasions for the time being. He may be considered as the **Founder of our Navy**.

901   **Alfred died** and was succeeded by his son Edward the Elder.

NOTE.—Summary of Alfred's work. " No man ever combined in his own person so much excellence in war, legislation, and learning." (1) He saved England from the ravages of the Danes. (2) He collected and arranged the laws of his predecessors and framed new laws of his own. (3) He was a strict administrator of justice and punished evil-doers (especially corrupt judges and robbers) with the greatest severity. (4) He restored monasteries, appointed the best men he could find as bishops and priests, encouraged learning by founding schools, and invited learned men from other countries to come and teach in them. (5) He translated Bede's History and other books into English. (6) He built and kept up a navy to protect the coast, and encouraged commerce. (7) He reorganized the fyrd or militia, and ordered that one half of it should always be ready and under arms to defend the country, and the other half left at home to till the fields. (8) Lastly, under his direction, the famous Anglo-Saxon Chronicle was compiled: " the earliest history, which any European nation possesses in its own tongue."

THE RECONQUEST OF THE DANELAW

EDWARD I (CALLED THE ELDER), SON OF ALFRED, 901–925 (24 YEARS)

905   **Edward called himself King of the English.** His aim was to bring the whole of England south of the Humber under his rule. In this he was assisted by his sister **Ethelfleda**, called the " Lady of Mercia."

(1) They built a line of forts across the country from Bedford to Runcorn, she beginning from the west, and he from the east.

921   (2) **Edward invaded East Anglia.** The last Danish King of that country was slain in battle at **Tempsford,** near Bedford, and his territory annexed to Wessex.

(3) Town after town was captured, and the **subjugation of the Five Danish Boroughs** completed the conquest of England south of the Humber.

924   Terrified by Edward's successes, the Danes of Northumbria, the Scots, and the Welsh of Strathclyde did homage to Edward and chose him as " *father and lord* " at a great meeting held at **Dore** near Sheffield.

NOTE.—The invasion of the Danes had at least one beneficial effect on England. It helped to unite the English in their efforts against a common foe.

925   **Death of Edward**

ATHELSTAN, SON OF EDWARD I,
925–940 (15 YEARS)

926   Athelstan compelled the Welsh, Scottish, and Danish under-kings to renew to him the oaths of allegiance which they had taken to his father.

937   **At Brunanburgh** (*Lancashire*), Athelstan utterly defeated a great confederation formed against him, consisting of **Anlaf** King of the Danes of Ireland, **Constantine** King of the Scots, **Owen** King of Cumbria, and the **Northumbrian Danes.**

NOTE.—This was the greatest victory that the Kings of Wessex had as yet won. Its results: (1) The Scots, the Welsh, and the Northumbrian Danes all did homage to Athelstan, who thus once more became the Overlord of Britain.

(2) It settled the fact that the Danelaw was to be incorporated with the realm of the Wessex overkings, and that there was to be but one nation, the English, between the Firth of Forth and the English Channel.

(3) After this battle Athelstan was considered the most powerful monarch in the West of Europe, and many of the neighbouring Kings and Princes sought his friendship and alliance.

940   **Death of Athelstan**

EDMUND, HALF-BROTHER OF ATHELSTAN,
940–946 (6 YEARS)

945   Edmund suppressed a rebellion of the Danes of Northumbria and Mercia, subdued the Welsh Kingdom of Strathclyde, the district between the river Derwent in Cumberland and the Firth of Clyde, and secured the friendship of Malcolm, King of the Scots, by granting him the conquered district, as a fief, " *on condition that he should be his faithful fellow-worker by sea and land.*"

946   **Edmund was assassinated** at a feast in his hall at Pucklechurch (*Gloucestershire*) by a notorious outlaw named *Leofa.*

EDRED, BROTHER OF EDMUND,
946–955 (9 YEARS)

955   **Edred** quelled the *last rising of the Danes in Northumbria,* who had proclaimed a son of the King of the Norwegians as their King. He divided Northumbria into three districts, one of which he gave to the King of the Scots, the other two to Englishmen, who were called Earldormen (i.e., Earls).

The **Rise of Dunstan,** the first of our great ecclesiastical statesmen. Under Edmund, he had been made **Abbot of Glastonbury,** and on the death of that King became Edred's chief adviser.

NOTE.—Edred took the title not only of King of the Anglo-Saxons but also that of Cæsar of Britain.

Death of Edred

EDWY, SON OF EDMUND, 955-949 (4 YEARS)

956 Edwy having married the lady Elgiva, who was his near kins-woman, and within the " prohibited degrees " of the Church, incurred the displeasure of Dunstan, Odo the Archbishop of Canterbury, and the Church generally. *Dunstan was driven into exile by the King.*

957 Assisted by the Church, all the English north of the Thames revolted against Edwy and set up **Edgar**, the King's brother, as King, who immediately recalled Dunstan.

NOTE.—Elgiva, having fallen into the hands of Odo, was cruelly branded with hot irons and sent to Ireland.

959 **Death of Edwy**

EDGAR THE PEACEABLE, BROTHER OF EDWY, 959-975 (16 YEARS)

Edgar was chosen King of all the English.

960 **Dunstan** became **Archbishop of Canterbury**, and for sixteen years **Edgar's chief adviser.**

His Work: (1) He reformed the monasteries and tried to enforce the rule ›˙ St. Benedict—" poverty, chastity, and obedience " on the monks, and celibacy on the secular clergy (i.e., the parish priests).

(2) He did much to unite the English and the Danish races by giving the men of the Danelaw equal social advantages with the men of Essex, making them bishops, earldormen, and members of the Witan.

973 At **Chester** the Kings of Scotland, Cumbria, and the Isle of Man, as well as three Welsh Chiefs, did homage to Edgar. He was one of the most prosperous of the old English Kings, and the pros-perity of his reign was largely due to the wisdom of his minister Dunstan.

NOTE 1.—Edgar was said to have instituted the **Ordinance of the Hundred.** By this arrangement, the shires were divided into smaller districts called Hundreds, and the inhabitants of each Hundred were made responsible for the suppression of theft, robbery, violence, and murder in that district.

NOTE 2.—In Edgar's reign the country was first called **Engla-land,** i.e., the land of the Angles or English.

975 **Edgar died** and was succeeded by his son Edward.

EDWARD THE MARTYR, SON OF EDGAR, 975-979 (4 YEARS)

979 Edward was cruelly murdered near Corfe at the instigation of his step-mother Elfthryth, who was anxious to secure the throne for her son **Ethelred.**

NOTE.—Edward was only thirteen when he ascended the throne. The great earldormen would not obey him because of his youth, and they disliked Dunstan, who upheld the strong-handed government of the late King. After the murder of Edward, Dunstan lost all his political influence.

THE DANISH CONQUEST

ETHELRED THE UNREADY, SON OF EDGAR, 979–1016 (37 YEARS)

980   The **Invasions of the Northmen began again, and continued with increased severity for 36 years.**

NOTE.—Ethelred gained the title of " Unready," which means "uncounselled," because he would not listen to the " rede " or counsel of others. His long reign was nothing but a series of disasters, which plunged England into the deepest misery and ultimately laid her at the feet of a foreign conqueror.

991   The weakness of the King and the disunion existing among the earldormen assisted the Danes in their work of conquest. At **Maldon** they gained a great victory over the English. To buy off the invaders Ethelred and the Witan levied a tax called Danegeld to the amount of £10,000.

994   New swarms of invaders appeared under **Sweyn,** King of the Danes, and **Anlaf,** King of the Norwegians. They attacked London, but were again bought off for the sum of £16,000.

1002   The sum of £24,000 was paid to the Danes to leave the country. Ethelred married **Emma,** daughter of Richard I Duke of Normandy, in the hope that the Normans would help him against the Danes.

The **Massacre of St. Brice's Day.** By Ethelred's orders *all the Danes in England were massacred on St. Brice's Day.* Among the slain were **Gunhild,** sister of **Sweyn,** her husband, and child.

1003   Sweyn returned to England with a powerful army *to avenge the death of his countrymen and to conquer England.*

1008   The Witan imposed a tax to build a fleet, which, however, proved useless on account of the quarrels among the leaders.

1011   The sum of £48,000 was paid to the Danes, but in the following year the invaders took Canterbury and murdered **St. Alphege,** the Archbishop, because he refused to pay an exorbitant ransom.

1013   **Sweyn was chosen King**
Sweyn ravaged the whole of England. Northumbria and Mercia flocked to his standard and even the thegns (*thanes*) of Wessex submitted to him.
Ethelred fled to Normandy, *and the Witan acknowledged Sweyn as King.*

1014   **The Restoration of Ethelred**
On the death of Sweyn, the Danish warriors chose **Canute,** his son, as King of England, *while the Witan sent for Ethelred to return.*

1016   **Death of Ethelred**

EDMUND IRONSIDE, SON OF ETHELRED,
1016 (7 MONTHS)

1016   The **people of London** chose **Edmund Ironside** as King, those of other parts chose **Canute.**

> NOTE.—In a single year Edmund fought no less than five pitched battles with Canute with various success, but at **Assandun** (Ashington, Essex), he was defeated owing to the treachery of Edric Streona, "the Grasper," a powerful English chief, who had first joined him with a body of Mercian troops, and in the midst of the fight turned against him. Edmund and Canute recognizing each other's greatness then agreed to divide the kingdom between them:
> (1) **Edmund** was to hold Wessex, Essex, and East Anglia.
> (2) **Canute,** Mercia and Northumbria.

Edmund reigned only seven months, when he was murdered, probably at the instigation of Edric Streona, *and the Witan then chose Canute as King of all England.*

THE DANISH KINGS

CANUTE, SON OF SWEYN, 1017–1035 (18 YEARS)

1017   **Canute** resolved to rule as an English King.

To conciliate the English:

(1) He married Emma, widow of the late King Ethelred.

(2) He sent home his Danish fleet and army except a bodyguard of 2,000 men.

(3) He established the laws of the great English King, Edgar.

(4) Although he was King of Denmark and Norway, he regarded England as his home, and the centre of his great Empire.

(5) He divided England into four great earldoms: Northumbria, East Anglia, Mercia, and Wessex, and while giving the first and second to men of Danish blood, he gave the third and fourth to two Englishmen, Leofric and Godwin, as a reward for their services.

> NOTE.—It is worthy of notice that the **Danes,** like their predecessors the **Saxons,** at first came to England only to plunder, then they began to settle, and lastly they conquered and ruled the whole land.

1027   The land had now settled down to such a state of quiet, that Canute was able to undertake a pilgrimage to Rome, leaving the cares of the state in the hands of Godwin, Earl of Wessex.

1031   **Canute went to Scotland,** and to protect England from the inroads of the Scots, compelled Malcolm to do homage to him as overlord.

1035   **Death of Canute.** On the death of Canute, his extensive dominions were divided between his three sons: (1) **Norway** fell to the lot of *Sweyn*; (2) **Denmark** and **England, south of the Thames,** to *Hardicanute*; (3) **England, north of the Thames,** to *Harold Harefoot.*

> NOTE.—Canute's reign was one of profound peace and continued prosperity.

A.D.

HAROLD I, CALLED HAREFOOT, SON OF CANUTE, 1035–1040 (5 YEARS)

1036   **Alfred** and **Edward,** sons of Ethelred the Unready, and Emma, returned to England from Normandy. Alfred was seized by Harold's orders, and blinded with such cruelty that he died at Ely. Edward returned to Normandy.

1040   **Death of Harold Harefoot.** Hardicanute came over from Denmark with a large army and took possession of the whole of England.

HARDICANUTE, SON OF CANUTE AND EMMA, 1040–1042 (2 YEARS)

1041   Hardicanute sent to Normandy for his half-brother Edward to return to England.

1042   **Hardicanute died** suddenly, while celebrating the marriage feast of one of his followers. The people chose Edward as King, and so the *Royal House of Alfred was restored.*

NOTE.—" From this time the Danes who lived in England were gradually absorbed into the English nation."

THE NORMAN CONQUEST

EDWARD THE CONFESSOR, SON OF ETHELRED II AND EMMA, 1042–1066 (24 YEARS)

1044   Edward appointed Robert of Jumièges, a Norman priest, as Bishop of London, and afterwards as Archbishop of Canterbury. He also filled his court with Norman favourites.

1045   Edward married **Edith,** daughter of Earl Godwin, and the Earl became the real governor of the Kingdom.

1051   The King's *extreme partiality for Norman priests and favourites* caused a rupture between himself and Earl Godwin; and at a meeting of the Witan, the Earl was outlawed, and banished together with all his family.
William of Normandy visited England, and was said to have received a promise of the Crown of England from Edward.

1052   Godwin returned to England, and was restored by the Witan to his earldom and former position of power. All the Norman bishops and knights were outlawed, and fled the country, and Stigand was made Archbishop of Canterbury in the place of Robert of Jumièges.

1053   Death of Godwin. His son Harold became Earl of Wessex.

NOTE.—In 1054, **Macbeth,** the Lord of Moray, who had murdered Duncan, King of Scotland, and seized the throne, was slain by Siward, Earl of Northumbria, and Malcolm, the son of Duncan, restored to the throne.

A.D.

1063   **Harold** and **Tostig** suppressed a rebellion raised by Griffith, King of North Wales.   Griffith was slain by his own followers.

1065   The Anglo-Danes of Northumbria rose against **Tostig** on account of his unjust government, and expelled him from his earldom. **Morcar,** the grandson of Leofric, was made Earl of Northumbria, and his brother, **Edwin,** Earl of Mercia.

1066   **Death of Edward the Confessor**

NOTE.—Edward gained the title of " Confessor " on account of his piety.

HAROLD II, SON OF GODWIN,
1066 (10 MONTHS)

1066   The Witan passed over **Edgar Atheling,** a grandson of Edmund Ironside, and chose **Harold,** the son of Godwin, as King.
William of Normandy sent ambassadors to claim the Crown of England, but his claim was rejected, and he prepared to invade the country.

NOTE.—His pretexts for the invasion were:

(1) That Edward the Confessor had promised him the Crown at his death.

(2) That Harold had solemnly sworn not to stand in the way of his claim to the Crown, and as he had now broken his oath, William considered himself bound to punish him as a perjurer.

(3) That the Pope had sanctioned his claim, because he considered that Robert of Canterbury had been wrongfully expelled from his see, and he looked to William to uphold the power and laws of the Church.

(4) That Harold and his brothers had harshly treated the Norman priests, and noblemen, who had been invited to England by Edward the Confessor.

Harold made preparations to resist the invaders.   He collected the " fyrd," and fortified some of the most important points on the south coast.

Tostig, Harold's brother, joined Harold Hardrada, King of Norway, and made an attempt to recover his lost earldom of Northumbria. They defeated Morcar and his brother Edwin at the battle of **Fulford.**

Harold marched north and met the invaders at **Stamford Bridge,** where Tostig and Hardrada were both defeated and slain.

William of Normandy landed at Pevensey, and Harold hurried southward to oppose him.   At the **Battle of Hastings,** or **Senlac,** Harold was defeated and slain.

NOTE 1.—The Battle of Hastings.   Harold had posted his men on the brow of a hill, behind a strong palisade, and William, finding that he could not break through the English line, ordered his left wing to turn and fly.   Immediately the English followed in hot pursuit.   The Normans suddenly turned round and charged their pursuers with such fury that they were either slain or scattered in all directions.

Harold, surrounded by a few thousands of his brave retainers, still maintained the fight, until he was pierced by an arrow in his right eye, and stretched lifeless on the ground.

NOTE 2.—The Normans were Northmen or Danes, who in the time of Alfred the Great invaded France, under a famous Viking called Rollo.   Charles the Simple, King of France, made a treaty with Rollo, and gave him land round the Seine, and his daughter in marriage.   The territory in which these Northmen settled, was known as Normandy (i.e., Northman's Land).

The Government of the English

(1) The **Village** or **Township.** The English were a nation of " franklins " or " freeholders," every man living in his own homestead on the produce of his land and cattle. *A group of these homesteads* formed a village or township. The franklins of the village assembled at the *village-moot* (i.e., the meeting of the village) under the presidency of the *village or town-reeve*.

(2) The **Hundred.** A number of townships, from 100 to 120, grouped together, constituted a hundred. Like the township, the hundred had a meeting for the management of its own affairs. This meeting was called the *hundred-moot*, and was presided over by the *hundred-man* or *hundred-elder*.

(3) The **Shire.** This embraced a number of hundreds. Its meeting was called the *shire-moot*, and was held under the presidency of an *earldorman*, appointed by the King and the Witan. *Every shire had to raise a certain number of men towards the fyrd or militia for national defence.*

(4) The **Kingdom.** This was made up of a number of shires, and was ruled conjointly by the **Witenagemot** and the **King.**
The **Witenagemot,** or " *Meeting of the Wise Men*," consisted of the King, his adult sons, the earldormen, bishops, and the King's thegns or chosen warriors. It could elect and depose the King, make and amend the laws, decide questions of peace and war, confirm the appointment of earldormen and bishops, and settle disputes between the great men.

The **King** was regarded with the greatest reverence by the people as being the descendant of their principal god, Woden. He was the leader of the army in war, and had great power, but could not make a grant of land, alter the laws, or levy a tax without the consent of the Witenagemot.

When the King died the Witan generally elected his eldest son King, but if he was young, foolish, or otherwise incapable of ruling he was passed over, and the late King's brother elected King.

NOTE.—The Old English and Norman systems of Government compared.

(1) The **Old English System,** worked from below, upwards, from the freeman to the King, every man holding his own land as his right, choosing his own earldormen, who in turn helped to choose the King.

(2) The **Norman System** (i.e., the Feudal System of the Conqueror) on the contrary, worked from above, downwards. The King owned all the land, and gave it to his knights, earls, and barons under certain mutual conditions. In this way he gathered up, and concentrated in himself, the whole power of the state.

THE NORMAN LINE 1066–1154
(88 YEARS)

WILLIAM I 1066–1087 (21 YEARS)

Title: By conquest, *but he wished to rule England as a King, and not as a conqueror.*

Married Matilda of Flanders.

Children: Robert, William II, Henry I, and Adela.

1066   **Accession.** After the **Battle of Hastings,** or **Senlac,** in which Harold was killed, Edgar Atheling was chosen King by the Witan. William advanced along the coast, took Dover, and marched towards London. Crossing the Thames at Wallingford, he pitched his camp at **Berkhampstead** to cut off all communication between London and the unconquered North. At Berkhampstead Edgar and the leading Saxons offered the crown to William, whose coronation took place at Westminster on Christmas Day.

The **Struggle with Saxons and Completion of the Conquest of England**

NOTE.—The want of unity on the part of the Saxon leaders weakened their cause.

1067   (*a*) The **First Revolt of the Saxons.** William visited Normandy, leaving **Odo** Bishop of Bayeux and **William Fitz-Osbern** as Regents. The Saxons, being oppressed, revolted in the West and South-west. William returned, captured Exeter, and subdued all the country south of the Thames.

1068– 1069   (*b*) The **Great Rising of the Saxons** in the North under the two great Saxon chiefs, Edwin and Morcar, assisted by the Danes under Sweyn. William re-took York, bought off the Danish fleet, and ravaged the country between the Humber and the Tees. He then took Chester, the last town which held out against him, and subdued the Welsh Borders. *Most of the land belonging to the Saxons was confiscated and given to the Norman Barons.*

1071   (*c*) The **Last struggle of the Saxons** for independence. The **Camp of Refuge** was formed under Hereward and Morcar in the Fen District. William constructed a causeway two miles long across the fens, and, after a desperate and prolonged resistance on the part of its defenders, took this stronghold. *This completed the conquest of England.*

NOTE 1.—It is from William's successful conflicts with the English that he has gained the name of " the Conqueror."

NOTE 2.—In 1072 William invaded Scotland and compelled Malcolm III to do homage.

1074   **William's troubles with the Barons and his son Robert**

(*a*) The **Bridal of Norwich.** This was a conspiracy of the Norman Barons against William under Roger Earl of Hereford and Ralph Gwader, who disliked the strong hand which William kept over them.

Waltheof, a Saxon noble who had been well treated by William, and had married his niece Judith, being implicated, was executed at Winchester in 1076, and the conspiracy was suppressed.

NOTE.—This was the only execution in the reign.

1079   (*b*) **Robert,** anxious to possess Normandy, rebelled again his father. He was besieged by William at **Gerberoi,** but subsequently was reconciled to his father.

1082   (*c*) **Odo** was apprehended by William, and his possessions taken from him, on account of his extortion during William's absence in Normandy.

1087   **William's death.** William invaded France, and, while burning **Mantes,** met with an accident which caused his death.

On his death-bed he bequeathed **Normandy** to Robert, **England** to William, and a large **sum of money** to Henry.

1079   **Memorable Events**

(*a*) The **New Forest,** comprising many thousand acres in Hampshire, was enclosed as a royal hunting ground, and Forest Laws were enacted.

1085   (*b*) The **Feudal System** was completely established. Under this system all the land belonged to the Sovereign as lord paramount, who divided it into " *fiefs* " and gave them to his nobles (*tenants-in-capite*) to be held by them under certain mutual conditions:

(1) The lord undertook to afford protection to his vassal.

(2) The vassal undertook to serve his lord at his own expense in the field for forty days in the year (called military tenure or knight service), to pay certain dues (such as aids, reliefs, etc.). The tenants-in-capite sub-let their lands on the same terms to other tenants called *mesne-tenants*, who, in their turn, held the right to sub-let under similar conditions. Thus, whenever the king needed an army, he summoned his tenants-in-capite, these called their vassals, and in this manner an army of 60,000 men could be gathered round the Royal standard.

NOTE 1.—One peculiar feature of the Feudal System of England, and one which restrained the growth of the power of the Barons, was that all landowners, whether tenants-in-capite or sub-tenants, took the oath of allegiance for the land they held, not only to their immediate lord, but also to the King.

NOTE 2.—In England there were 60,215 fiefs, and many of the Norman Barons held a great number of these.

NOTE 3.—Means adopted by William to keep his Barons in subjection:
(1) He took care that the grants of land made to them should be scattered all over the country, rather than in one continuous whole. (2) He abolished all the great Earldoms with the exception of three—the Bishopric of Durham and the Earldoms of Chester and Kent.

1086   (*c*) The **Domesday Book** was completed. This book was the result of a general survey of England made in 1085, and stated the *extent, value, population, state of cultivation, and ownership of the land.* It was the natural outcome of the Feudal System, and was a kind of rent-roll by which the King knew the exact strength of his resources.

NOTE 1.—The population of England at this time was, according to the Domesday Book, about 2,000,000.

NOTE 2.—At a great Gemot or court held at Salisbury all landowners, whether Norman or English, did homage directly to William for the land they held. It had the effect of increasing William's power as King, strengthening his hand against his turbulent barons, and uniting Normans and English into one nation.

(d) **William's Church Policy.** William's policy towards the Church was *to keep it completely under his control, but at the same time to uphold its power.*

(1) In 1070 he disposed Stigand and made Lanfranc, Abbot of Bec (Normandy), Archbishop of Canterbury. He also displaced several English Bishops and filled their sees with Normans (most of whom were learned and pious men), and made them do homage for their lands like the temporal barons.

(2) He claimed and exercised for himself absolute authority over the Church, and passed laws to the effect: (a) that no Pope should be recognized in England unless by his authority, and that no Papal Bull should have any force which had not first met with his approval; (b) that no Council of the Clergy should be held and no laws enacted without his consent; (c) that no tenant-in-capite should be excommunicated without his permission; (d) lastly, that the right of investing the Bishops with the ring and crozier should belong to the crown.

(3) He refused to do homage to the Pope for his English Crown on the ground that none of his predecessors had done so.

(4) He allowed the Bishops to withdraw from the county courts and establish courts of their own where only cases strictly ecclesiastical should be tried.

Results of the Norman Conquest: (1) A strong Norman Government superseded the weak Saxon rule. (2) Nearly all the land was confiscated to the Normans. (3) The Feudal System was completely established. (4) Relations with the Continent were opened, civilization and commerce extended. (5) Norman-French language, manners, and architecture were introduced. (6) The Church was brought into closer connection with Rome, and the ecclesiastical jurisdiction was separated from the secular. (7) There were no more Danish invasions.

WILLIAM II 1087–1100 (13 YEARS)

Title: Second son of William I. He was never married.

1087   **Accession.** Securing the support of **Lanfranc,** William was crowned King. He won over the English by a promise of laws " *more just and mild than their forefathers had known.*"

1088   **The Rebellion of the Norman Barons** under Odo, who were in favour of the careless and easy-going Robert and disliked the separation of their possessions in France from those in England. By the aid of the English the rebellion was crushed, and Odo retired to France.

A.D.

William's oppressive rule, and the Extortions of Flambard.

1089   Lanfranc died, and the see of Canterbury was vacant four years. **Ralph Flambard,** a man of low origin, became Justiciar, and raised money for William, by: (1) keeping vacant the sees of the Abbots and Bishops so that the King might receive their revenues; (2) exacting heavy feudal dues from the barons; (3) levying unjust taxes from the people.

NOTE.—The **Justiciar** was the King's representative. He acted as regent when the King was out of England, and administered all the legal and financial business of the State.

1090   **William's Wars.** (a) With **Robert.** William made war on Robert in Normandy, but the brothers made a treaty at **Caen,** 1091, by which it was agreed *that the survivor should succeed to the dominions of his brother.* In 1096 Robert, being anxious to join the **First Crusade,** pledged Normandy to William for 10,000 marks. (b) With **Wales.** William granted lands in Wales to those barons who would undertake to conquer them. In this way the English frontier was considerably extended, and many new castles were built.

1091   (c) With **Scotland.** Malcolm III of Scotland invaded England, and William marched northward with a large army to punish the invader. Malcolm was so overawed by the presence of so powerful a neighbour that he readily consented to do homage to William for his Crown. William took possession of Cumberland, and having fortified Carlisle, settled there a body of colonists said to have been brought from Hampshire.

NOTE.—In 1093 a new quarrel broke out with Scotland, and Malcolm, while invading England, was killed at Alnwick by Robert Mowbray, Earl of Northumberland.

(d) The **Rebellion of Robert Mowbray.** This was a great rebellion of the northern Barons to dethrone William. The leader, Robert Mowbray, took refuge in Bamborough Castle, but venturing outside its wall, he was taken prisoner and condemned to life-long imprisonment.

1093   The **Dispute with Anselm.** The King, falling ill, in a moment of repentance vowed to make amends to the Church for the wrongs he had done to her, and appointed Anselm, Abbot of Bec, as Archbishop of Canterbury. Anselm opposed the King in his rapacious policy towards the Church, and in 1097, being unable to withstand his violence, retired to Rome. He did not return until the next reign.

1100   **William's Death.** William was killed by an arrow from the bow of Sir Walter Tyrrel while hunting in the New Forest, but whether accidentally or by design is uncertain.

HENRY I 1100–1135 (35 YEARS)

Title: Third son of William I.

Married Matilda, daughter of Malcolm III of Scotland.

NOTE.—By this marriage Henry united the Saxon and Norman lines.

Children: William and Matilda.

1100   **Accession.** To conciliate all parties, and make his position as a usurper secure, he granted a " Charter of Liberties."

In this Charter he promised:

(1) To the **Church**, that he would fill up all the vacant sees and benefices. (2) To the **Barons**, that he would abolish all oppressive feudal laws, and that lands held by knight-service shall be free from all other imposts. (3) To the **People**, that he would restore the laws of Edward the Confessor.

Further conciliatory measures: (1) He married Matilda, a Princess of English descent, the niece of **Edgar Atheling** and daughter of Malcolm III. (2) Imprisoned Flambard, thus showing his disapproval of his brother's rapacious policy. (3) Recalled Anselm.

1101   The **Contest with Robert and subjugation of Normandy.** Robert returned to England and claimed the Crown. The English supported Henry and a treaty was made, *in virtue of which Robert withdrew with a pension of 3,000 marks a year.*

1102   **Robert Belesme,** a Norman baron, having sided with Robert against Henry, was expelled from England and retired to Normandy.

1106   Prince Robert had received the exiles from England contrary to the treaty, and war broke out. Henry invaded Normandy, took Robert prisoner at **Tenchebrai,** and reduced the whole province. Robert was confined for the rest of his life (28 years) in Cardiff Castle.

1118   At **Brenville** Henry defeated his rebellious barons and Louis VI of France, who had supported the cause of William, son of Prince Robert (the " Clito " as he was called). Subsequently William Clito was fatally wounded at Alost, and by his death, Henry became undisputed master of Normandy.

1107   The **Quarrel with Anselm and the Pope** about the **Investiture of Bishops**

Anselm had refused to *consecrate the Bishops who had received their investitures from Henry.* A dispute arose about the Right of Investiture. This was referred to Pope Pascal II and finally ended in a compromise at Bec (Normandy), by which Henry retained the really important part of investiture, i.e., the claims to the oaths of fealty and homage from the new prelates for their temporal possessions, but resigned the right of granting investiture, i.e., the ring and crozier.

1116   Henry's aim was to secure the Succession in his family

(*a*) In favour of **his son William.** He induced the barons, both of England and Normandy, to promise their allegiance to his son William.

A.D.

1120   Prince William, his son, was drowned in the shipwreck of the **White Ship.** This was not only a domestic misfortune but also a *national calamity, as it was the cause of the Civil War in Stephen's reign.*

1126   (*b*) In favour of **his daughter Matilda.** Henry caused the Barons of the Great Council, including his nephew Stephen of Boulogne, to swear fealty to Matilda as future Sovereign.

> NOTE.—In 1131 the Barons again swore fealty to Matilda after her marriage with Geoffrey of Anjou, and again in 1133, after the birth of her son Henry II.

1135   **Death of Henry**

Henry's administrative Government

(*a*) The **Great Council,** or **Magnum Concilium,** was a court of the tenants-in-capite, and included the Archbishops and Bishops. It appears to have been summoned only on great occasions.

(*b*) The **Curia Regis,** or **King's Court,** was a committee of the King's Great Council with the King at its head, or in his absence the Justiciar, who was the King's chief minister. It settled disputes between the tenants-in-capite and the Crown, and tried and punished those who opposed the King's Government.

(*c*) The **Court of the Exchequer** (so called from the chequered cloth which covered the table round which the Barons sat) was the Court which managed the financial matters of the Government, and received the taxes from the sheriffs of the counties.

> NOTE 1.—These two latter Courts were organized under the direction of Roger, Bishop of Salisbury.

> NOTE 2.—The King's Revenue was derived from: (*a*) the Ferm, i.e., money raised in the counties by the sheriffs from the rents of Royal land; (*b*) fines; (*c*) The Danegeld, originally levied to raise money to buy off the Danes; (*d*) the feudal dues.

The **Crusades,** so called because its votaries wore a coloured cross on their left arm, lasted 174 years (1096–1270).

Object: *To recover the Holy Land from the Turks.* Pope Urban II encouraged Peter the Hermit to preach the First Crusade. The search for lands and wealth was partly a motive for later Crusades. Comparatively few nobles from England went on the Crusades.

Effects on Europe: (1) Commercial intercourse was established between Southern Europe and the Levant. (2) The power of the Church was greatly increased, since the Princes, who engaged in the Crusades, left their dominions under the protection of the Church. (3) A blow was given to the Feudal System, as the barons often sold or mortgaged their estates before joining the Crusades.

> NOTE.—Prince Robert was engaged in the First Crusade (1096), Richard I in the Third (1189), Edward I in the Seventh (1270).

STEPHEN 1135–1154 (19 YEARS)

Title: Son of Adela, daughter of William I.

Married Matilda of Boulogne.

Children: Eustace.

1135   **Accession.** Stephen, supported by his brother **Henry, Bishop of Winchester,** and the Church, gained the throne to the exclusion of Matilda, daughter of Henry I, although he had promised his allegiance to her as Queen of England.
He confirmed the charters by Henry I, and allowed the Barons to build castles on their own estates, which led to incessant warfare among them.

1138   **David I of Scotland** invaded England in support of his niece Matilda, but was defeated at **Northallerton,** or the " Battle of the Standard "; *so called because the English had hoisted on a tall mast a silver casket, containing a consecrated wafer, as a standard.*

     Results: (1) 10,000 Scots were killed. (2) Stephen's position as King was much strengthened. (3) There were no more Scottish invasions for nearly 200 years.
The **Civil War** (1139–1154) was a contest between Stephen and Matilda for the Crown.

1139   **Robert of Gloucester,** a natural son of Henry I, who had the previous year renounced his fealty to Stephen, now landed at Portsmouth with Matilda, and civil war broke out. *Stephen lost the support of his brother Henry, Bishop of Winchester, and of the Church by arresting Roger, Bishop of Salisbury, whom he suspected of disloyalty.*

1141   After a good deal of irregular fighting, Stephen was defeated and taken prisoner at **Lincoln.** Henry, Bishop of Winchester, joined Matilda, who was acknowledged Queen, but her haughty manner soon estranged her supporters.
Robert of Gloucester was captured and exchanged for Stephen, and the war was resumed.

1147   **The death of Robert** and withdrawal of Matilda to France caused the war to languish for a time.

1153   **Prince Henry** (Matilda's son) asserted his right to the throne, invaded England, and renewed the war.

     The **Treaty of Wallingford** was agreed to, by which **Prince Henry** was acknowledged as Stephen's successor.

1154   **Death of Stephen**

THE PLANTAGENET LINE 1154–1399
(245 YEARS)

HENRY II 1154–1189 (35 YEARS)

Title: Son of Matilda, daughter of Henry I.

NOTE.—With Henry II came in a new line of kings—" the Angevin Kings," so called because they were descended from Geoffrey of Anjou.

Married Eleanor of Guienne, divorced wife of Louis VII.

Children: Henry, Richard, Geoffrey, and John.

1154　**His extensive dominions:**

(*a*) From his **mother,** he inherited England, Normandy, and Maine.

(*b*) From his **father,** Anjou and Touraine.

(*c*) From his **wife,** Poitou and all the Provinces south of the Loire to the Pyrenees (including Saintonge, Limousin, Guienne, and Gascony).

NOTE.—His possessions in France were larger than all England.

His early measures to restore order in the kingdom.

(*a*) The Flemish auxiliaries hired by Stephen were compelled to leave England.

(*b*) Grants of Royal lands made by Stephen were recalled.

(*c*) Castles built in the late reign were demolished.

NOTE.—In 1157 Henry compelled Malcolm IV of Scotland to do homage.

The Rise of Becket. Becket was the son of a London citizen, and was brought to Henry's notice by Theobald, Archbishop of Canterbury. Henry made him Chancellor and Chief Clerk of the Curia Regis.

Henry, wishing to reform certain abuses in the Church government, insisted *that all clerks charged with criminal offences should be tried in the King's courts instead of in the Bishops courts.* These latter courts could punish only by means of censures, excommunications, and penance, and could not inflict corporal punishment. " Clerks " included thousands of servants, etc., who obtained " benefit of clergy " by knowing a few words of Latin.

1162　Henry made Becket Archbishop of Canterbury, thinking he would assist him in carrying out these reforms.

Henry's Quarrel with Becket, and the Constitutions of Clarendon

1164　(*a*) Becket changed his mode of life from that of a gay courtier to that of a rigid ecclesiastic, resigned his temporal offices, and opposed Henry in his Church reforms.

(*b*) A clerk, having committed a murder, was allowed to go unpunished; this brought matters to a crisis.

(*c*) Henry drew up the **Constitutions of Clarendon** (Wilts.), enacting: (1) That clerks charged with criminal offences should

A.D.

be tried in Civil Courts. (2) That no cleric of rank should leave the country without the King's consent. (3) That the King should enjoy the revenues of vacant sees. (4) That the Prelates as well as the Barons should be subject to feudal burdens. (5) That no appeal should be made to Rome without the King's consent. (6) That forfeited goods should not be protected in churches. (7) That no tenant-in-capite should be excommunicated without the King's consent.

Becket reluctantly signed the Constitutions, but shortly afterwards rejected them, and appealed to the Pope to free him from his promise.

(d) Becket defied the King at the Council of Northampton, and, fearing for his life, fled in the disguise of a monk to France, and was well received by Louis VII.

The Murder of Becket

1170 (a) Henry, to show his authority, caused his eldest son Henry to be crowned by Roger, Archbishop of York. Becket, Louis, and the Pope were most indignant, as this was a distinct invasion of the rights of the Archbishop of Canterbury.

(b) Henry was compelled to effect a reconciliation with Becket, who returned to England, *but renewed the struggle by excommunicating Roger and the other Bishops who had opposed him.*

(c) Four knights, encouraged by some hasty words of the King, hastened to England, and, on Becket's refusing to withdraw the excommunication, murdered him at the altar of his own cathedral.

NOTE.—Subsequently Henry, to satisfy public feeling, did penance at Becket's tomb.

The Conquest of Ireland

Early in the reign Henry had gained permission from Pope Adrian IV to conquer Ireland.

1166 Dermot, King of Leinster, having been expelled by a confederacy of Irish chiefs, sought the aid of Henry, who allowed Strongbow, Earl of Pembroke, to invade the country, and Leinster was reduced.

1171 On the death of Dermot, Strongbow succeeded to the Crown of Leinster. Henry, jealous of the success of his vassal, visited Ireland in person and received homage from Strongbow and the Irish Chiefs.

NOTE.—English law was only in force in the subdued part of the country, which was known as the " English Pale."

The Rebellions against Henry

1173 (1) A general league was formed against him:

(a) In France, by his sons Henry, Richard, and Geoffrey, who incited by their mother, each wished to gain independent dominions. They were joined by Louis VII and the Counts of Boulogne and Flanders. In 1174 Henry crushed the league.

A.D.

1174 (*b*) In **England,** by several powerful barons, who disliked his rigorous rule. William I, " the Lion " of Scotland, joined the league, and, having invaded England, was surprised and captured at Alnwick by Ralph de Glanville, and the rebellion was suppressed. William only regained his liberty by doing homage to Henry for Scotland.

1183 (2) The **Second Rebellion of Henry's sons**

(*a*) During this contest Prince Henry died of a fever, and subsequently Geoffrey was slain in a tournament.

1189 (*b*) **Death of Henry II.** Richard, assisted by Philip, expelled his father from Touraine. Henry, finding the name of his favourite son John at the head of the list of the conspirators, died of a broken heart.

Constitutional Changes

1159 **Scutage,** i.e., *a payment in money instead of military service*, was introduced. This, while it checked the power of the barons, enabled the King to hire mercenaries, and dispense with the services of his feudal followers.

1166 By the **Assize of Clarendon,** Trial by Grand Jury was established.

1176 By the **Assize of Northampton,** the country was divided into six circuits, and itinerant justices appointed to each, called " Justices in Eyre," i.e., *justices on journey.*

1181 The **Assize of Arms** was issued to reorganize the national militia, the old " fyrd " of the Saxons.

RICHARD I 1189–1199 (10 YEARS)

Title: Son of Henry II.

Married Berengaria of Navarre. Richard had no children.

1189 **Accession** and **Preparations for a Crusade**

(*a*) Being the eldest surviving son of Henry II, he was crowned without opposition.

Some Jews, having presented themselves at his coronation contrary to the Royal command, were cruelly massacred. This was followed by similar massacres at Norwich, Stamford, and York.

(*b*) Richard being desirous of joining the Crusade, raised money for the expedition by: (1) putting up for sale offices in Church and State; (2) selling Church and Crown lands; (3) releasing William the Lion from obligations imposed on him by Henry II on payment of 10,000 marks; (4) selling charters of self-government to towns.

NOTE.—To William Longchamp he sold the Bishopric of Ely for £3,000, and to Hugh de Puiset, the Earldom of Northumberland for £1,000.

(*c*) **William Longchamp,** Bishop of Ely, was appointed Justiciar, and Richard joined the Third Crusade.

A.D.

Events in the Third Crusade (1189–1192)

1190 (a) Richard joined Philip of France, reduced **Cyprus,** and, proceeding to Palestine, took **Acre** (1191).

1191 (b) He defeated the Saracens under Saladin at the battle of **Arsoof,** near Jaffa.

1192 (c) Philip returned home, and Richard, having quarrelled with Leopold, Archduke of Austria, and disunion having crept in among his allies, concluded a peace with Saladin, *which guaranteed that the pilgrims should have free access to Jerusalem.*

 On his way home Richard was made prisoner by the Archduke and handed over to Henry VI, Emperor of Germany.

1194 Richard was liberated on payment of 100,000 marks (a sum more than twice the whole revenue of the Crown), and returned to England, although John his brother had treacherously tried to persuade the Emperor to keep him prisoner.

1199 **Richard's death.** Richard was mortally wounded while besieging the **Castle of Chaluz,** where the Count of Limoges was said to be keeping some treasure, which Richard claimed.

JOHN 1199–1216 (17 YEARS)

Title: Fourth son of Henry II.

Married: (1) Hadwisa of Gloucester; (2) Isabella of Angoulême.

Children: By Isabella of Angoulême, Henry.

His reign may be divided into three parts: (1) The **Contest with Prince Arthur,** son of Geoffrey, *who claimed the Crown of England.*

(a) Philip II supported Arthur's cause, and in conjunction with Arthur attacked John's dominions.

Arthur, while attempting to capture the Castle of Mirabeau, where his grandmother Eleanor was staying, was taken prisoner by John and thrown into the dungeons of Rouen Castle, where it is generally supposed he was murdered by John's own hand.

1204 (b) The **Loss of Normandy.** Philip, having summoned John as his vassal to Paris to answer for Arthur's death, in default of his appearance, took all his French possessions except the Channel Islands, Rochelle, and a few towns in Poitou.

Note 1.—John made several attempts to regain Normandy, but was unsuccessful.

Note 2.—The loss of Normandy proved beneficial to England. (1) It had the effect of gradually uniting Normans and English into one nation. (2) Both king and nobles now began to regard England as their home.

(2) The **Contest with Pope Innocent III,** *about the election of an Archbishop of Canterbury.*

1205 On the death of Hubert, the younger monks of Canterbury elected Reginald, their sub-prior, as Archbishop; the elder monks, by John's order, elected John de Grey, Bishop of Norwich. To settle the dispute both parties appealed to Rome.

A.D.

1206　　The Pope set aside both elections, and ordered the election of **Stephen Langton.**

1208　　John refused to receive Langton, and the Pope proceeded to punish John for his obstinacy:

(*a*) By an **interdict.** England for four years was laid under an interdict, i.e., all services of the Church with the exception of baptism and extreme unction were forbidden, as well as the burial of the dead in consecrated ground. By this means the Pope hoped to rouse the national feeling against John.

1209　　(*b*) By **excommunication.** John still refusing to yield, the Pope excommunicated him, and John, by way of revenge, seized the property of the bishops and the clergy.

1212　　(*c*) By **deposition.** Finally, the Pope declared that John had forfeited his throne and should be deposed, and called on Philip of France, John's old enemy, to carry out the sentence.

1213　　John submitted, and did homage for England at Dover to Pandulf, the Pope's legate, promising: (1) to receive Langton as Archbishop; (2) to restore Church property; (3) to pay an annual tribute of 1,000 marks to the Pope. Men said that "*John had forfeited the name of King, and had become the Pope's man.*"
The Pope ordered Philip not to make war on his faithful vassal John, whereupon Philip, angry at being thus duped, directed his army against the Count of Flanders, John's ally.

1214　　John allied himself with Otto, Emperor of Germany, and the Count of Flanders and sent an army under the Earl of Salisbury to crush Philip.

The **Battle of Bouvines.** Their united armies were defeated by Philip at Bouvines.

NOTE.—It is to this defeat, and the consequent weakness of John's power, that England owes her great Charter.

(3) The **Contest with the Barons** under the leadership of Stephen Langton and Fitz-Walter.

Causes: (1) The heavy taxation with which John oppressed every class of the people. (2) His insolent and tyrannical conduct towards the barons.

The **Meetings of the Barons**

1213　　(*a*) At **St. Albans,** where a declaration of the grievances of all classes was brought forward.

NOTE.—These barons were chiefly those of the North, called "the Northerners. They were not the descendants of the old baronial families which came over with the Conqueror, but "new-made men." They demanded that the power of the King and the rights and liberties of the subject should be more accurately defined.

(*b*) At **St. Paul's** Stephen Langton laid before the opposition barons the Coronation Charter of Henry I. This was accepted as the basis of their demands from the King.

1214   (c) At **Bury St. Edmunds** the barons took an oath that they would compel John to grant them a sealed charter of rights and liberties, or take up arms against him if he refused.

John demanded three months for consideration. Meanwhile he: (1) Tried to separate the Church from the barons by granting the clergy freedom of election to bishoprics and abbeys. (2) Took the oath of the Crusaders so as to put himself under the immediate protection of the Church. (3) Summoned mercenaries from Poitou.

1215   (d) At **Brackley** the barons again assembled and renewed their claims.

Marching towards London, the Barons were well received by the Londoners. The support of the Londoners decided the contest. Meanwhile John's army was deserting him, and he found himself face to face with a whole nation in arms.

(e) At **Runnymede** John summoned the barons to meet him, and there signed the **Magna Charta.**

The **Clauses of the Magna Charta** (63 in all) relating:

I. To the **Church.** That the Church should possess all its rights, together with freedom of elections.

II. To **Feudal Tenants.** (1) That reliefs, i.e., money paid by an heir on taking possession of his fief, should be raised according to the rank of the tenant; (2) That aid should be demanded in three cases only: (a) ransoming the King; (b) the knighthood of his eldest son; (c) the marriage of his eldest daughter.

III. To **Traders.** (1) That London and other towns should retain their ancient rights and privileges. (2) That there should be the same weight and measures throughout the realm. (3) That foreign merchants might enter the country and leave when they pleased, except in time of war.

IV. To **all classes of persons.** (1) That justice should not be sold, delayed, or refused to anyone. (2) That no person should be imprisoned, deprived of his property, or outlawed but by the judgment of his equals, or by the law of the land. (3) That no person should be fined to his utter ruin, but in proportion to his offence. (4) That no person should be deprived of his means of livelihood. (5) That the Court of Common Pleas should be stationary (at Westminster), and no longer follow the King's person.

NOTE 1.—A Council of twenty-five barons (" Over-kings " John contemptuously called them) was chosen to enforce on John the observance of the Charter, with the right of declaring war on him should he infringe its provisions.

NOTE 2.—This Charter has been ratified no less than thirty-eight times.

Remarks on the Magna Charta:

1. The Magna Charta is the first definite statement in writing of the duties of the King, and the rights and liberties of the subject. Viewed in this light, it is a " treaty of peace " between the King and his people.

2. It is, moreover, the first constitutional document which recognizes the people of England as one united whole.

3. Its importance is seen from the fact that " if all other subsequent laws are repealed the Magna Charta would prove England to be a free country."

The Wars between John and his Barons

The Pope disallowed the Great Charter, and suspended Langton. John defied the barons, collected mercenary troops, and ravaged the North of England.

1216   Driven to despair, the barons invited Louis, Philip's son, to take the Crown. Louis was well received by the Londoners, and most of the barons deserted John.

Death of John. John prepared to march on London, but while crossing the Wash, lost all his treasure and baggage. He retired to Swinestead Abbey near Newark, where he died.

HENRY III 1216–1272 (56 YEARS)

Title: Son of John.

Married Eleanor of Provence.

Children: Edward I.

The Regency of Pembroke

1216   The King being a minor, the Earl of Pembroke was appointed " Governor of the King and Kingdom," and ruled well.

Most of the Barons deserted Louis, and rallied round the King.

1217   The question whether Henry of England or Louis of France was to be King of England was decided by two battles.
(1) The **Fair of Lincoln,** where Louis was defeated. (2) The **Battle off Dover,** where the French fleet which was bringing Louis assistance was destroyed by Hubert de Burgh. Louis made a treaty with Pembroke at Lambeth and left England.

1219   The death of Pembroke. **Hubert de Burgh** became Justiciar and the King's chief counsellor, but in 1232 he was superseded by **Peter des Roches,** Bishop of Winchester, whose friends from Poitou, " the Poitevins," were appointed to many of the highest offices in the kingdom.

Twenty-six years (1232–1258) of **misrule** under Henry followed.

1236   (a) The King married Eleanor of Provence. In consequence of this marriage, swarms of foreigners from Provence flocked to England, where they acquired great influence by marrying rich English heiresses or by holding the most important offices in Church and State.

The most powerful of these were the Queen's three uncles, William, Bishop of Valence, Peter of Savoy, and Boniface of Savoy; the latter became Archbishop of Canterbury on the death of Edmund Rich.

NOTE.—The whole administration thus passed into the hands of men utterly ignorant of the principles of English government and English law, and their rule became mere anarchy.

A.D.

1242   (b) **The French War.** Henry undertook an expensive war to regain the French possessions, but was unsuccessful, and having been disgracefully defeated at Taillebourg and Saintes, was compelled to accept a peace which deprived him of the whole of Poitou.

1258   (c) The **Rebellion of the Barons** took place. It was in reality a continuation of the great struggle between the King and his Barons in the last reign. **Simon de Montfort,** brother-in-law to the King, having quarrelled with William of Valence, assumed the leadership of the rebellious barons.

The **causes** of this discontent were: (1) the King's extreme partiality for foreigners, to whom he gave all the highest offices in Church and State; (2) his lavish expenditure of public money on foreign favourites; (3) his unsuccessful war with France; (4) his foolish and unsuccessful attempt to win the Crown of Sicily for his son Edmund.

(d) The **Mad Parliament,** including 100 Barons " *in arms,*" met at Oxford, presented the King with a list of grievances, and drew up a new constitution, called the **Provisions of Oxford,** which Henry and his son Prince Edward swore to accept: (1) that twenty-four Barons should be appointed to reform the Government; (2) that there should be three Parliaments every year; (3) that the King should have a permanent body of fifteen to advise him, without whose authority the King could not act; (4) that another committee should be appointed to manage financial affairs.

NOTE.—The proclamation of the King's assent to these Provisions was the first document issued in the English language.

1261   (e) The Pope absolved Henry from his oath to keep the Provisions.

1264   The **Barons' War**

(1) Henry having refused to confirm the Provisions, the quarrel was referred to Louis IX, *who by the Mise* (i.e., *arbitration*) *of Amiens set aside the Provisions*, and civil war broke out.

(2) At the battle of **Lewes** the King was defeated by De Montfort and taken prisoner, together with his brother Richard, **Earl of Cornwall.**

(3) A treaty was made, called the **Mise of Lewes,** *by which Prince Edward gave himself up as a ransom for his father.*

Simon de Montfort now became sole master of the kingdom.

1265   The **First House of Commons.** Finding that he was losing the support of many of the barons, De Montfort threw himself upon the towns and summoned his famous Parliament of 1265, including the **Barons,** the **Clergy, two Knights** from each county, and, for the first time, *two representatives* from each of the chief cities and boroughs. As it represented *all classes*, it was in this sense the fullest representation of England that had ever been summoned.

NOTE.—Only twenty-three Earls, friends of De Montfort, sat in this Parliament, and it was probably to strengthen his position that he introduced representatives from the towns

A **reaction** now set in in favour of the King, and De Clare, Earl of Gloucester, and other nobles deserted De Montfort.

The **causes** of this reaction were: (1) jealousy of Montfort's power; (2) Montfort's ambition and self-aggrandizement; (3) the popular nature of his policy, with which the Barons had little sympathy; (4) the introduction of the " *town element* " into his Parliament, to the disgust of the Baronial party; (5) the imprisonment of Prince Edward.

The battle of **Evesham.** Prince Edward escaped from confinement, raised an army, and defeated De Montfort at Evesham, where the latter, " *fighting bravely like a giant*," was slain.

1266 The **Dictum of Kenilworth** was signed: (1) it restored Henry to his full authority; (2) annulled the Provisions of Oxford; (3) provided that the King should keep the Great Charter. In 1270 the country had settled down so peaceably that Prince Edward joined the Seventh and last Crusade.

1272 **Death of Henry**

NOTE 1.—The **Coming of the Friars.** The evil state of the Church in the thirteenth century led to the coming into England of two new orders of Mendicant Friars:

(1) The **Dominicans,** or **Black Friars** founded by St. Dominic, a Spanish Canon, who directed all their energies towards raising the spiritual and moral life of men.

(2) The **Franciscans,** or **Grey Friars,** founded by St. Francis of Assisi, who devoted their whole life towards alleviating the miseries of mankind.

NOTE 2.—**The Chroniclers.** The reign of Henry III is remarkable for its Chroniclers. First and foremost stands Matthew Paris, who gives us in his writing a vivid picture of the troublesome times of Henry III. After him came Adam Marsh, a learned Franciscan Monk, Thomas of Wykes, William of Rishanger and Robert of Gloucester.

EDWARD I 1272–1307 (35 YEARS)

Title: Son of Henry III.

Married: (1) Eleanor of Castile; (2) Margaret of France.

Children: Edward II.

1272 **Accession.** Edward was proclaimed King, although absent on a Crusade.

1274 Edward was crowned at Westminster, and at his coronation received the homage of Alexander III of Scotland for his English fiefs.

His **aims** were: (1) to consolidate his kingdom by adding Wales and Scotland; (2) to reform abuses in the government; (3) to give his people good laws and see that they were carefully kept; (4) to give all classes a greater share in the Government than they had hitherto enjoyed. " *Edward was by instinct a lawgiver.*"

A.D.

The Conquest of Wales (1277–1284)

1277 The First Rising of the Welsh

(*a*) **Llewellyn,** the reigning Prince of Wales, had allied himself to Simon de Montfort during the late civil war, and now refused to swear allegiance to Edward.

(*b*) With a view to continue the disturbance of the last reign a marriage was arranged between Llewellyn and the daughter of de Montfort, but the lady was captured and detained in England by Edward, and war broke out.

(*c*) Edward invaded Wales, and Llewellyn was compelled to submit. He was allowed to retain only Anglesey and the district round Snowdon.

1282 The Second Rising of the Welsh

David, Llewellyn's brother, who had fought for Edward, now deserted to his fellow-countrymen.

Edward advanced against the brothers, Llewellyn was surprised and killed at **Builth,** on the river Wye, and shortly after David was captured, condemned by a Parliament called at Shrewsbury, and executed.

1284 **The Statute of Wales was enacted at Rhuddlan,** *by which Wales was annexed to England and placed under the same laws.*

NOTE 1.—Edward completed the conquest of Wales by presenting the new-born heir to the Welsh, under the title of Prince of Wales.

NOTE 2.—It was not until the reign of Henry VII that Wales was represented in the English Parliament.

The Struggle with Scotland (1291–1307)

Alexander III had died in 1286, leaving his little grand-daughter Margaret, called the " Maid of Norway," as the only direct heir to the throne.

A treaty was arranged by Edward with the Scots, by which " the Maid " was betrothed to his son Edward, Prince of Wales. Her death at the Orkneys, on her way to Scotland, set aside this treaty, and three claimants appeared for the Scottish Crown, **John Balliol, Robert Bruce,** and **John Hastings,** all of whom were descended from **David I.**

1291 (*a*) The **Struggle under Balliol.** Edward, being appealed to by the Scotch Council as " Overlord," to settle the dispute, met the Scotch Parliament at **Norham** (near Berwick), and gave a just verdict in favour of Balliol, who accepted the kingdom as Edward's vassal, did homage to him, and was crowned at Scone.

NOTE.—The claim of English kings to Overlordship goes back to Edward the Elder, who was accepted by the Scots as " Father and Lord "; but the question was constantly disputed from the time of the Norman Conquest.

1296 **War broke out.** The **causes were:** (1) Edward had insisted that the nobles and citizens might appeal to him against decisions made by Balliol in the Scotch law courts. (2) Edward had become involved in a war with France, and Balliol, thinking that his opportunity had come for making a bold strike for independence, made a secret treaty with France, crossed the Border, and ravaged Cumberland.

Edward invaded Scotland, captured Berwick, and defeated the Scots at **Dunbar,** after which Balliol surrendered and was sent a prisoner to England.

Scotland ceased to be a kingdom, and became a dependency of England: (1) De Warrenne was made Guardian, Cressingham Treasurer, and Ormsby Justiciar of Scotland. (2) At Berwick Edward received the fealty of the clergy, gentry, and barons. (3) The Crown jewels, and sacred stone of Scone were carried to England, the latter being placed in Westminster Abbey, where it still remains.

1297 (b) The **Struggle under Wallace.** The **cause:** The oppressive government of Edward's officers incited the Scots to rise in rebellion under Sir William Wallace, an outlawed knight, who inflicted a terrible defeat on the English at **Cambuskenneth** (Stirling), invaded England, and from Newcastle to Carlisle " left nothing behind him but blood and ashes."
Wallace now unwisely took the title of " Guardian of the Kingdom " for Balliol. This step excited the jealousy of the nobles.

1298 Edward again invaded Scotland, defeated Wallace at Falkirk. Wallace was later betrayed and executed.

NOTE.—The battle of Falkirk was won by the English archers, whose arrows broke up the solid squares of Scottish spearmen, and the English cavalry then dashed in and cut them to pieces.

1299 (c) The **Struggle under John Comyn,** who was placed by the Scots at the head of a Regency for his uncle Balliol.

1303 Comyn defeated the English at Roslin. Edward a third time reduced the country, and made a treaty with Comyn, by which the Government was placed in Edward's hands.

1306 (d) The **Struggle under Robert Bruce,** grandson of the rival of Balliol, who had hitherto remained faithful to Edward.
Bruce murdered Comyn in the Church of Dumfries, because he refused to assist him, raised the standard of revolt, and was crowned at Scone.

At **Methven,** near Perth, Bruce was defeated by the Earl of Pembroke and became a fugitive.

Edward's last invasion of Scotland and **Death.** At a banquet held at Westminster, Edward took a solemn oath to avenge Comyn's death, set out for Scotland with an immense army, but died while on the march at **Burgh-on-Sands** (1307).

Constitutional Changes

1278 (1) **Writs of Quo Warranto** were issued, *to inquire into the titles of lands.* Its objects were: (a) to establish the rights of landed property which had been disturbed in the last reign; (b) to define clearly the revenue due to the Crown.

1279 (2) The **Statute of Mortmain** was passed, *to prevent men from giving their lands to the Church, so as to avoid rendering feudal service for them.*

1285   (3) The **Statute De Donis,** or the Second Statute of Westminster, was passed. It enacted that the owner of an estate had but a life interest in it, and that if his children were not living at his death it returned to the original grantor. *In this way the law of entail* i.e., *the fixing of the estate to some particular line of heirs, was established.*

     (4) The **Statute of Winchester,** a re-enactment and completion of the Assize of Arms established by Henry II, was passed. It enacted: (1) that each class of persons should provide themselves with certain kinds of arms for the defence of the country; (2) that the gates of every walled town should be closed at sunset, and that all strangers should give an account of themselves before the magistrate; (3) that every district should be answerable for the crimes committed in it; (4) that a space of 200 feet should be cleared on each side of the highway for the safety of travellers; (5) that officers should be appointed to see that the statute was duly observed. These officers were afterwards known as the " *Justices of the Peace.*"

NOTE.—England was at this time infested with riotous bands of robbers called trail-bâtons, who hired themselves out either for robbery or private outrage.

1290   (5) The **Statute of " Quia Emptores "** was passed, *to prevent sub-infeudation (or sub-letting), and the formation of new manors.*

1295   (6) The **First Complete Parliament** was summoned. Edward's extensive wars compelled him to raise supplies from all classes of his subjects. He said, " *That it was right that what concerned all, should be approved by all.*" This led him to summon the First Complete Parliament, representing the three estates of the realm, **Lords, Commons, and Clergy.**

NOTE.—This is generally considered as the " true origin of Parliament as it now exists."

1297   (7) The **Statute called " De Tallagio non concedendo "** was passed. Edward's excessive and arbitrary taxation induced the Barons to insist upon his signing this Charter while he was at Ghent. It enacted: (1) that no aids or tallage should be levied but by the common consent of the realm, and for the common profit thereof; (2) that the maletote of wool, i.e., a toll of 40*s.* per sack, should be discontinued.

NOTE 1.—Edward had raised the duty on wool to six times what it had been before.

NOTE 2.—The Clergy under Archbishop Winchelsea refused to make any grant to the king, whereupon Edward seized all the lands belonging to the Archbishop's See.

1300   (8) The **Organization of the Law Courts** took place. The Law Courts, which had been previously united under the Justiciar, were now divided into three: (*a*) the King's Bench; (*b*) the Court of Common Pleas; (*c*) the Court of the Exchequer.

1307   **Death of Edward I**

EDWARD II 1307–1327 (20 YEARS)

Title: Son of Edward I.

Married Isabella of France.

Children: Edward III.

The **Rule of Favourites**

(1) **Piers Gaveston,** a Gascon knight, who had been previously banished by Edward I, was now recalled and created Earl of Cornwall.

1308 The Barons, headed by **Thomas, Earl of Lancaster,** demanded the dismissal of Gaveston. Edward consented, but made Gaveston Lord-Deputy of Ireland.

> NOTE.—This Lancaster was the eldest son of Edmund, brother of Edward I, and so cousin to the King. His power in England was enormous; he was Earl of five counties. " Distantly following out the policy of Simon de Montfort, he had set himself up as a friend of the clergy and of the liberties of the people."— (Stubbs).

1310 Parliament, following the lines laid down in the Provisions of Oxford, appointed the **Lords Ordainers,** consisting of twenty-one Bishops and Peers, to regulate the King's household and reform the Government.

These Ordainers drew up a series of ordinances, enacting: (1) that the King should not make war without the consent of Parliament; (2) that the great officers of state should be nominated by Parliament; (3) that no gifts should be made by the King without the consent of the Ordainers; (4) that the taxes on wool and cloth should be abolished; (5) that the Parliament should be held at least once a year.

1312 Gaveston was again recalled, but having been seized by the Earl of Warwick (the " Black Dog " as Gaveston had nicknamed him), was executed.

1314 The **Scottish War** was resumed.

Robert Bruce had taken fortress after fortress from the English, but **Stirling Castle** still held out. The Governor promised to capitulate unless relieved before St. John's Day, June 24th. Edward marched to its relief with an army of 100,000 men, but was totally defeated by Bruce at **Bannockburn** and escaped with difficulty to Dunbar, whence he took ship to Berwick.

Scotland regained its independence

1320 (2) **Hugh Despenser** and his son became the King's favourites.
Disgusted at the King's misrule, the Barons under the leadership of Lancaster rebelled, but were defeated by Edward at **Borough-bridge** (1322), and Lancaster was beheaded at Pontefract.

1326 **Edward's Deposition and Death**
Roger Mortimer, having joined the Queen in France, landed in Suffolk, accompanied by the Queen and the Prince of Wales.
The Queen and Mortimer now assumed the Royal power. Both the Despensers were captured and hanged.

A.D.

1327 The Parliament met and declared Prince Edward King.

Edward II was deposed on the following charges: (1) " that he was incompetent or too indolent to judge between right and wrong; (2) that he had obstinately refused the advice of the wise, and listened to evil counsel; (3) that he had lost Ireland, Scotland and Gascony; (4) that he had injured the Church and oppressed the Barons; (5) that he had broken his coronation oath and was ruining the land."— (Stubbs). The King confessed that these articles were true, and that he was unworthy to reign.

Death of Edward II. Edward was subsequently murdered in Berkeley Castle (1327).

EDWARD III 1327–1377 (50 YEARS)

Title: Son of Edward II.

Married Philippa of Hainault.

Children: Edward, the Black Prince, Lionel, John of Gaunt, and Edmund.

1327 **The Government** was in the **hands of Isabella and Mortimer.**

1330 Edward now took the Royal power, seized Nottingham Castle, and arrested Mortimer, who was condemned and executed.

His mother, Isabella, was confined at Castle Rising, Norfolk, for the rest of her life.

1333 **The First Scottish War**

David Bruce, son of Robert Bruce, was crowned King, as David II.

Edward supported the cause of Edward Balliol, son of John Balliol, defeated the Scots under Douglas the Regent at **Halidon Hill,** and placed Edward Balliol on the throne.

NOTE.—In the following year Edward Balliol was compelled to fly the country and David II was re-established as King.

The **Hundred Years' War with France** (1337–1453). **First Stage.**

1337 Edward, *in spite of the Salic Law which debarred females from the succession*, claimed the French Crown by right of his mother Isabella, daughter of Philip IV, and the Hundred Years' War began in 1338. (*See Table page 173.*)

1339 **The First Campaign.** Edward, in alliance with the States on the North-east of France, invaded France unsuccessfully, but in 1340 he won the great naval battle of **Sluys.**

1346 The **Second Campaign.** Edward invaded Normandy with 30,000 men, advanced almost to the gates of Paris, and, crossing the Seine, retreated towards Calais, pursued by Philip VI with an army of 100,000 men.

At **Crecy** the French were routed with terrible slaughter, more than 30,000 being killed, including the Duke of Alençon, Philip's brother.

NOTE.—The English gained this great victory owing: (a) to the superior skill of their archers; (b) to the more effective organization of their army, consisting as it did of regularly trained men, while the French army was organized on the old Feudal model.

1347 **Calais** capitulated after a siege of eleven months. After its surrender Calais became to all intents and purposes an English town. Subsequently the town became an important depot for English goods and in time enjoyed great prosperity.
Philip died in 1350 and was succeeded by his son John II.

(The **Second Scottish War.** In 1346 the Scots, in alliance with France, invaded England, but were defeated at **Neville's Cross** by Henry Percy and Ralph Neville, and David II was taken prisoner.)

1356 The **Third Campaign.** The Black Prince, living at Bordeaux as Governor of Gascony, advanced northwards, ravaging the country. The French King opposed him on his return, but was totally defeated at **Poitiers,** and taken prisoner.

1360 The **Peace of Bretigny,** the " Great Peace," was signed; on the whole, very favourable to the English. It stated: (1) that Edward should give up all claim to the Crown of France, but retain Calais, Poitou, Guienne, Gascony, and several other provinces free from feudal claims; (2) that King John should be liberated on payment of three million golden crowns.

NOTE.—Failing to raise the money for his ransom, John returned to England, and died a prisoner in the Savoy.

1367 The **Expedition into Spain.** The Black Prince went into Spain to support Pedro the Cruel, King of Castile, against his brother Henry, *who was an ally of the French.*   He won the battle of **Navarette,** and Pedro regained the throne.

1369 The **Fourth Campaign.** Charles V, son of John, renewed the war, generally to the disadvantage of the English.

The **Massacre at Limoges.** In 1370 the inhabitants of Limoges, who had deserted the English cause, were cruelly massacred, to the number of 3,000, by the Black Prince.

1371 The **Black Prince,** shattered in health, returned to England, *and in 1374 the English lost all their French dominions except Bordeaux, Bayonne, and Calais.*

1376 The **Good Parliament,** supported by the Black Prince and William of Wykeham, impeached Alice Perrers, a favourite of the King, and the Lords Latimer and Neville.
This is the first instance of an **impeachment** in our history.

NOTE.—In an impeachment the House of Commons, acting as the representatives of the nation and as accusers, bring to trial before the House of Lords, who act as judges, any servant of the Crown who seems to them to have done wrong.

Death of the Black Prince.

1377 **Death of the King**

Memorable Events

1332 The **Knights of the Shire** were for the first time recorded as deliberating apart from the lords and bishops, and in the next year as sitting with the citizens and burgesses. The knights had 4s. a day during sitting, the burgesses 2s.

1340 The power of levying tallage was finally abolished.

1341 The **Trial of Peers.** The King, having accused John Stratford, Archbishop of Canterbury, of wasting his money, ordered him to answer in the Court of Exchequer. The Lords demanded that no peer should be tried except by his Peers in Parliament, to which Edward consented.

1349 The **Black Death** ravaged England, *carrying off little less than one-half of the population.* In Norwich alone 60,000 people are said to have perished.

 The **First Statute of Labourers** was passed. It: (1) fixed the amount of wages to be paid to labourers; (2) forbade the giving of alms to sturdy beggars.

 NOTE.—" The Black Death made labour scarce, and held out a prospect of better wages, but this Statute offered the labourer wages that it was worse than slavery to accept."—(Stubbs).

1351 The **First Statute of Provisors,** *to check Papal influence in England* was passed. It enacted that all persons receiving papal provisions (i.e., grants of living) should be liable to punishment, and all preferments nominated by the Pope should be forfeited to the King.

1352 The **First Statute of Treason,** " *the chief enactment of the reign,*" was passed, defining it to be high treason: (1) to compass the death of the King or his eldest son; (2) to levy war against the King; (3) to aid the King's enemies; (4) to utter counterfeit coin; (5) to kill the chancellor, treasurer, or any of the judges while in the discharge of their duties. This Act was considered so great a boon that the Parliament which passed it was called the **Blessed Parliament.**

1362 An enactment was passed that no subsidy should be set on wool without the consent of Parliament.

 Purveyance was also forbidden, except for the personal wants of the King and Queen.

 NOTE 1.—Purveyance was the right claimed by the King on his travels, and transferred to any of his suite, of seizing horses, carriages, or food, and paying what he liked for them, or nothing.

 NOTE 2.—Hallam says that three essential principles of our Government were established on a firm footing in this reign: (*a*) the illegality of raising money without consent of Parliament; (*b*) the necessity that the two Houses should concur for any alterations of the law; (*c*) the right of the Commons to inquire into public abuses, and to impeach counsellors.

RICHARD II 1377–1399 (22 YEARS)

Title: Son of the Black Prince, eldest son of Edward III.

Married: (1) Anne of Bohemia; (2) Isabella of France. Richard II had no children.

A.D.

1381   The **Great Revolt of the Peasants** or " Commons " took place.

Immediate Cause: The imposition of a poll-tax of not less than 1*s.* and not more than £1 on every person above the age of 15.

NOTE.—The growing ideas of liberty and equality, fostered by the teaching of the Lollards, played a large part in producing this revolt. John Ball, " the mad priest of Kent," as the landowners called him, had for twenty years preached these doctrines.

(1) The revolt extended over the East and South-east counties from Winchester to Scarborough. In Essex, Jack Straw was chosen leader; and in Kent, **Wat Tyler.** The rebels, amounting to 100,000 men, marched upon London; they pillaged and destroyed manor-houses, burnt the court-rolls containing the villeins' names, so as to destroy every record of their bondage, and put to death lawyers, justices, and other officials.

(2) The King met the men of Essex at Mile End, and on granting their demands they dispersed.
These **demands** were: (1) *abolition of villeinage*; (2) *reduction of rent to fourpence an acre*; (3) *free access to all fairs and markets*; (4) *a general pardon.*

(3) Meanwhile, the Kentish men broke into the Tower and murdered Simon of Sudbury, the Primate and Chancellor. Richard met them at Smithfield, where Tyler was slain, but on receiving written charters of freedom from the King, the insurgents dispersed to their homes, and the rebellion was suppressed.
Results. Many hundreds of the rebels were put to death by Richard as he passed triumphantly with an army of 40,000 men through Kent and Essex, but the landowners did not from this time so rigidly enforce villein service, and so villeinage gradually died out.

1386   The **Council of Eleven** was appointed. The King, being ruled by favourites, was compelled to entrust the Government to a Council of Eleven, with his uncle, Thomas, Duke of Gloucester, at its head.

1388   The **Merciless** or **Wonderful Parliament** met, and the **Five Lords Appellant**, Gloucester, Arundel, Warwick, Nottingham, and Derby (the King's cousin) impeached the King's favourites De Vere, Michael de la Pole (Earl of Suffolk), and others, several of whom were executed. These nobles were called " appellant," *because they " appealed " some of the King's counsellors of high treason.*

NOTE.—This Parliament was called the " Wonderful Parliament " by its supporters and the " Merciless Parliament " by those who opposed it.

1389   **Richard's personal Government**

Richard, being now twenty-three years of age, dismissed his guardians, and assumed the sole authority. He ruled well for eight years.

1397   He now made himself an absolute monarch, and took vengeance on three of the Lords Appellant: Gloucester, who died in custody at Calais, Arundel, who was beheaded, and Warwick, imprisoned for life.

A.D.

A **quarrel arose** between **Norfolk** (formerly Nottingham), and **Hereford** (formerly Derby), the latter accusing the former of having uttered treasonable words.
Parliament agreed that the dispute should be settled by the arbitration of single combat. As the combatants were about to engage at Coventry *the King took the matter into his own hands, and banished Hereford for ten years, Norfolk for life.*

1398   The **Parliament of Shrewsbury** annulled the acts of the Merciless Parliament, and granted the King customs for life.

1399   Hereford landed at Ravenspur to claim his father's estates, which Richard had unjustly seized. He was supported by the Percies, the Duke of York, and the mass of the people.

     Parliament imprisoned Richard and **compelled him to resign his Crown,** on the ground of tyranny and misgovernment. Hereford, now Duke of Lancaster, was declared King.

     NOTE.—The usurpation of Henry IV is called the "Lancastrian Revolution."

Memorable Events

1388   Henry Percy was defeated by the Scots at **Otterburn,** in a battle called " Chevy Chase."

     The **Statute of Præmunire** (so called from the first word in the Act) was passed. Object: *To lessen the Papal authority in England.* It enacted that whoever procured at Rome or elsewhere any processes, bulls, or excommunications against the King, or the realm, should be outlawed, and their goods and lands forfeited.

THE HOUSE OF LANCASTER 1399–1461
(62 YEARS)

HENRY IV 1399–1413 (14 YEARS)

Title: Son of John of Gaunt, third son of Edward III.

Married: (1) Mary de Bohun; (2) Joan of Navarre.

Children: Henry V, John, Duke of Bedford, Humphrey, Duke of Gloucester.

1400   A **Rebellion of the Earls of Kent and Huntingdon** (half-brother of Richard II), **Rutland** and **Salisbury,** to restore Richard, was betrayed by Rutland, and soon suppressed. Kent, Huntingdon, and Salisbury, with many others, were executed. Richard mysteriously disappeared. A report was spread that he was dead, and his corpse was exhibited in London.

A.D.

1401   The **Persecution of the Lollards.** The Act " **De Heretico combu-rendo** " was passed at the instigation of Archbishop Arundel. This is the first time in our history we read of " heretics."

William Sawtre, at one time Rector of Lynn, who had gone to London to preach Lollard doctrines, was burnt by Royal command.

NOTE 1.—This was the first execution for Lollard heresy in England.

NOTE 2.—Henry, probably feeling the weakness of his claim to the Crown, was compelled to lean on the Parliament and the Church for support, and so he approved of the Lollard persecution.

1402   The **War with Scotland.** The Scots, under the Duke of Albany, invaded England. On returning home heavily laden with booty, they were totally routed at Homildon Hill by the Percies, and many Scottish nobles, including Earl Douglas, taken prisoner.

1403   The **Rebellions of the Percies,** Earl of Northumberland and his son Henry, surnamed " Hotspur," took place.

(1) **Causes:** (*a*) The King owed the Percies a debt of £20,000, due to them as Wardens of the Borders, and was unable to pay it. (*b*) He claimed the ransom on the prisoners taken in the late Scottish war. (*c*) He refused to ransom Sir Edmund Mortimer, Hotspur's brother-in-law, who was at that time a prisoner in the hands of Glendower, a Welsh chief.

(2) The **First Rebellion.** The Percies allied themselves with Owen Glendower, the Mortimers, and the Scottish Earl Douglas, to whom they granted his liberty.

NOTE.—Owen Glendower had been a squire in the Court of Richard II, and on the deposition of Richard, raised a rebellion in Wales. Henry made several attempts to subdue him without success.

(3) The **Battle of Shrewsbury.** Hotspur, *advancing towards Shrewsbury to effect a juncture with the Welsh troops,* was met by Henry near that town, and defeated and slain. Northumberland submitted and was pardoned with a fine.

1405   (4) The **Second Rebellion,** under Northumberland, Archbishop Scrope, and Thomas Mowbray, in favour of Edmund Mortimer, fifth Earl of March, the rightful heir to the English Crown, and at that time a prisoner in Henry's power.

The rebellion was suppressed, Mowbray and Scrope were captured and executed, while Northumberland fled to Scotland.

1408   (5) The **Third Rebellion.** Northumberland again took up arms, but was defeated at **Bramham Moor** (near Tadcaster) and slain.

1413   **Death of Henry**

     Memorable Events

1407   **Constitutional Points**

(1) The King conceded to the Commons *the exclusive right of originating grants of money.*

(2) Henry was compelled to name 16 counsellors, by whose advice he was to be guided.

1411
(3) Retainers were for a third time prohibited by Parliament. These retainers were the followers of the Barons, and wore their badge or livery. By their assistance the Barons could easily make war on each other or on the King.

HENRY V 1413–1422 (9 YEARS)

Title: Son of Henry IV.

Married Catherine of France.

Children: Henry VI.

1413
Persecution of the Lollards

Sir John Oldcastle (Lord Cobham), a leading Lollard, was arrested, condemned to death, and thrown into the Tower, but escaped into Wales.

Roused by the ill-treatment of their leader, the Lollards entered into a plot to seize the King. They met in St. Giles' Field, but were soon dispersed by the royal forces.

NOTE.—Lord Cobham was captured in 1417, hung in chains, and burnt.

1415
A **Conspiracy** in favour of **Edmund Mortimer**, fifth Earl of March, was discovered. The chief conspirators, Richard, Earl of Cambridge (who had married Ann Mortimer, the sister of the Earl of March), Lord Scrope, and Sir Thomas Grey, were executed.

The **Hundred Years' War** was resumed. The **Second Stage.**

Henry revived the claim made by Edward III to the French Crown, and invaded France with 30,000 men.

(1) The **circumstances** which rendered this war **favourable to the English** were: (a) The Church wished to divert the attention of the Parliament from the confiscation of Church Property, and urged on the war. (b) The Barons were restless and tired of peace. (c) The existence of two rival factions in France, the Houses of Orleans and Burgundy, disorganized the country, and offered advantages to an invader.

(2) The **First Campaign.** Harfleur surrendered after a terrible siege of five weeks, during which time the English army was reduced by privation and sickness to half its number. Henry retreated to Calais.

(3) The **Battle of Agincourt.** The French, numbering 50,000 men, under the Constable of France, were defeated with the loss of 10,000 men (of whom more than 100 were princes and nobles); 15,000 were taken prisoners, while the loss on the side of the English was only 1,600. The battle lasted only three hours.

NOTE.—The English won this great victory, like that of Crecy, owing to the skill of their bowmen, and the superior discipline and organization of their army. It showed clearly that small but well-trained bodies of infantry were infinitely superior to undisciplined masses of mail-clad cavalry.

A.D.

1417   (4) The **Second Campaign** and **Conquest of Normandy.**
Henry again invaded France, and took many towns in Normandy.

1419   (5) **Rouen,** after a gallant defence of six months, was starved into surrender.

(6) An **Alliance was made with Burgundy.** John, Duke of Burgundy, having gone to a conference with Charles, the Dauphin, was treacherously assassinated by some Orleanists in the Dauphin's presence, *and the Burgundians, under the Duke's son, Philip the Good, joined the English to avenge the Duke's death.*

This event brought about the Treaty of Troyes.

1420   (7) The **Treaty of Troyes,** called the " Perpetual Peace," stated:
(1) that Henry should marry Catherine, daughter of the French King, Charles VI; (2) that he should be Regent during Charles VI's life, and King after his death.

1421   Henry returned to England with his Queen Catherine.
The Duke of Clarence, Henry's brother, was defeated and slain at Beaugé by the French, who were assisted by Scotch auxiliaries. Henry again invaded France, and captured Dreux, *and all France north of the Loire* submitted.

1422   **Death of Henry at Vincennes**

Memorable Events

1415   **A Great Council,** " Magnum Concilium regis et regni," was summoned, and determined that the French war should begin. " *This is generally considered either as a sort of enlarged Privy Council, or as the House of Lords sitting out of Parliament.*"

HENRY VI 1422–1461 (39 YEARS)

Title: Son of Henry V.

Married Margaret of Anjou.

Children: Prince Edward.

1422   The **Hundred Years' War (Third Stage)** was continued under **Bedford,** as Protector of England and Regent of France.
Humphrey, Duke of Gloucester, his brother, was made Protector during Bedford's absence in France.

1423   (1) The **Alliance with Burgundy** was strengthened by the marriage of Bedford with Anne, sister of Philip the Good.

(2) The French were defeated at the **Battles of Crevant** and **Verneuil.** The former secured the communication between Burgundy and the English, the latter between Brittany and the English.

1428   (3) The **Siege of Orleans.** With a view to extending their conquests beyond the Loire, the English generals laid siege to Orleans, the key to the southern provinces of France.

A.D.

1429

The **Battle of Herrings.** This was the name given to an unsuccessful attack made by the French on a convoy under Sir John Fastolf, which was carrying provisions of herrings to the besieged.

(4) **Joan of Arc,** a peasant maid of Domremi, appeared on the scene with 6,000 men, raised the siege of Orleans, and compelled the English to retire. She thus fulfilled one part of her promise to Charles VII; the other was *that he should be crowned at Rheims.*

At **Pataye** she defeated and took prisoner **Talbot** (thought to be the greatest soldier of his time), and conquering all before her, conducted Charles successfully through the very heart of the enemy's country to Rheims, where he was crowned. Her mission being now accomplished, she wished to return home, but Charles denied her request.

NOTE.—The unparalleled success of the Maid of Orleans is attributed to: (1) the belief that her mission was divine, and the patriotic enthusiasm such a belief inspired in her countrymen and a corresponding superstitious terror in the English; (2) the guidance of experienced generals, such as Dunois and La Hire, who had taken the place of court favourites in the army; (3) her cause being a national one, not a party struggle.

1430

(5) At **Compiegne** Joan was captured by the Burgundians and sold to the English. Charles made no effort to save her.
She was burnt the following year for sorcery and witchcraft at Rouen.

Gradual loss of the whole of France, except Calais.

1435

(1) By the **Congress of Arras** the French offered to give up Normandy and Guienne, if the English King would renounce the claim to the Crown of France.
The terms were rejected by the English.

(2) The **Death of Bedford,** the **secession of Burgundy,** and the **frequent quarrels** at home between **Gloucester** (who represented the war party) and **Cardinal Beaufort** (the head of the peace party) weakened the English cause in France.

1445

(3) The **Marriage of the King.** William de la Pole, Duke of Suffolk, negotiated the marriage of the King with Margaret of Anjou. It was agreed that Anjou and Maine should be given up to René, Margaret's father.
This arrangement caused great dissatisfaction in England.

1453

(4) Defeat and death of Sir John Talbot at **Châtillon,** and **end of the Hundred Years' War.**

NOTE.—England had now nothing left but Calais.

Home Affairs

1447

(1) The **Death of Gloucester.** Having opposed Suffolk's policy in the matter of the King's marriage, Gloucester was arrested, charged with high treason, and shortly afterwards found dead in his bed. He had probably been murdered.

A.D.

1450 (2) The **Death of Suffolk.** Suffolk now became the King's chief minister. He was impeached *on the ground of having treated treacherously with France*, and banished for five years, but was overtaken by his enemies on his way to France, and beheaded in an open boat off Calais.

(3) **Cade's Rebellion.** The men of Kent, hearing that the King was preparing to take vengeance on them for having furnished ships to seize Suffolk, rose in arms. Jack Cade, assuming the name of Mortimer, and the title " Captain of Kent," marched towards London at the head of 20,000 rebels.

Their petitions were rejected, and after a victory over the Royal forces at Sevenoaks, the rebels then entered London, but were repulsed with great slaughter, and on receiving a promise of general pardon, dispersed. Cade was subsequently slain near Lewes by Iden, Sheriff of Kent.

NOTE 1.—No bloody retaliation followed this movement on the death of its leader.

NOTE 2.—The rebels demanded the return to favour of Richard Duke of York, and more careful expenditure of the Royal revenue. This rebellion is important as throwing some light on the condition of the " commons ": (a) Lollardism was so utterly extinguished that none of the demands of the rebels touched on religious reforms; (b) the question of villeinage and wages had so completely died out since the rebel rising in 1381, that it had no place in the complaints; (c) the Sumptuary Statutes (i.e., laws regulating apparel) which crowd the Statute Book show that the social condition of the labourer and farmer had greatly improved.

1454 (4) The King becoming an imbecile, York was made **Protector,** but was displaced the following year by John Beaufort, Duke of Somerset, a favourite of the Queen, and in consequence took up arms.

NOTE.—York was the heir presumptive to the throne after Gloucester's death, and this may possibly have caused his dislike of Somerset.

1455 The **Wars of the Roses** began. **Causes:** (1) The dissatisfaction arising from the feeble government of Henry VI, and the consequent loss of France. (2) The rivalry between Somerset and York, resulting in the dismissal of York from power. (3) The birth of Edward, Prince of Wales, thus depriving York of all chance of a peaceful succession to the throne.

NOTE.—The chief leader of the Yorkist party was Richard, Duke of York; of the Lancastrian party, John Beaufort, Duke of Somerset. The badge of the Yorkists was a white rose, that of the Lancastrians a red rose.

Battles

(1) **1st St. Albans;** Yorkists victorious. Somerset was slain, and the King taken prisoner.

1459 (2) **Bloreheath;** Yorkists victorious. Bills of Attainder were passed against the Duke of York and his friends by the Parliament.

1460 (3) **Northampton;** The Yorkists under the Earl of Warwick, the " King-maker," defeated the Lancastrians. The King was again taken prisoner; Margaret fled with her son to Scotland.

A.D.

Richard, Duke of York, now for the first time publicly claimed the throne, and the Lords agreed to a compromise: (*a*) that the King should hold the Crown for life; (*b*) that the Crown should then pass to the Duke of York and his heirs; (*c*) that he should be created Prince of Wales and ruler of the Kingdom.

Queen Margaret was highly indignant at this arrangement, *as it set aside her son from the succession.*

NOTE.—The Duke of York had undoubtedly more right to the throne than Henry VI, as being descended from Lionel, Duke of Clarence, second son of Edward III, while Henry was descended from John of Gaunt, the third son.

(4) **Wakefield;** Lancastrians victorious. The Duke of York was taken prisoner, crowned in mockery with " a wreath of grass," and beheaded. His son, the Earl of Rutland, shared the same fate.

1461 (5) **Mortimer's Cross;** Yorkists victorious. Edward, Earl of March, son of Duke of York, defeated the Lancastrians under Pembroke. Owen Tudor was taken prisoner and beheaded by Edward's orders.

(6) **2nd St. Albans;** Lancastrians victorious. Margaret, marching towards London, met the Earl of Warwick, and defeated him. The King again fell into her hands.

NOTE.—The devastation caused by Margaret's wild and disorderly troops roused the people of London, and they refused her admittance.

Meanwhile, the Earl of March, taking advantage of the ill-feeling towards the Queen, entered the capital in triumph, and was proclaimed as Edward IV.

Memorable Events

1425 The **Parliament of Bats**

During this reign the power of Parliament had much declined. It had become, in fact, a mere instrument in the hands of the King's ministers, and when these happened to disagree, the members took up the quarrel and attended Parliament armed. The Parliament of Bats was so called because the members, having been forbidden to carry arms, brought clubs and " bats " instead.

THE HOUSE OF YORK 1461–1485
(24 YEARS)

EDWARD IV 1461–1483 (22 YEARS)

Title: Descended from Lionel, second son of Edward III.

Married Elizabeth Woodville.

Children: Edward V, Richard, Duke of York, and Elizabeth.

1461 The **Wars of the Roses** continued:
(1) **Towton:** Edward defeated the Earl of Somerset, the leader of the Lancastrians in the bloodiest battle of the Wars.
Edward was now crowned King.

A.D.

1464   (2) **Hedgely Moor** and **Hexham**; Lancastrians defeated.

The **Marriage of Edward with Elizabeth Woodville.** This marriage and the consequent rise of the whole of the Woodville family to some of the highest positions in the kingdom gave great offence to Warwick, " the King-maker."

1469   **Clarence,** Edward's brother, married Isabella Neville, daughter of the Earl of Warwick, and joined his father-in-law in the disaffection.

An insurrection occurred in the North under Robin of Redesdale, probably inspired by Warwick.

The rebels defeated the royal forces, and the Queen's father and brother were captured and executed. *Edward was also imprisoned for a time, but subsequently released, and a reconciliation with Warwick was effected.*

Alienation of Warwick

1470   A fresh rebellion broke out in Lincolnshire, under the leadership of Sir Robert Wells, caused by the oppression of the royal tax-gatherers. Edward defeated the insurgents near **Empingham** (in Rutland), in a battle known as " Lose Coat Field."

Warwick and Clarence, *finding that the King had proofs of their treachery,* fled to France, where they were reconciled to Margaret, the late Queen, by Louis XI.

A **Treaty** was made by which: (1) Anne Neville, daughter of Warwick, was to marry the Prince of Wales, upon whom the Crown was settled; (2) failing him, it was to pass to Clarence.

NOTE.—This treaty put Clarence's claim in the background, and consequently displeased him.

Henry VI was re-crowned

Warwick, Clarence, and Queen Margaret landed at Dartmouth; Edward fled to Flanders, and Henry VI was restored to the throne.

Edward IV regained the throne

1471   Edward, assisted by the Duke of Burgundy his brother-in-law, landed at Ravenspur, was joined by Clarence, and advanced towards London.

At **Barnet** he defeated Warwick, where the latter was slain.

Margaret landed at Weymouth the same day as that on which the Battle of Barnet was fought. She advanced northwards, but was overtaken and defeated by Edward at **Tewkesbury.** *After the battle her son, Prince Edward, was stabbed in the King's presence by Clarence and Gloucester.*

Henry VI was secretly murdered in the Tower.

NOTE.—The rapid success of these revolutions is explained by the fact that the nation was weary of the struggle, and cared little who possessed the Crown.

The War with France

'1475   Edward made a league with the Duke of Burgundy against Louis XI, and revived the old claim to the French Crown.

The **Treaty of Pecquigny** was made between Edward and Louis: (1) that Louis should pay a yearly pension to Edward, the expenses of the war, and 50,000 crowns as a ransom for Margaret; (2) that the Dauphin should marry Edward's eldest daughter.

Clarence quarrelled with his **brother Gloucester,** and with the **King.**

(1) With **Gloucester.** Clarence had married Isabel Neville, the eldest daughter of the late Earl of Warwick, and on the death of his father-in-law he was anxious to possess the whole of his vast possessions. Gloucester, who had married Anne Neville, the younger daughter of Warwick, claimed his wife's portion, and the King favoured his claim. The result was a fierce quarrel arose between the two brothers.
Parliament caused an equitable division of the property to be made, but Clarence retired in anger from the Court.

(2) With the **King.** Being distrusted by Edward, Clarence was tried before the House of Lords, found guilty of treason, and drowned, it is said, in a butt of Malmsey wine (1478).

1483   Louis broke off the marriage contract made in the Treaty of Pecquigny, and Edward prepared for a new invasion of France, but died shortly afterwards.

Memorable Events

Edward IV was the first English King who extorted benevolences (i.e., forced loans) from his subjects.

EDWARD V (REIGNED TWO MONTHS)

Title: Son of Edward IV.

(1) A struggle of parties arose for the **guardianship of the King,** who was a minor, between:

(*a*) The **New Nobility,** led by the Queen and her party, including Lords Rivers and Hastings, and Grey, Earl of Dorset.

(*b*) The **Old Nobility,** represented by Richard, Duke of Gloucester, uncle of the young King, and the Duke of Buckingham.
At Stony Stratford Gloucester met the young King; Rivers and Grey, who were his escort, were arrested, and sent as prisoners to Pontefract Castle. The King was conducted to the Tower.
The Queen and her son Richard took refuge in the Sanctuary at Westminster.

(2) **Gloucester** gained the support of Hastings, and was made **Protector.** He then accused the Queen and Hastings of aiming at his life by sorcery; the latter was beheaded on Tower Green without trial.

The Queen was persuaded to give up her son Richard, who was placed in the palace of the Tower with his brother.

(3) Gloucester now gained the Crown.

Dr. Shaw, Richard's chaplain, appeared at St. Paul's Cross and Buckingham at Guildhall, and attempted to prove that Elizabeth Woodville was not Edward IV's lawful wife, *as he had been betrothed to Lady Eleanor Talbot before he married her, and that therefore the two young princes were illegitimate, and had no right to the Crown.*

A body of Lords and Commons, acting for the " Three Estates of the Realm," offered the Crown to Gloucester, which he accepted.

NOTE.—The young Earl of Warwick, son of Clarence, was set aside because his father had been attainted.

RICHARD III 1483–1485 (2 YEARS)

Title: Brother of Edward IV.

Married Anne Neville.   Richard III had no surviving children.

1483   (1) **Accession.**   Richard was crowned with great pomp.   He went on Royal progress, and was everywhere well received.

The young King Edward V and his brother, Richard Duke of York, mysteriously disappeared.   They were probably murdered in the Tower.

(2) The **Defection of Buckingham.**   Buckingham, Henry Tudor, Earl of Richmond, and Morton, Bishop of Ely formed a conspiracy against Richard.

NOTE.—Buckingham was a thoroughly selfish and unprincipled man, and probably wished to be the chief means of restoring the exiled House of Lancaster to the throne.

Buckingham raised the standard of rebellion in Wales, but owing to the swollen state of the rivers, known as " Buckingham's flood," he was prevented from joining the rebel leaders in the South.   His followers deserted him, and he was captured, and executed at Salisbury.

1484   (3) On the death of Richard's son, **John de la Pole,** Earl of Lincoln, was declared heir to the throne.

1485   (4) Death of the Queen.   Richard, *to strengthen his position, proposed a marriage with his niece, Elizabeth of York.*

(5) The **Invasion of Henry Richmond.**   Supported by France, Richmond set sail from Harfleur, and landed at Milford Haven.   The **Battle of Bosworth.**   Richmond engaged Richard at Bosworth. The desertion of Lord Stanley and his retainers during the battle turned the fortune of the day.   Richard fell, fighting bravely.   His Crown, which was found under a hawthorn bush, was placed on Richmond's head by Lord Stanley.

1484   **Miscellaneous Events**

Parliament passed a statute abolishing the illegal practice of exacting benevolences.

Remarks on the Wars of the Roses

(1) The Wars of the Roses were in the main a great contest for the Crown between the rival houses of York and Lancaster. But the real cause is to be found in the domestic policy of Edward III, who allowed the various members of his family to form marriage connections with his nobles.

(2) Besides being a struggle between two rival factions, the wars were in a broader sense the " *result of a general demand for reforms in the Government.*"

(3) They point to the fact that " *hereditary claim* " to the throne was stronger in men's minds than " *parliamentary election.*"

(4) The persons most engaged in them were the nobles and their retainers, the towns as a rule took but little part in them. *It is stated that no less than eighty nobles of royal blood fell in the struggle.*

(5) The main characteristics of these Wars were the ruthless executions, which took place after the battles, " shameless treason, and the utter want of nobleness and chivalry."

(6) From these Wars Feudalism received its death blow. The King's power now became supreme, since the nobles had so decreased in numbers that they were no longer able to offer him any opposition.

(7) Learning still flourished, and it is interesting to record that amidst these troublesome times Eton College was founded.

THE TUDOR LINE 1485–1603
(118 YEARS)

HENRY VII 1485–1509 (24 YEARS)

Title: Based on: (1) his descent from John of Gaunt, third son of Edward III; (2) his marriage with Elizabeth of York, daughter of Edward IV, thereby uniting the rival houses of York and Lancaster; (3) the right of conquest; (4) the sanction of Parliament.

Henry's chief aim was to put down all rivals, and secure the throne for himself and his descendants.

NOTE.—His descent from John of Gaunt was not worth much, seeing that the Beaufort line had been declared illegitimate, and consequently excluded from the succession.

Married Elizabeth of York.

Children: Arthur, Henry VIII, Margaret, and Mary.

A.D.

The Yorkist Rebellions

Causes: (1) Henry's partiality for the Lancastrians, and marked aversion towards the Yorkist party; (2) his delaying the coronation of Queen Elizabeth, whose title he would not recognize.

1486   (a) **Lord Lovel's.** This was a feeble rising under Lord Lovel and the Staffords, which was soon suppressed.

1487   (b) **Lambert Simnel's.** Simnel was the son of a joiner at Oxford. *He called himself the Earl of Warwick, son of the Duke of Clarence, and was therefore a possible rival of Henry.* To expose the imposture, Henry caused the real Earl of Warwick, then a prisoner in the Tower, to be led through the streets of London.

Simnel appeared in **Ireland,** and being supported by the Earl of Kildare, the Lord Deputy, was crowned in Dublin as Edward VI. Assisted by the Duchess of Burgundy, Simnel landed in Lancashire, but was defeated by the King's forces at **Stoke** (Nottinghamshire), where John de la Pole, Earl of Lincoln, who had joined his standard, was slain and the rebellion suppressed.

1492   (c) **Perkin Warbeck's.** Warbeck was the son of a citizen of Tournay. *He called himself Richard, Duke of York, son of Edward IV.*

(1) In **Ireland** and **France.** Warbeck first appeared in Ireland, and subsequently sought refuge with Charles VIII of France, who acknowledged him as the rightful heir to the English throne. By the Treaty of Etaples, *Warbeck was compelled to withdraw from France.*

1493   (2) In **Burgundy.** Margaret, Duchess of Burgundy received Warbeck as her nephew, and called him the " White Rose of England."

1494   **Sir William Stanley** (brother of Lord Stanley, who had won for Henry the Battle of Bosworth) and other nobles were arrested on a charge of complicity in the plot, and executed.

1496   The **Great Intercourse** (Magnus Intercursus) was agreed to between Henry and Philip, Duke of Burgundy, and while stipulating a reciprocal liberty of trading " in all commodities to each other's ports, without pass or license," *provided that Warbeck should not be received in Burgundy.*

(3) In **Scotland.** Warbeck was well received by James IV of Scotland, who gave him his own kinswoman, Lady Catherine Gordon, in marriage.

1497   (4) In **Cornwall.** Warbeck landed in Cornwall, then in an unsettled state owing to the heavy taxation. Failing to take Exeter, he lost courage, fled to Beaulieu Abbey, where he was captured, and finally executed with the Earl of Warwick (1499).

NOTE.—Warbeck was probably executed because Henry was at this time negotiating a marriage between his eldest son Prince Arthur and Catherine of Aragon, daughter of Ferdinand and Isabella of Spain, and Ferdinand insisted that all rivals to the throne should be removed.

Matrimonial Alliances, made by Henry to secure peace with foreign countries, and strengthen his position as King of England.

A.D.

1501   (*a*) **Prince Arthur** married Catherine of Aragon, but died the next year. Both Henry and Ferdinand were unwilling to break off the alliance, and so a dispensation was obtained from Pope Julius II, by which Catherine was espoused to Prince Henry, then only eleven years old.

1502   (*b*) **Princess Margaret** married James IV of Scotland, and *thus became the maternal ancestor of the Stuart line.*

1509   **Death of Henry**

Memorable Events

1487   (1) The Court subsequently known as the **Court of Star Chamber** was established by Henry. (*a*) It consisted of the Lord Chancellor, the Treasurer, the Keeper of the Privy Seal, one bishop, one temporal peer, and the chief judges. (*b*) It dispensed with juries, and punished offenders by fines, imprisonment, and mutilation, but had not the power of life and death. (*c*) Its main object was to bring to trial and punish all nobles who broke the laws against Maintenance. (*d*) It also took cognizance of riots, unlawful assemblies, conspiracy, perjury, fraud, and libel. (*e*) Though perhaps necessary at the time for the maintenance of order, under future kings its power became most tyrannical, and it tried and punished men who offended the King or his ministers by writing or by word.

NOTE 1.—Maintenance was a system by which the nobles retained their liveried attendants, who were bound by oath to fight in their quarrels.

NOTE 2.—The Court of Star Chamber punished " without the intervention of a jury," because in those times " juries were afraid to convict."

NOTE 3.—For breaking this law the Earl of Oxford was on one occasion fined £10,000.

1491   (2) **War with France.** Charles VIII had annexed Brittany to France by compelling Anne, Duchess of Brittany, to marry him. Henry sided with the Duchess, and, having levied a benevolence and obtained a subsidy from Parliament, invested Boulogne.

By the **Treaty of Etaples**, Henry agreed to withdraw his forces on promise of a payment of £149,000, *thus " making profit upon his subjects for the war, and upon his enemies for the peace."*

1495   (3) **Poyning's Law,** or Statute of Drogheda, passed by Sir Edward Poyning, who was acting as deputy for Prince Henry in Ireland. It stated *that no Irish Parliament should be held, and no law brought forward without the consent of the English Parliament.*

NOTE.—This Act tended in a great measure to settle the disturbed state of Ireland, and bring the country more directly under the King's power than it had been before.

(4) Henry's means of **raising money:** (*a*) by subsidies, i.e., sums of money granted by Parliament, and levied on all men's property; (*b*) by benevolences, or forced loans; (*c*) by fines inflicted by the Star Chamber.

NOTE.—In extorting money from his subjects Henry was assisted by Archbishop Morton, the Chancellor, and by Empson and Dudley, the former the Speaker of the House of Commons, the latter a famous lawyer. He is said to have amassed the sum of £1,800,000.

(5) The **Law of Entail** was abolished in this reign, i.e., *the fixing of an estate to some particular line of heirs, none of whom had the power either to sell or bequeath it.* Henry's object in allowing the barons to sell their estates, regardless of the entail, was to lessen their power.

(6) **Feudalism** had now come to its **last days,** and the spirit of industry and commercial enterprise was occupying men's minds.

(7) This was the age of great **geographical discoveries.**

(a) In 1492 Columbus, a native of Genoa, was sent out by Spain and discovered the Bahamas.

(b) In 1497 John Cabot, together with his son Sebastian, was sent out by Henry VII and discovered Labrador.

(c) In 1498 Vasco da Gama, a Portuguese, rounded the Cape of Good Hope and discovered the sea-route to India.

(d) In 1499 Americus Vespuccius, a native of Florence, explored the coast of South America and gave his name to the New World.

HENRY VIII 1509–1547 (38 YEARS)

Title: Son of Henry VII.

Married: (1) Catherine of Aragon (*divorced*); (2) Anne Boleyn (*beheaded*); (3) Jane Seymour (*died*); (4) Anne of Cleves (*divorced*); (5) Catherine Howard (*beheaded*); (6) Catherine Parr (*outlived him*).

Children: By Catherine of Aragon, Mary; by Anne Boleyn, Elizabeth; by Jane Seymour, Edward VI.

1510   **Accession.** Uniting in his person the claims of the rival Houses of York and Lancaster, Henry came to the throne without opposition. To gain popularity, **Empson** and **Dudley** were executed on a frivolous charge of treason.

The **War** of the **Holy League**

1511   Henry joined Spain and Germany in the Holy League *to protect the Pope's dominions against France.*

The **First Campaign.** An English expedition was sent to co-operate with Ferdinand of Spain in the conquest of Navarre in the South of France. Ferdinand did not send the assistance he had promised, and the English army, becoming disorganized from inactivity and sickness, returned to England.

The **Second Campaign.** Henry attacked France in person. He defeated the French at **Guinegate** (called the Battle of the Spurs, 1513), and took the towns of Terouenne and Tournay.

1513   **The Scots,** in pursuance of their old policy, formed an alliance with France, and taking advantage of the French War, invaded England, but were defeated with terrible slaughter at **Flodden Field** by Thomas Howard, Earl of Surrey. James IV, the flower of his nobility, and 10,000 Scots lay dead on the field.

A.D.

1514 **Peace** was made with **Scotland** and **France.** Mary, Henry VIII's youngest sister, married Louis XII of France, who, however, died three months afterwards, and Mary then married Charles Brandon, Duke of Suffolk.

The **Rise** and **Administration of Wolsey** (1515–1530).

1515 **Wolsey** was made Archbishop of York and Lord Chancellor, and in the following year became Papal Legate. *He was thus the most powerful man in the kingdom, both in Church and State*; in fact, it was said, " that no subject had ever been so powerful."

1520 (1) The **Field of the Cloth of Gold.** Francis I of France, and Charles V of Spain, lately chosen Emperor of Germany, were both anxious to secure the alliance of Henry. A meeting took place between Henry and Francis, on the Field of the Cloth of Gold (so called from its magnificence), but with no definite result. Shortly afterwards Henry met and formed an alliance with Charles at Gravelines.

1521 (2) Pope Leo X conferred the title of **Defender of the Faith** on Henry for having written a work defending the Seven Sacraments against the German reformer, Luther.

1527 (3) The **Divorce Question.** Henry, having no male heir by Queen Catherine, wished to divorce her, and marry Anne Boleyn to legitimize the child she was bearing. The Pope, Clement VII, who alone could grant a dispensation, was at this time a prisoner in the hands of Charles V, Catherine's nephew.

1529 The Pope, afraid of offending Charles V, ordered the court, which was being held in London under Cardinals Wolsey and Campeggio to try the divorce, to be transferred to Rome.

(4) The **Fall of Wolsey.** Wolsey's neutral conduct in the matter of the divorce greatly displeased the King, and his disgrace at Court followed. He was indicted under the Act of Præmunire *charging him with having received papal bulls*, and having resigned the Great Seal, finally retired to his see at York.

Sir Thomas More was made Lord Chancellor.

1530 Wolsey was arrested for high treason, but died at Leicester Abbey on his way to the Tower.

The **Administration of Thomas Cromwell** (1530–1540).

The **First stage of the Reformation** in England was brought about mainly by the Pope's refusal to grant a divorce to Henry, and thereby caused a separation from Rome. *It was a political rather than a religious movement, a change of doctrine being at first scarcely thought of.*

1533 (1) All **appeals to Rome** were forbidden by Parliament. Cranmer became Archbishop of Canterbury.

1534 (2) The **Payment of Annates** (i.e., the first year's income of a benefice to the Pope) was forbidden.

(3) The **authority of the Pope** in England was abolished by Act of Parliament.

A.D.

(4) The **Act of Succession** was passed, declaring the King's marriage with Catherine absolutely invalid, and his marriage with Anne Boleyn " true, sincere, and perfect."

1535 (5) The **Act of Supremacy** was passed, declaring Henry to be the only **Supreme Head of the Church of England.**

Fisher, Bishop of Rochester, and Sir Thomas More were imprisoned for refusing to swear to the Act of Succession, and subsequently executed *for denying the King's supremacy.*

1536 (6) The **Suppression of the smaller Monasteries.** A Commission had been appointed to visit the lesser monasteries. Their report, alleging much wickedness and immorality, was made the pretext for their dissolution.

Cromwell, having complete control of the Church under the title of **Vicar-General,** carried out the suppression of the smaller monasteries, the incomes of which were less than £200. Their revenues were transferred to the Crown, and the monks were either pensioned off or taken into the larger monasteries.

The **Pilgrimage of Grace.** The suppression of the smaller monasteries was followed by several insurrections in the North and West. The most formidable of these was in Yorkshire, and was led by a young lawyer named **Robert Aske.** It was called by the rebels the " *Pilgrimage of Grace.*"

The rebels demanded: (1) the restoration of the Old Religion; (2) the removal of Cromwell from office. On receiving the promise of a general pardon from the Duke of Norfolk, they dispersed. A fresh insurrection which was set on foot in Cumberland and Westmorland was made the pretext for taking vengeance on the rebels, and the leaders, Aske, Darcy, and Constable, were arrested, condemned, and executed.

The **Council of the North,** on the model of the Star Chamber, was instituted to keep order.

(7) A copy of the **English Bible** was ordered to be placed in every Church.

NOTE.—The Parliament which carried out these important changes is called the Seven Years' Parliament (1529–1536).

1539 (8) The **Suppression of the larger Monasteries.** Most of the property belonging to the larger monasteries passed into the hands of the King. Six new Bishoprics were founded.

NOTE.—The total number of religious houses thus destroyed is estimated at upwards of 3,000.

(9) Although Henry had severed England from Rome, he had no intention of forsaking the doctrines and practices of the Roman Catholic Church. Accordingly, he caused the Statute called the Six Articles (sometimes known as the " Bloody Statute " or the " Whip with Six Strings ") to be passed. It declared to be necessary: (1) the doctrine of Transubstantiation; (2) Communion in one kind only; (3) celibacy of the clergy; (4) vows of chastity; (5) private masses; (6) auricular confession.

NOTE 1.—Under this Act no less than 500 persons were thrown into prison in a fortnight, but only twenty-eight actually suffered death.

A.D.

NOTE 2.—Henry put to death Roman Catholics for denying the Act of Supremacy, and Protestants for refusing to believe in the Roman Catholic doctrine of Transubstantiation.

1540 **Cromwell's Fall.** After the death of Jane Seymour, Henry, on the advice of Cromwell, married Anne of Cleves, a Protestant princess, with a view to strengthening the Protestant cause in England by an alliance with Germany.

Disappointed in her appearance and manners, Henry persuaded Parliament to abrogate the marriage. Cromwell's disgrace followed, *and he was condemned for treason by a Bill of Attainder without being allowed to speak in his own defence*, and was executed on Tower Hill.

A Reaction in favour of the Old Religion set in. Henry's marriage with Catherine Howard, niece of the Duke of Norfolk, was followed by a reaction in favour of the Old Religion, and the triumph of the party opposed to Cromwell.

NOTE.—Catherine Howard was executed on a charge of immorality, and the King married Catherine Parr.

The **Second War** with **Scotland** and **France**

1542 (1) With **Scotland**. The **Cause** of this war was the frequent depredations made by the Scots on the English Borders. At **Solway Moss** they were defeated with great loss, and James V was so affected by the disaster that he died, leaving his Crown to his infant daughter, Mary, Queen of Scots.

1543 A treaty was concluded with Scotland, *by which Prince Edward was to marry Mary, Queen of Scots.*

1544 (2) With **France**. Henry invaded France because that country was in secret alliance with Scotland, and captured Boulogne.

1546 The **Peace of Boulogne** was concluded, by which the French were to pay two million crowns within eight years, and Boulogne was to be held by the English as a security for the payment of this sum.

The **Rule of Earl of Hertford** and the **rise of the Protestant Party.** Influenced by the Earl of Hertford, Prince Edward's uncle, Henry apprehended **Thomas, Duke of Norfolk,** and his son **Henry, Earl of Surrey,** on a charge of treason.

The Duke of Norfolk was suspected of wishing to seize the Regency while the young King was under age, and Surrey had made a change in his coat-of-arms, which implied a close connection with Royalty.

Surrey was executed, but Norfolk was only saved by the **death of the King.**

Important Acts of Parliament

1539 The King's proclamations were declared by Parliament to be as valid as Acts of Parliament.

1544 An Act was passed releasing the King from his debts.

NOTE.—These Acts show the subserviency of Parliament to the King's will.

EDWARD VI 1547–1553 (6 YEARS)

Title: Son of Henry VIII.

The **Protectorship of Hertford,** now **Duke of Somerset** (1547–1549).

1547 **Somerset,** the King's maternal uncle, was made Protector. He was assisted by a council of 16.

(*a*) The **War with Scotland,** *to enforce the Marriage Treaty made in 1543.* The Scots were defeated at **Pinkie,** and Mary was subsequently sent to France, where she was contracted in marriage to the Dauphin, afterwards Francis II.

(*b*) The **Second Stage of the Reformation** *brought about several Protestant reforms*, which were vigorously carried out by Somerset and Archbishop Cranmer.

(1) The **Statutes of Henry IV (1401)** against the Lollards and the **Six Articles** were repealed. Images of saints, and paintings were ordered to be removed from churches. A Book of Homilies (a kind of authorized sermons) was appointed to be read by the clergy to their congregations.

1549 (2) The **First Act of Uniformity** was passed: (*a*) forbidding the use of the Roman Catholic Mass; (*b*) enforcing the use of the **First Prayer Book of Edward VI.** Gardiner and Bonner protested against these innovations and were imprisoned.

NOTE.—In 1552 a second Act of Uniformity and a second Prayer Book were issued.

(3) Perfect liberty was granted for the use of the English Bible.

(*c*) **Troubles and Insurrections followed these changes.**

(1) The **Execution of Lord Seymour.** Taking advantage of the popular discontent, Lord Seymour plotted against his brother, the Protector, with a view to thrust him from the Regency. He was arrested, condemned for treason, and executed.

(2) The Rebellion under **Kett in Norfolk,** was the most formidable of these rebellions. *Strictly speaking, it was a social rebellion*, caused by the distress which followed on the destruction of the monasteries and the enclosure of common land. 16,000 men, well trained and disciplined, assembled under the leadership of Kett, a tanner, who, assisted by the Mayor of Norwich, administered justice under the " Oak of the Reformation " near Norwich. The rebellion was suppressed by the Earl of Warwick, and its leaders hanged.

(3) In **Devonshire** and **Cornwall** the rebellion was caused by the people's dislike of the Protestant reforms, especially the disuse of the Roman Catholic Mass and the substitution of the English Liturgy. *It was a religious movement*, and was suppressed by Lord Russell.

The **Fall of Somerset.** Somerset, becoming very unpopular with all parties, was forced to resign his Protectorship. The **Causes** of his unpopularity were: (1) his unsuccessful war with Scot-

A.D.

land; (2) his overbearing conduct; (3) the execution of his brother, Admiral Seymour, on a charge of treason; (4) the violent and sudden changes he had made in the religious services; (5) the destruction of several religious houses in the Strand for the erection of a grand palace called Somerset House; (6) a supposed sympathy with the people in the matter of the " enclosure of common lands."

1552 The **Protectorship of Warwick,** now Duke of Northumberland. Somerset was allowed to retain his seat in the Council and, gathering his old friends around him, plotted to regain his authority.

Northumberland, fearing his influence, caused him to be arrested at the council board. He was tried, condemned for treason, and executed.

1553 Edward, now 16 years of age, fell dangerously ill.

Northumberland's plan to change the line of succession. Under the pretext of upholding the Protestant Religion, Northumberland persuaded the King to sign a declaration naming **Lady Jane Grey** as his successor to the exclusion of his sisters Mary and Elizabeth. Meanwhile, for his own advancement he married his son, Lord Guildford, to Lady Jane Grey.

Death of the King

Memorable Events

1547 The **Vagrant Act** enacted " that any determinately idle and able-bodied vagrant might be adjudged by two magistrates to anyone wanting him as a slave, branded with a letter V, and kept in slavery for two years."

This was a most oppressive Act, because at the time " *there was neither work to be done, nor money to be had.*"

MARY 1553–1558 (5 YEARS)

Title: Elder daughter of Henry VIII.

Married Philip II of Spain. Mary had no children.

1553 The **Settlement of the Succession.** Lady Jane Grey was proclaimed Queen, but as the people generally were not disposed to sanction the change of the succession, they recognized Mary as the lawful Sovereign.

Mary withdrew to Norfolk. Northumberland was anxious to capture Mary, but his army deserted him. He retreated to Cambridge, where he was compelled to acknowledge Mary as Queen, on her being proclaimed in that city. Mary advanced towards London and was received with joy by the Londoners and proclaimed Queen. Northumberland, Lady Jane Grey, and her husband were committed to the Tower, and Northumberland was executed.

A.D.

The **Roman Catholic Religion was restored.**

(1) The Duke of Norfolk, Bishops Bonner and Gardiner were all released from the Tower, and the Protestant Bishops Cranmer and Latimer and others imprisoned. Bonner was made Bishop of London, and Gardiner Lord Chancellor.

(2) All the Statutes relating to religious matters passed in Edward VI's reign were annulled.

(3) Married priests were driven from their livings, the new Prayer Book was forbidden, and the Mass restored.

(4) In the following year **Cardinal Pole** came to England as Papal Legate, and on St. Andrew's Day, November 30, granted absolution " *for the sin of heresy and schism* " to the King and Queen and both Houses of Parliament, assembled at Whitehall.
All the Statutes passed against the Pope since the 20th year of Henry VIII's reign were repealed.

NOTE.—The Queen was much influenced in carrying out these measures by Simon Renard, the Spanish Ambassador.

Mary's Marriage with Philip II of Spain

1554   Mary's great object was *to restore the Pope's authority in England*, and as a step towards the attainment of this object, she was advised by Renard to marry her cousin Philip II of Spain. Negotiations at once opened for the marriage.

Wyatt's Rebellion. The **Cause** of this rebellion was: *The unpopularity of the Queen's projected marriage.* People thought that the Spanish King would claim too much power in England, or even conquer the realm, and introduce the cruel Inquisition.

(1) The *men of Kent* rose in rebellion under Sir Thomas Wyatt and seized the cannon and ships in the Thames, and having been joined by the train-bands of London, who had deserted the Duke of Norfolk, marched on London.

(2) **Mary's courage saved the day.** At Guildhall she boldly appealed to the loyalty of the citizens and promised not to marry without the consent of Parliament. 25,000 men were at once enrolled under her standard, and London Bridge was secured.

(3) Wyatt crossed the Thames at Kingston and entered London on the North. With only a handful of followers he pushed madly on to Temple Bar, where he was taken prisoner and sent to the Tower.

Results: (1) Sir Thomas Wyatt, Lady Jane Grey, her husband, father, and uncle were executed, and more than 100 commoners hanged. (2) The Princess Elizabeth was sent to the Tower.

Marriage of the Queen with Philip II of Spain took place. *Parliament would not allow Philip to be crowned King.*

The **Marian Persecution began.** Its object was *to enforce conformity to the Roman Catholic Religion.*

A.D.

1555 The **Persecuting Statutes** of Henry IV and Henry V against heretics were revived, so as to give a legal appearance to the persecution.

A Commission, with Bishop Gardiner at its head, was opened at St. Mary Overy's, Southwark, for the trial of heretics, *and the tests proposed were the doctrine of Transubstantiation and the Pope's supremacy.*

Rogers, Prebendary of St. Paul's, the first victim, was burnt at Smithfield; **Hooper,** Bishop of Gloucester, was burnt in his own cathedral city; **Rowland Taylor,** Vicar of Hadleigh, suffered on the same day as Hooper; **Ridley** and **Latimer** were burnt at the same stake at Oxford.

1556 **Cranmer** was burnt at Oxford. Having been degraded from office, Cranmer signed a recantation under a promise that his life should be spared, but his enemies had determined that he should die. He afterwards publicly withdrew his recantation in St. Mary's, Oxford, and while at the stake held "the unworthy hand," which had signed it, in the flames so that it should be first burnt.

NOTE.—It is estimated that upwards of 280 persons were brought to the stake, besides those who were punished by imprisonment, fines, and confiscation.

The War with France

1557 Philip visited England a second time, and persuaded Mary to declare war against France.

The **Battle of St. Quentin.** In this battle the French suffered a disastrous defeat from the united English and Spanish forces.

1558 **Loss of Calais.** Calais, "the key to France," and "the brightest jewel in the English Crown," was attacked by sea and land, and taken from the English by the Duke of Guise. It had been in our possession for 210 years, and after its loss *the English no longer held a foot of land on the Continent.*

Death of Mary

ELIZABETH I 1558–1603 (45 YEARS)

Title: Younger daughter of Henry VIII. Elizabeth was never married.

1558 **Accession.** Elizabeth ascended the throne amidst the joy of all parties.

Elizabeth retained Mary's council, but added to it **Sir William Cecil** (afterwards Lord Burleigh), who became her chief adviser. **Sir Francis Walsingham** was appointed her private secretary, **and Sir Nicolas Bacon,** Lord Keeper of the Great Seal.

1559 The **Third Stage of the Reformation** and *gradual establishment of the Church of England.*

The Protestant Religion was restored. Parliament passed the following important Acts:

(1) The **Second Act of Supremacy,** declaring: (*a*) that no foreign Potentate should exercise any power or authority in England; (*b*) that the Sovereign is the supreme head of the Church.
Only two Bishops took the Oath of Supremacy; the rest were deprived of their sees. Parker was made Archbishop of Canterbury.

(2) The **Second Act of Uniformity,** enacting: (1) that the Second Prayer Book of Edward VI should be used in the Church of England; (2) that all persons inhabiting the realm should attend the Church of England, under a fine of 1*s.* Those Roman Catholics who refused were called " Recusants."

NOTE.—In 1563 the Thirty-nine Articles of Religion were ratified.

NOTE 2.—In religious matters Elizabeth desired " that there should be outward conformity to the Established religion, but that opinion should be left free."

The Rivalry between Elizabeth and Mary Queen of Scots, and the Roman Catholic Plots against Elizabeth

1561

(1) Mary Queen of Scots returned to Scotland, and in 1565 married her cousin, Lord Darnley. Rizzio was Mary's private secretary, and Darnley being jealous of his intimacy with the Queen, formed a plot against the favourite and caused him to be assassinated.

1567

Darnley was mysteriously murdered at Kirk-o-field, and Mary then married Bothwell, whereupon the nobles, believing that Darnley had been murdered by Bothwell and that the Queen herself was an accomplice, raised a rebellion under the Earl of Murray.

Mary was defeated at **Carberry Hill,** imprisoned in Loch Leven Castle, and compelled to abdicate in favour of her son, James VI. Murray was appointed Regent of Scotland.

1568

She escaped and again took the field, but was defeated at **Langside,** and, taking refuge in England, was detained a prisoner by Elizabeth.

(2) The **Roman Catholic Plots against Elizabeth.** The chief **Causes** of these plots were: (1) Mary was considered by some to be the rightful heir to the English throne, and nearly everyone regarded her as the rightful successor to Elizabeth. (2) In 1570 Pope Pius V excommunicated Elizabeth, declaring her to be no longer Queen of England, *and released all her English subjects from their allegiance to her.*

Mary wished Elizabeth to name her as her successor, but she refused, saying " she did not wish to hang a winding-sheet before her eyes."

NOTE.—These plots were fomented by Jesuits from the Continent; the most noted was Edward Campion, who was executed in 1581.

A.D.

1569   An insurrection was set on foot in the North under the Earls of Northumberland and Westmorland *in favour of the Old Religion and of the release of Mary*, but was suppressed with great cruelty.

1572   (*a*) **Ridolfi's Plot.** The conspirators arranged that: (1) the Duke of Norfolk, the head of the Roman Catholic party in England should marry Mary; (2) there should be a general rising of the Roman Catholics; (3) with the aid of a Spanish army Elizabeth was to be dethroned. The plot was discovered by Cecil.

Results: (1) Norfolk was tried and executed. (2) The plot proved beyond a doubt that Philip of Spain was Elizabeth's greatest enemy.

(*b*) **Throgmorton's Plot.** This was a plot to murder Elizabeth and place Mary on the throne. Thomas Throgmorton was arrested and executed. It was clear from his papers that the Spanish Ambassador Mendoza was implicated in it, and he was ordered to leave England.

1584   An **Association** was formed by the chief nobles in England, with the sanction of Parliament, " *to pursue to the death anyone plotting against the Queen, as well as any person in whose behalf they plotted.*" Protestants and Catholics alike joined it, *and even Mary signed it.*

1586   (*c*) **Babington's conspiracy.** Anthony Babington formed a plot to kill Elizabeth, liberate Mary with the assistance of Spain, and place her on the throne. To this plot Mary gave her consent, but the whole affair was discovered by Walsingham, and Mary was made a strict prisoner at Fotheringay Castle. Babington and others were executed.

Mary's trial and death. A Commission of peers and lawyers was appointed to try Mary for complicity in Babington's plot; she was found guilty and executed (1587).

NOTE.—To the great bulk of the nation Mary's execution appeared a necessity.

1585   **Spain and the Invincible Armada**

The people of the Netherlands had revolted against the Spaniards in consequence of the cruel persecutions of the Duke of Alva. They offered the Crown to Elizabeth, who, however, declined it, but assisted them with money and troops, under the command of the Earl of Leicester. Owing to the incompetence of the general and ill-support received from England, the expedition failed.

At the **Battle of Zutphen** Sir Philip Sidney was killed (1586).

1588   **The Invincible Armada**

(*a*) The **Causes:** (1) the assistance Elizabeth had sent to the Protestants in the Spanish Netherlands; (2) the plundering of the gold ships of Spain by Drake in his voyage round the world; (3) the devastation done to Spanish ships by the English privateers called " Sea Dogs "; (4) while the Armada was preparing, Drake had sailed into the harbour of Cadiz and destroyed forty Spanish ships;

(5) Philip wished to crush England, as she was considered the leading Protestant Power in Europe; (6) Philip wished to avenge the death of Mary Queen of Scots.

(b) The Armada consisted of a fleet of 129 immense ships manned by 8,000 seamen, and having on board upwards of 20,000 soldiers, under the command of Medina Sidonia.

(c) The **Plan of Invasion** was that the Armada should sail to Dunkirk, so as to protect the Duke of Parma's army of 30,000 in its passage across into England.

(d) The English fleet consisted of eighty comparatively small ships, manned by 9,000 seamen, under the command of Lord Howard, assisted by Frobisher, Drake, and Hawkins.

(e) **Defeat of the Armada.** The Armada sailed up the Channel, pursued by the English fleet, and anchored off Calais. Here the English sent fire-ships among the Spanish fleet, and the panic-stricken Spaniards slipped their cables and drifted out to sea.

A fierce battle ensued off **Gravelines,** ship after ship was riddled with English shot, and sunk or run aground. Meanwhile a strong gale was blowing from the south, rendering a return to Spain by way of the English Channel impossible, and so the Spaniards attempted to reach Spain by sailing round the North of Scotland. Many of the ships, however, were wrecked in their passage, and only fifty-three returned to Corunna.

Results: (1) It showed England's superiority as a naval power. (2) It completely crushed the maritime power of Spain, and enabled England to become a great trading and colonizing country. (3) The Roman Catholic party no longer plotted against Elizabeth. (4) It led to a continual warfare for some years between the two countries, generally to the advantage of England.

Irish Affairs

The **Desmonds of Munster,** assisted by a Spanish force, rose in rebellion, but were suppressed in 1580.

1599 **Hugh O'Neill,** Earl of Tyrone, with the help of Spain, rose against the English Government. **Sir Henry Bagenal** was sent against him, but was defeated near the **Blackwater.**

Essex with 20,000 men was sent to Ireland. He failed to put down the rebellion, and returned to England in disgrace, and having raised an insurrection in London against the Queen, was found guilty of treason and executed.

Finally, **Lord Mountjoy** subjugated the Island, and received the submission of O'Neill (1603).

1603 **Death of the Queen**

Memorable Events

1572 The **Massacre of the Huguenots** (as the Protestants in France were called) on St. Bartholomew's Day. No less than 20,000 were murdered.

1583   The **High Commission Court** was established. It consisted of forty-four members, twelve of whom were bishops, and was invested with almost unlimited authority on questions relating to Church government and discipline.

1601   The Parliament demanded the abolition of monopolies, to which the Queen consented.

The **First Regular Poor Law** was passed. It enacted that the Justices of the Peace should appoint overseers of the poor in each parish, with powers to raise money by taxation for the housing and feeding of the indigent and deserving poor. This system continued to be the basis of the Poor Law till 1834.

The **Puritans** first came into notice in this reign. They were the "Advanced Protestants" of the Established Church. *They held that the Reformation had not gone far enough from the Church of Rome, and from a desire to establish "a purer form of worship" they gained the name of "Puritans."* They objected to the government of the Church by bishops, set forms of prayer, kneeling at the Communion, and other observances. Many were fined and imprisoned in Elizabeth's reign for refusing to obey the Act of Uniformity.

The **Parliament** under the **Tudors.**

(1) The Parliament under the Tudors had less power than the King and his ministers had, and generally followed the monarch's wishes.

(2) The great changes which took place in England during the Tudor period rendered it necessary that there should be one head only: (*a*) Henry VII had destroyed the power of the Feudal nobles; (*b*) Henry VIII had separated England from the papal authority; (*c*) under Edward VI's rule the Reformation had been vigorously carried on; (*d*) Elizabeth had endeavoured to bring about uniformity in religion, and had strengthened the nation so as to withstand the power of Spain.

The **Attempts made at Colonization**

1583   **Sir Humphrey Gilbert,** "the pioneer of English Colonization," attempted to establish a colony on the shores of Newfoundland.

1584   **Sir Walter Raleigh,** Sir Humphrey's half-brother, established a colony in North America and called it "Virginia," but it failed.

1595   Raleigh sailed to Guiana in the hope of discovering a valuable gold mine, but the expedition was unsuccessful.

1600   The First Charter was granted to the **East India Company.**

THE STUART LINE 1603–1714
(111 YEARS)

JAMES I 1603–1625 (22 YEARS)

Title: Great-grandson of Margaret, daughter of Henry VII.

Married Anne of Denmark.

Children: Prince Henry, Charles I and Elizabeth.

Religious Affairs

1603   The **Millenary Petition** was presented to the King by the Puritans:
(1) demanding the abolition of certain ceremonies in the Church;
(2) objecting to pluralities, non-residence, and unpreaching ministers.

1604   The **Hampton Court Conference** took place. It was in reality the outcome of the Millenary Petition, and its **Object** was *to settle the disputes between the Episcopalians and the Puritans.* Four representatives of the Puritan party met the Bishops at Hampton Court, but very little was done to satisfy their objections, James declaring " *that he would make the Puritans conform or harry them out of the land.*"

Results: (1) Some slight changes, however, were made in the Book of Common Prayer. (2) A new translation of the Bible into English was made. This is called the " Authorized Version."

NOTE.—There were three strongly marked religious parties in England at this time: (1) the Episcopalians, who wished matters in the Church to remain as Elizabeth had left them; (2) the Puritans (see under Elizabeth); (3) the Roman Catholics, who wished to restore the Mass and the Pope's power in England.

The **Conspiracies against James**

1603   (1) The **Main** or **Cobham's Plot.** This was a plot *to dethrone James and place Arabella Stuart on the throne.*

(2) The **Surprise** or **Bye Plot,** was a *plot to seize the King and obtain from him toleration for Roman Catholics.* **Cobham** and **Grey** were imprisoned. **Raleigh,** who was also supposed to be implicated, was sent to the Tower, where he remained 13 years.

1605   (3) The **Gunpowder Plot.** The Roman Catholics, failing to obtain religious toleration from James, formed a plot under Robert Catesby, Wright, Fawkes, and others, *to destroy the King and Parliament and re-establish the Roman Catholic Religion.*

NOTE.—In one year only, as many as 6,000 Roman Catholic Recusants are said to have been punished.

The plot was discovered by means of a mysterious letter, sent to Monteagle warning him not to attend Parliament. James, on seeing the letter, ordered a search to be made, and Guy Fawkes was discovered in a vault under the Houses of Parliament with thirty-six barrels of gun-powder stacked ready to be fired.

Results: (1) Some of the conspirators, including Catesby, were killed at Holbeach House, whither they had fled after the discovery of the plot; others, including Fawkes, were seized and perished on the scaffold. (2) Very severe laws were passed against the Roman Catholics.

James's **Contests** with his **Parliaments:** a beginning of the great struggle which reached a climax in Charles I's reign.

1604 His **First Parliament** met and asserted: (1) its right to control its own elections; (2) the right of its members to freedom from arrest; (3) that its privileges are " *of right and not grace.*"

1610 The Commons refused to give James money till he had given up *impositions* (i.e., increase of customs and duties). James would not consent to this arrangement.

The **Great Contract** between the King and Commons was drawn up by the younger Cecil. The terms were that the King should give up purveyance and certain feudal rights, and the Commons should allow him £200,000 a year for life. The Commons would not consent to this arrangement, and Parliament was dissolved.

1614 His **Second Parliament,** or the **Addled Parliament,** *so named because it did not pass a single act.* It had been packed by the " Undertakers," i.e., those who " undertook " to manage the Commons for the King.

It refused to grant a supply till the impositions were discontinued. Several members were imprisoned.

NOTE.—For seven years (1614–1621) James summoned no Parliament.

The Rule of Favourites

1612 On the death of the younger Cecil (Earl of Salisbury), **Robert Carr,** Viscount Rochester (afterwards Earl of Somerset), became the King's chief adviser.

Somerset subsequently married the divorced wife of the Earl of Essex, but having been convicted, together with his wife, of the murder of **Sir Thomas Overbury** (his secretary, who had opposed his marriage), was disgraced at Court (1616).

1616 **George Villiers,** afterwards Duke of Buckingham, became the King's chief favourite.

1620 Negotiations were opened with Spain with a view to arranging the **marriage** between **Prince Charles** and the **Infanta Maria.** In 1623 Prince Charles and Buckingham visited Madrid in disguise, but the Infanta did not like Charles, and the Spanish King wished him to become a Roman Catholic, and so on their return the match was broken off.

1621 His **Third Parliament.** (1) The Commons impeached: (*a*) **Sir Giles Mompesson** for holding the monopoly of manufacturing gold and silver thread; (*b*) **Lord Bacon** for bribery and corruption. Mompesson fled the country, and Bacon was condemned, deprived of his offices, and heavily fined.

(2) The Commons made a " **protest** " in which they declared: (a) that their privileges were not the gift of the Crown, but the natural birthright of English subjects; (b) that matters of public interest were proper subjects for them to discuss; (c) that they had a right to liberty of speech.

James tore out the protest from the Journal of the House with his own hand.

On the dissolution of Parliament, Pym, Coke, and Selden were imprisoned.

1624   His **Fourth Parliament.** War was declared with Spain, and supplies were voted to carry it on. Monopolies were declared illegal.

NOTE.—James's policy was to govern without a Parliament. He raised money by impositions, monopolies, benevolences, sale of honours, and the heavy fines inflicted by the Star Chamber.

1625   **Death of the King**

Memorable Events

1611   The **Colonization of Ulster** began. After the suppression of the Earl of Tyrone's rebellion in the last reign, the estates of the rebel lords were confiscated. *In this reign these lands were parcelled out among English and Scotch emigrants.* This is known as the Colonization of Ulster.

1616   The **Story of Raleigh.** James, being in want of money, released Raleigh from the Tower and gave him command of an expedition to sail to Guiana in search of a gold mine, with orders not to molest the Spaniards in that region. The expedition proved unsuccessful, and on his return in 1618 Raleigh was executed, *nominally for treason, but in reality for having attacked the Spaniards.*

1618   The **Thirty Years' War.** The people of Bohemia, being Protestants, had revolted against Ferdinand, the Roman Catholic Emperor of Germany, and had chosen as their King, Frederick, Elector Palatine, who had married Elizabeth, eldest daughter of James. The King of Spain and other Roman Catholic princes joined Ferdinand against the Protestants, and the terrible Thirty Years' War began. James, whose policy was never in favour of war, refused to assist his son-in-law, who lost not only Bohemia but also the Palatinate, and he and his wife became fugitives.

1620   The **Pilgrim Fathers.** Many Puritans who had despaired of being allowed to worship in their own way had left England for Holland. In 1620 a small band of these Puritans, numbering 120, called the Pilgrim Fathers, sailed from Holland in the *Mayflower*, and founded a colony at New Plymouth in America.

CHARLES I 1625–1649 (24 YEARS)

Title: Son of James I.

Married Henrietta Maria of France.

Children: Charles II, James II, Mary.

A.D.

Charles's Contests with his Parliaments

1625   His **First Parliament.** To carry on the war with Spain, Parliament granted two subsidies, and " Tonnage " and " Poundage " for one year only instead of for life. The tonnage and poundage Charles refused to accept.

NOTE.—Tonnage was a tax varying from 1s. 6d. to 3s. upon every tun of wine or beer; poundage a tax from 6d. to 1s. on every pound of merchandise imported or exported. They realized about £160,000 a year.

The **War with Spain** (declared in 1624). **Causes:** (1) the refusal of Spain to help England in winning back the Palatinate for Frederick; (2) the failure of the negotiations for the marriage between Charles and the Infanta.

(Eight ships, which had been fitted out ostensibly to act against Spain, were used against the Huguenots at **Rochelle,** who were in rebellion against the French Government. This gave rise to great dissatisfaction in England.)

Meanwhile a fleet of ninety ships was sent out under the command of Lord Wimbledon to take Cadiz, but the expedition ended most disastrously.

Parliament refused to grant supplies without a redress of grievances, and was dissolved.

1626   His **Second Parliament** met; many obnoxious members, including Wentworth and Coke, were excluded by being appointed sheriffs by the King. Buckingham was impeached, and Digges and Eliot, who conducted the impeachment, were sent to the Tower, but the Commons refused to proceed with business, and so they were released. Charles dissolved the Parliament.

To carry on the war with Spain, Charles raised money by benevolences.

1627   **War was declared** against **France,** *arising out of a personal pique between Buckingham and Richelieu.* Buckingham attempted to relieve the Huguenots at **Rochelle,** who, suspecting treachery, refused to admit his fleet, and so the expedition failed.

1628   His **Third Parliament.** The **Petition of Right** drawn up by Pym and Wentworth stated *the grievances under which the country was then suffering*: it requested that: (1) no man be compelled to pay loan, benevolence, or tax, levied without consent of Parliament; (2) no subject be imprisoned without cause shown; (3) soldiers and sailors be not billeted in private houses; (4) no person be tried by martial law. The King, being in great financial difficulty, accepted the Petition.

NOTE.—It is second in importance to Magna Charta.

Buckingham, while fitting out another expedition to aid Rochelle, was **assassinated** at Portsmouth by Felton, an officer who had been refused promotion in the army.

On Buckingham's death, **Wentworth** deserted the popular party and became the King's chief adviser and President of the Council of the North.

A.D.

1629   **Parliament defied the King's authority** on this occasion. A scene of tumult occurred in the House. The speaker was forcibly held in the chair while Eliot's resolutions against illegal taxation and innovations in religion were read and passed, although the King had expressly forbidden that they should be brought forward. Parliament was dissolved. Hollis, Valentine, and Eliot were sent to the Tower, where the latter died in 1632.

Charles ruled without a Parliament (1629–1640). His chief advisers were **Sir Thomas Wentworth** and **Laud.**

(1) The **Star Chamber** and **High Commission Court** exercised arbitrary power.

Charles raised money by the following means, *all more or less illegal*: (1) tonnage and poundage; (2) fines exacted from Roman Catholics; (3) all persons with a yearly income of £40 were compelled to take up their knighthood or pay a fine; (4) sale of monopolies; (5) the ancient forest land was reclaimed; (6) fines inflicted by the Star Chamber.

1630   (2) **Dr. Leighton** was fined, mutilated, and imprisoned for life by the Star Chamber *for writing a book against the prelates, called* Sion's Plea against Prelacy.

1633   (3) Wentworth was appointed Lord-Deputy of Ireland, and Laud became Archbishop of Canterbury and the King's chief adviser in Church matters.

NOTE.—Wentworth's principle in government was " Thorough," i.e., suppressing with a strong hand all attempts to oppose the King's power.

1634   (4) **Ship-money** was imposed by the advice of Noy. At first it was a tax on seaports and maritime counties only, nominally to raise a fleet for the defence of the country. The following year, Charles, acting on the advice of Finch, extended it to all inland towns and counties.

NOTE.—Its real object was to raise a fixed revenue.

1637   **John Hampden** refused to pay ship-money: judgment was given against him by a majority of the judges.

(5) **Prynne,** a barrister, *having published a book* Histrio-Mastix *against stage-plays, which was held to reflect upon the character of the Queen,* was sentenced by the Star Chamber to undergo punishment similar to Leighton's.

Scotland was the first to resist Charles's arbitrary rule.

Charles, by the advice of Laud, tried to enforce the use of the English Liturgy in Scotland. The Scots, however, organized " Four Tables " or Committees representing four classes of the people—the barons, lesser barons, clergy, and burgesses—to oppose the King's attempt. When Charles threatened to suppress the movement by force, nearly the whole of Scotland signed the **National Covenant,** binding themselves *to resist the introduction of Popery and Episcopacy.* The " Covenanters," as they were called, formed an army of 16,000 men under Alexander Leslie to defend their rights.

A.D.

1639 The **Pacification of Berwick.** To suppress this rising Charles advanced to Scotland with an army of 20,000, but as he could not trust his men, he was compelled to conclude a treaty with the Covenanters known as the *Pacification of Berwick.* It enacted that all civil and religious grievances should be settled by a General Assembly. But when the Assembly met it condemned the English Prayer Book and abolished Episcopacy.

NOTE.—This short and bloodless campaign is called the First Bishops' War because it was waged in the cause of the Bishops.

1640 **Charles's Fourth** or **Short Parliament.** Charles, being in great financial difficulties, summoned his Fourth or Short Parliament. It sat only three weeks. Charles dissolved it because it refused to grant subsidy without a redress of grievances.

Invasion of the Scots. Meanwhile the Scots invaded England, and defeated the royal forces at **Newburn.**

NOTE.—This invasion of the Scots is known as the Second Bishops' War.

The **Treaty of Ripon.** Charles, being aware of his weak and critical position, concluded a treaty with the Scots at **Ripon,** by which it was agreed that the Scots should abstain from all acts of hostility and Charles should pay £850 a day for the maintenance of the Scottish army, until the differences between them and the King should be settled.

The **Great Council.** Charles was now convinced of the hopelessness of his cause, and so he summoned a **Great Council of Peers** to meet at York. This council was in fact a revival of the " Great Council of the Plantagenets," but being afraid to act apart from the Commons, it advised the King to summon another Parliament. This advice Charles was obliged to follow.

Charles's Fifth or **Long Parliament.** Charles, being still in want of money and fearing a second invasion of the Scots, called his Fifth Parliament, sometimes called the Long Parliament. *It lasted 20 years* (1640–1660), and was in many respects the most famous in our history. Its first work was to remove the King's obnoxious ministers, Strafford and Laud.

(1) **Strafford** was impeached on the grounds: (*a*) that he had advised the King to employ his army in Ireland to reduce England to obedience; (*b*) that he had acted illegally and tyrannically as President of the Council of the North. The impeachment having fallen through, a *Bill of Attainder was passed against him, and he was executed* (1641).

NOTE.—In a Bill of Attainder the Commons act as judges as well as the Lords. It may be introduced into either House, and passes through the same stages as any other Bill, and when agreed to by both Houses receives the assent of the Crown. " It is in fact an Act of Parliament made for the occasion, to inflict pains and penalties beyond or contrary to the common law."

(2) **Laud** was impeached and imprisoned. (His execution took place in 1645.)

(3) **Leighton, Prynne,** and other victims of the Star Chamber were released.

A.D.

1641 (4) The **Triennial Bill** was passed, enacting: (*a*) that every Parliament should be dissolved at the end of three years; (*b*) that a Parliament should be summoned within three years from the dissolution of the last Parliament.

(5) A Bill was passed enacting *that the Parliament should not be dissolved without its own consent.* This Bill was a necessary safeguard for its own existence.

(6) The **Root and Branch Bill was brought forward** *demanding the complete abolition of Episcopacy.* The Bill, however, never got beyond its second reading. But it had the effect of splitting up the Parliament into two parties, the Episcopalians and the Puritans.

(7) The Star Chamber, High Commission Court, and Council of the North were abolished.

(8) The Grand Remonstrance was passed and published by the Commons, *because they saw that the King was regaining his popularity.* It contained 204 clauses, and stated: (1) all the unconstitutional acts of Charles since the beginning of the reign; (2) the good work the Parliament had done, and (3) demanded the appointment of ministers by the Parliament.

1642 Charles failed in his attempt to arrest the **Five Members,** Hollis, Haselrig, Hampden, Pym, and Strode—leaders of the party opposed to the King. He then left London (and did not return until just before his execution). After this both King and Parliament began to prepare for war.

Irish Affairs

NOTE.—In 1641 Ireland was the scene of a terrible rebellion. There were in Ireland two chief parties, the descendants of the old Norman settlers, mostly Roman Catholics, who wanted religious toleration, and the native Irish landowners, who wanted to regain those lands, which had been taken from them by the English settlers. The removal of Strafford and the dissensions between Charles and the Parliament offered a favourable opportunity to each party for gaining their ends. These two parties, having formed an alliance, plotted to seize Dublin and overthrow the Government. The plot, however, was detected, and the conspirators then turned savagely upon the English and Scottish colonists of Ulster In the massacre which followed it is estimated that no less than 30,000 persons perished. In England the news of these atrocities excited the greatest horror, and served to increase the King's unpopularity, while the majority of the nation believed that Charles had intrigued with the Irish Roman Catholics and encouraged the massacre.

The Civil War, or **Great Rebellion** (1642–1648).

Causes: (1) the determined opposition offered to Charles's arbitrary government by the Long Parliament; (2) the supposed encouragement given by Charles and his Queen to Popery; (3) illegal taxation; (4) the unpopularity of the King's advisers.

The more **immediate causes** were: (1) the attempt made by Charles to seize the Five Members; (2) the refusal of Charles to give up to the Commons the command of the militia and of the chief fortresses.

Division into Parties: (1) London and the counties round it belonged to the Parliamentary party, the North and West, and the counties near Wales were inclined towards the King. (2) Many nobles and gentry, bringing with them a train of dependants, gathered round the King, while the Parliamentary army was made up of yeoman farmers, middle-class townspeople, and artisans, " poor tapsters and town apprentices, raw and untrained." (3) The Universities of Oxford and Cambridge, the Church party, were on the side of the King, the Presbyterians on the side of the Parliament.

NOTE 1.—It was now to be decided whether the King or the Parliament should rule England.

NOTE 2.—The King's party received the name of " Cavaliers " from their gallant bearing and skill in horsemanship; the Parliamentarians were called " Roundheads," because they wore their hair cut short.

The First Civil War. Leaders: (1) Royalist—the King himself, Prince Rupert, Newcastle, Hopton, and Wilmot; (2) Parliamentary—Essex, commander-in-chief, Manchester, Waller, Fairfax, and Cromwell.

The First Campaign. Edgehill: between the King and Essex; both parties claimed the victory.

1643   **The Second Campaign.** (1) **Chalgrove Field:** Prince Rupert defeated Hampden (Parl.), who was mortally wounded.

(2) **Atherton Moor:** Newcastle (Roy.) defeated Fairfax (Parl.).

(3) **Roundway Down:** Hopton (Roy.) defeated Waller (Parl.). Bristol was stormed by Prince Rupert.

(4) **Gainsborough:** Cromwell (Parl.) defeated Newcastle (Roy.).

(5) **First Newbury:** the King engaged Essex; indecisive. Lord Falkland was killed.

(6) **Winceby Fight:** Cromwell (Parl.) defeated Newcastle.

NOTE.—The events of the second campaign clearly proved that both parties were fairly matched, and so both the King and the Parliament began to seek aid outside England: (1) The King concluded a treaty with the Roman Catholic Irish, called " the Cessation," by which it was arranged that 10,000 Papists should cross over into England and assist him against the Parliament. (2) The **Parliament**, at Pym's suggestion, made an alliance with the Scots and signed the Solemn League and Covenant binding: (a) the Parliament to adopt the Presbyterian Religion; (b) the Scots to assist the Parliament with 20,000 men in the war against Charles.

The Third Campaign. (1) **Nantwich:** Fairfax (Parl.) defeated the Irish Contingent.

1644   (2) **Cropredy Bridge:** the King defeated Waller.

(3) **Marston Moor:** Manchester and Cromwell (Parl.) defeated Newcastle (Roy.). The victory was mainly owing to Cromwell's splendid troops, " The Ironsides." " *We never charged,*" he said, " *but we routed them.*"

NOTE.—In this battle the Scots for the first time assisted the Parliamentary forces. " It was the first decisive battle of the war."

(4) **At Lostwithiel:** Essex's army surrendered to Charles.

(5) **Second Newbury:** Charles engaged Manchester; the battle was indecisive, owing to the inertness of Manchester. Charles escaped to Oxford. Cromwell accused Manchester in the House *of having wilfully neglected to render the battle decisive.*

A.D.

1645

To remove the half-hearted generals from their posts in the army the Independents passed the **Self-denying Ordinance** by which *all members of both Houses were compelled to resign their commissions in the army within forty days*. Essex, Manchester, and Waller at once gave up their commissions; but Fairfax, as Commander-in-Chief, and **Cromwell**, as his Lieutenant-General, retained theirs by a special Act of Parliament.

The **New Model Army** was organized by Cromwell, on the plan of his Ironsides. It was in fact the foundation of a large standing army, and its ranks were filled with "*men of religion, who would*," as Cromwell said, "*withstand the gentlemen of honour of the Royalist army.*"

The Fourth Campaign and End of the War

Naseby: Fairfax and Cromwell utterly defeated Charles, and the First Civil War was ended at a blow. The result of the battle proved the efficient character of the New Model Army.
Montrose, rising in favour of Charles in Scotland, was defeated by Leslie at **Philiphaugh.**

Charles's subsequent movements

1646

Charles betook himself to the Scottish army at **Newark,** and the following year was surrendered by the Scots to the Parliamentary Commissioners at **Newcastle,** on payment of the arrears due to them. He was taken from **Holmby House** to **Hampton Court,** but, fearing for his life, escaped to Carisbrook, where he was kept a prisoner. Meanwhile he carried on intrigues with the Scots, Presbyterians, and Independents.

1648

The **Second Civil War.** Induced by Charles, the Scots rose in his favour under Hamilton, and invaded England, but were defeated by Cromwell at **Preston** and **Warrington.** The army returned to London, and clamoured for the death of the King, who was now brought from **Hurst Castle** to **Whitehall.**

Trial and Execution of the King

By **Pride's Purge above** 100 Presbyterian members *who refused to sit in judgment on the King* were excluded from the House. The remaining members (fifty-three Independents), called the "Rump," voted for the trial of the King.

1649

Charles was tried by a High Court of Justice, found guilty of *having levied war against his kingdom and the Parliament*, condemned to death, and executed.

NOTE 1.—The Presbyterians were so called because they were governed by Presbyters or Elders, and not by Bishops.

NOTE 2.—The Independents held that every Christian congregation formed an independent Church of itself, and was not bound in obedience to any higher power. They wished to see the Monarchy overthrown and a Republic established in its place.

NOTE 3.—Both Presbyterians and Independents were offshoots of the Puritan Party, and held religious opinions much the same as those held by the Puritans.

THE COMMONWEALTH 1649–1653 (4 years)

1649   The **Rump** took the Government into its own hands and passed the following sweeping measures: (1) that the **office of King** and the **House of Lords** should be abolished as being " useless, burdensome, and dangerous "; (2) that England should be a **Commonwealth** and a **Free State**; (3) that a **Council of State** of 41 members should be appointed, with *Bradshaw* as President and *Milton* as Latin Secretary.

Opposition to the Commonwealth

(1) **In England.** The " Levellers," as the extreme Republicans in the army were called, rose in rebellion against the Commonwealth. They were dissatisfied with the results of the Civil War, and denounced the half-heartedness of Cromwell and the other generals of the army. They were suppressed by Cromwell and Fairfax, and their leaders executed.

(2) **In Ireland.** The English Royalist Protestants joined the Irish Roman Catholics and refused to acknowledge the Commonwealth. Cromwell undertook to suppress the rebels. He stormed Drogheda and put to the sword the whole of the garrison numbering upwards of 3,000. Wexford shared the same fate. His excuse for these atrocities was " *to prevent the effusion of blood for the future.*"

After taking several other towns he was recalled, and left Ireton to complete the conquest.

(3) **In Scotland.** The whole of Scotland had denounced the execution of Charles I and proclaimed Prince Charles as King. **Montrose** rose in his favour, but was captured and executed by Covenanters. Charles landed in Scotland, and pledged himself to uphold the Covenant and the Presbyterian Religion. Fairfax, being himself a Presbyterian, refused to march against the Scots, " the godly party," as he called them, and Cromwell accepted command of the army. He defeated the Scots under Leslie at **Dunbar.** Edinburgh opened its gates to the victor.

1651   Charles was crowned at Scone, but being weary of the strict Presbyterian restraint, resolved to try his fortune in England. Eluding Cromwell, he marched into England; Cromwell pursued and defeated him at **Worcester**—" *the crowning mercy* " of the war, as he called it. Charles, after many romantic adventures, reached Brighton, and finally escaped to France. Scotland was placed under the charge of Monk, and kept in good order.

(4) **Opposition to the Commonwealth in Holland** and the **First Dutch War** (1652–1653).

Causes: (1) the refusal of the Dutch to enter into alliance with the Commonwealth, and to salute the English flag in the Channel; (2) the assassination of Dr. Dorislaus, the English ambassador at The Hague, by some Scotch refugees whom the Dutch had allowed to escape; (3) the attempts made on the lives of the subsequent ambassadors, St. John and Strickland, by the Royalists; (4) the **Navigation Act, passed in 1651,** *inflicting a severe blow on the Dutch carrying trade.* This Act forbade the importation of any goods into England except by English vessels, or by vessels belonging to the country which produced the goods.

Battles:

1652   (1) The English, under Blake, were defeated **off the Naze** by Van Tromp.

1653   (2) The Dutch were defeated **off Portland** and the **North Foreland,** by Blake, and **The Texel** by Monk, *where Van Tromp was killed.* Peace was concluded in 1654 by the **Treaty of Westminster,** in which the Dutch promised: (1) to give no countenance to English Royalists; (2) to pay the usual honours to the flag of the Commonwealth; (3) to make compensation for damage done to English merchants.

Expulsion of the Rump

Cromwell, wishing to bring about certain reforms in the Government, desired a new Parliament. The Rump, however, fearing that if a new Parliament was elected the army would get the upper hand and the Commonwealth be destroyed, *tried to pass a Bill by which its members were to keep their seats without re-election and also to have the right to exclude all newly elected members.*

Cromwell, hearing of this proceeding, forcibly dissolved the House.

THE PROTECTORATE 1653–1660 (7 YEARS)

1653   The **Barebone's Parliament.** An Assembly of Nominees of about 140 members (sometimes called the Little or Barebone's Parliament) was summoned by Cromwell, *from a list of the names of men,* " *faithful, fearing God and hating covetousness,*" *sent in by the various Independent ministers.*

Instead of attempting to reform existing institutions, they proceeded to abolish the Court of Chancery, Tithes, and Church patronage, but being unable to carry out these measures and the army becoming dissatisfied, after sitting five months they gave back their power to Cromwell.

NOTE 1.—This Parliament was so called from Praise-God Barebone, junior member for London.

NOTE 2.—Some good Acts, however, were passed: (1) for the relief of debtors; (2) for the registration of births, deaths, and marriages.

The **Instrument of Government.** *Cromwell was anxious to have a settled form of government, which should be as much like the old state of things as possible,* and with this end in view the " Instrument of Government " was drawn up. It stated that: (1) The supreme authority should be vested in the Lord Protector and a Council of

A.D.

State of fifteen members. (2) A Parliament of 400 members should be summoned every three years and sit not less than five months. (3) An army of 30,000 men should be retained. (4) The office of Protector should be for life.

1654 The **First Parliament** summoned under the authority of the " Instrument." It was fairly elected, *except that Roman Catholics and declared Royalists were excluded.*

As soon as it assembled, the Republican party, headed by Vane, opposed Cromwell by calling in question: (1) *The legality of " the Instrument ";* (2) *the advantage of a government by Parliament and a single person.* This greatly displeased Cromwell, and in five " lunar " months he dissolved Parliament.

1655 Appointment of **Major-Generals.** The disputes between Cromwell and his Parliaments encouraged the Royalists to plot against Cromwell's life and overthrow the Protectorate. To crush these plots Cromwell was compelled to divide the country into twelve military districts, each under a major-general, with almost absolute power.

NOTE.—The expenses, entailed upon the Government in keeping down these plots, led Cromwell to levy from the Royalists an income tax of 10 per cent., known as " The Decimation."

Relations with foreign countries

Cromwell's foreign policy was " to set England at the head of the Protestant cause in Europe." *In this he was following Elizabeth's line of policy.*

(1) With **Spain.** War was declared against Spain, which country Cromwell regarded as the head of the Catholic powers. The **real object** of the war, however, was to gain freedom of trade and greater liberty of religious worship for the English merchants trading with Spanish America.

Events in the War:

(*a*) **Jamaica** was captured by Penn and Venables.

NOTE.—This expedition caused so much dissatisfaction that its leaders were imprisoned on their return to England.

(*b*) **Blake** captured the Spanish Plate Fleet **off Cadiz.** Subsequently Blake gained a glorious victory over the Spaniards in the **Bay of Santa Cruz** in Teneriffe, but died soon afterwards.

1658 (*c*) **France** joined England **against Spain.** The allied armies of England and France defeated the Spaniards at the **Dunes,** and captured Dunkirk. The town was made over to the English.

1656 (2) With **Savoy.** Louis XIV wished to make an alliance with England, but Cromwell would sign no treaty unless Louis compelled the Duke of Savoy to put a stop to the cruel persecutions of the Protestants in the Vaudois. Louis agreed to these terms.

A.D.

(3) With **Algiers.** Blake sailed into the Mediterranean and taught the Bey of Algiers to restrain his subjects from doing further violence to English ships and merchants.

NOTE.—Cromwell's foreign policy has been described "as magnanimous, enterprising, and successful. Europe regarded him with terror and admiration."

Cromwell's **Second Parliament**

Cromwell, being in want of money and fearing an invasion in favour of Charles II, as well as the plots of the Royalists, summoned his Second Parliament. He was also anxious to secure for the Protectorate the sanction of Parliament.

NOTE.—To secure some unity of action he excluded about 100 of his most violent enemies.

1657 The **Humble Petition and Advice.** The discovery of a plot to murder the Protector induced the Parliament to draw up an "improved constitution," known as the " *Humble Petition and Advice.*" It stated: (1) that the Executive Government should be vested in the Protector and a Council of State; (2) that the Protector should take the name of King; (3) that he should have the power of nominating his successor; (4) that there should be a " Second House of Parliament."

NOTE 1.—This practically restored the ancient Constitution of the country, and gave to Cromwell all the powers belonging to the Sovereign.

NOTE 2.—Cromwell accepted the Petition and Advice, but rejected the title of King by the request of the army. The title of " Lord Protector " was substituted for it.

1658 Cromwell's **Third and last Parliament** assembled in its reconstructed form, i.e., with its " Second House " of sixty members.

NOTE.—Only six of the ancient peers were summoned, and only one of these took his seat. The Commons refused to acknowledge the "Other House," as they called it, and Parliament, after sitting only sixteen days, was dissolved by Cromwell, who for the remainder of his life ruled without a Parliament.

Death of Cromwell. On 3rd September, *the anniversary of his two great victories, Dunbar and Worcester,* Cromwell died. His son, Richard Cromwell, was declared Protector, but being unpopular with the army because he was no soldier and with the " godly party " from his dislike to the outward show of religion, he resigned and retired into private life.

1659 **Events** immediately preceding the **Restoration.**

The **Rump** was recalled by the army, *but on trying to bring the army under its power,* it was forcibly dismissed by Lambert.

A Committee of Safety, consisting of officers of the army, was formed by the soldiers.

Monk marched from Scotland. Lambert hastened to oppose him, but his army gradually deserted him, and he himself was taken prisoner.

1660 Monk now entered London and recalled the " Long Parliament," which, having summoned a Convention, dissolved itself, and *thus the Long Parliament came to an end.*

Meeting of the **Convention,** in which there were many Royalists and Presbyterians. *A resolution was passed to restore the old form of government and invite Charles II to return.*

Meanwhile Charles II, who had been in secret correspondence with Monk, issued the **Declaration of Breda,** which promised: (1) a general pardon to all persons except those who should be exempted by Parliament; (2) such liberty of conscience in religious matter as Parliament should allow; (3) that Parliament should settle all claims to landed property and pay the arrears due to Monk's army.

The **Restoration.** Charles was recalled by the Convention and restored to the throne. *With the return of Charles II the Puritan Revolution was at an end.*

NOTE.—A " Convention " is a Parliament not summoned by the Sovereign.

CHARLES II 1660–1685 (25 YEARS)

Title: Son of Charles I.

Married Catherine of Portugal. He had no children.

Proceedings of the Convention Parliament

1660

(1) **Hyde** was created Lord Clarendon and became the King's leading minister; **Monk** was made Duke of Albemarle.

(2) An Act of **Indemnity and Oblivion** for all offences committed during the recent troubles was passed, *excepting the regicides and five others, including Sir Harry Vane and Lambert.*

NOTE.—In 1662 Sir Harry Vane was executed for treason, " a man," as Charles said, " too dangerous to live."

(3) **Settlement of the King's Revenue.** The Convention granted the King a fixed income of £1,200,000 for life, to be raised from tonnage and poundage, and abolished military tenures, feudal dues, and purveyance.

(4) The **Army was disbanded,** except two regiments amounting to about 5,000 men. *These regiments were the beginning of a standing army.*

(5) All **Lands** were restored to the **Crown,** the **Church,** and the **Cavaliers.** The Convention, having completed its work, was dissolved by the King.

1661

Administration of Clarendon

Charles's First Parliament, sometimes called the " Cavalier Parliament," met. It consisted for the most part of old Cavaliers and their sons, *and was eminently Royalist in character.*

NOTE.—This Parliament is sometimes called the **Pension Parliament,** because it was in the secret pay of Louis XIV. It lasted 18 years (1661–1679).

(1) It annulled all the Acts of Cromwell's Parliaments and confirmed the Acts of the Convention.

(2) A **reaction** now set in **against the Nonconformists,** and Clarendon passed the most severe laws against them, including the Corporation Act, Act of Uniformity, Conventicle Act, and Five Mile Act. These four Acts are sometimes called the **Clarendon Code.**

(a) The **Corporation Act.** Its object was to *weaken the power of Nonconformists in towns.* It enacted that every member of a Corporation should: (i) renounce the Solemn League and Covenant; (ii) declare it unlawful to bear arms against the King under any pretext whatever (called the doctrine of non-resistance); (iii) take the Sacrament according to the rites of the Church of England.

1662

(b) The third **Act of Uniformity.** Its object was to compel the Puritan Clergy to conform to or leave the English Church. It enacted: (i) that all ministers of the Church should be of episcopal ordination and use the Book of Common Prayer; (ii) that they should publicly declare their assent to everything contained in the same; (iii) that they should renounce the solemn League and Covenant, and take the oath of non-resistance.

NOTE.—About 2,000 ministers of good repute refused, and were ejected from their livings. These represented about one-fifth of the English Clergy, and were called Nonconformists.

1664

(c) The **Conventicle Act.** Its object was *to prevent Nonconformist clergymen from forming congregations of their own.*

It enacted that if five persons besides those of the same household should be present at a religious meeting, held not in accordance with the rites of the Church of England, such persons should be fined or imprisoned for the first and second offences, and transported for seven years for the third offence.

NOTE.—The gaols were filled with Nonconformists, including such men as Bunyan. By the Declaration of Indulgence, passed in 1672, as many as 12,000 persons were released from imprisonment.

1665

(d) The **Five Mile Act.** During the plague of London the clergy of the Established Church had deserted their churches and Nonconformist ministers had undertaken their duties. This conduct excited the anger and jealousy of the Episcopalians, and in the Parliament held at Oxford the Five Mile Act was passed.

It enacted: (a) that Nonconformist Clergymen should not come within five miles of any corporate town where they had ever preached, except when travelling; (b) that they should not act as schoolmasters.

(3) The **Second Dutch War** (1665–1667). **Causes:** (1) the Dutch had interfered with the trade of the African Company, and had been expelled by the English from their settlements on the African Coast, and from New Amsterdam (America); (2) the commercial jealousy between the two nations.

Battles:

(a) **Off Lowestoft:** the English under the Duke of York won a great victory over Admiral Opdam.

1666 (b) **In the Downs:** a terrible fight for two days, constantly to the disadvantage of the English under Prince Rupert and Albemarle.

1667 (c) **London was blockaded.** The Dutch under De Ruyter sailed up the Thames, burnt the dockyard and shipping at Chatham, *and held London in a state of blockade for some weeks.*

This disgrace to the English nation brought about the **Treaty of Breda.**

Fall of Clarendon

Causes: (1) the disastrous management of the Dutch war; (2) the heavy taxation and consequent distress; (3) the sale of Dunkirk to the French; (4) his severe laws against the Nonconformists and his illegal imprisonment of persons.

Having been impeached at the bar of the House of Lords, he fled from the kingdom on Charles's advice, and was ultimately banished for life.

The **Cabal Ministry,** a sort of Cabinet, was formed, comprising Clifford, Arlington, Buckingham, Ashley (afterwards Lord Shaftesbury), and Lauderdale.

NOTE.—The initial letters of the names of these ministers spelt the word " cabal," which originally meant nothing more than a club. They were, however, so odious. to the nation that ever since an evil meaning has been attached to the word.

1668 (1) The **Triple Alliance** was formed between England, Holland, and Sweden, *to check Louis XIV of France from encroaching on the Netherlands,* which belonged to Spain.

This alliance compelled Louis to make peace with Spain at the **Treaty of Aix-la-Chapelle.**

It was said of the Triple Alliance, " that it was the only good thing that had been done since Charles II came into England."

1670 (2) The **Secret Treaty of Dover** was concluded between Charles and Louis, by which it was agreed: (a) that Charles should declare himself a Roman Catholic, and help the French against Holland; (b) that Louis should give him £300,000 a year and send troops to England to crush any opposition to his plans.

1672 (3) The **first Declaration of Indulgence** was issued by Charles, who had given his promise to Louis XIV in the Secret Treaty of Dover that he would restore Romanism. It repealed *all Penal Laws against Nonconformists and Roman Catholics,* but in the following year Parliament compelled Charles to withdraw it.

NOTE.—This was the first step Charles took in his attempt towards the restoration of Romanism.

(4) The **Third Dutch War** (1672–1674).

(a) The English admirals, before war was declared, failed in their attempt to capture the Dutch Smyrna fleet on its way home.

(b) Charles now openly joined Louis and declared war against the Dutch.

(*c*) Battle of **Southwold Bay.** Here the Duke of York engaged De Ruyter in an obstinate but indecisive engagement.

(*d*) Peace was concluded in 1674.

1673 (5) The **Test Act** was passed. Its **object** was: *To keep Roman Catholics out of public offices.* It enacted: (1) that all persons holding any office under the Crown should receive the Sacrament in accordance with the rites of the Church of England; (2) that they should declare their disbelief in Transubstantiation.

Results: (*a*) the Duke of York was compelled to resign his post as High Admiral; (*b*) Clifford and Arlington also retired from office, thus breaking up the Cabal.

Note 1.—Shaftesbury, on quarrelling with the King, became the leader of the " Country " party, which formed the " Opposition " in Parliament. The party which supported the Government was called the " Court " party.

Note 2.—" This is the beginning of the division between ' Ministry ' and ' Opposition ' which has continued to our day."

Danby's Administration (1673–1679)

1677 Danby arranged a **marriage** between **William of Orange,** Louis' great opponent, and **Mary,** eldest daughter of James, Duke of York. *Louis regarded this as an act of treachery on the part of Charles,* and in 1678 disclosed a secret treaty signed by Charles, in which the latter had promised: (1) to disband the army; (2) and not to assist the Dutch, on payment of 6,000,000 livres from Louis.

Danby, who had written the treaty, was in consequence impeached by the Commons and committed to the Tower. Danby's impeachment and dismissal from office established the principle of the responsibility of ministers to Parliament.

1678 The **Popish Plot.** Titus Oates disclosed a " supposed " plot of the Roman Catholics: (1) to murder the King; (2) subvert the Government; (3) restore the Roman Catholic religion.

Results: (1) The nation was driven to a state of madness, and Oates, the " saviour of the nation," as he was called, was rewarded with a pension and lodged at Whitehall. (2) Upwards of 2,000 innocent Roman Catholics were imprisoned on information supplied by Oates. (3) *The Disabling Bill was passed " disabling " Roman Catholics from sitting in either House* (exception was made in the case of the Duke of York). (4) London was put into a state of siege, the trained bands were called out, streets guarded, and all Roman Catholics ordered to leave the city.

Note 1.—The aged Lord Stafford, the leader of the Roman Catholic party, was committed to the Tower, and executed in 1680.

Note 2.—After this no Roman Catholic sat in either House for 150 years.

Charles's **Second Parliament**

1679 (1) The **Council of Thirty.** Sir William Temple, author of the Triple Alliance, advised the formation of a Council of Thirty (a kind of Privy Council) to stand between the King and Parliament.

Note.—As, however, it did not represent the majority in the House, and was too large for practical purposes, it failed.

(2) The **Habeas Corpus Act** was brought in by Shaftesbury and passed. Its **object** was: *To prevent illegal and indefinite imprisonment*. It enacted: (1) that any unconvicted prisoner (except those charged with treason) could demand from one of the judges a writ of Habeas Corpus, by which the gaoler was directed to produce the body of the prisoner in court and certify the cause of his imprisonment; (2) that every person should be indicted the first term after his commitment and tried the subsequent term; (3) that no person should be recommitted for the same offence; (4) that no person should be imprisoned out of England.

NOTE 1.—This important statute contained no new principle. It simply made clear and effectual the exercise of an ancient right.

NOTE 2.—The arbitrary Government of Clarendon brought about this Act.

The **Struggle for the Exclusion Bill** (1679–1681)

Taking advantage of the ill-feeling against the Roman Catholics which had been caused by the Popish Plot, the Commons headed by Shaftesbury brought in the Exclusion Bill to *exclude James, Duke of York, from the succession to the throne, because he was a Roman Catholic*; but Charles, to save his brother's rights, dissolved Parliament after it had sat only two months.

1680 **The Petitioners**, representing the Shaftesbury party, sent " petitions " to the King urging him to assemble Parliament and pass the Exclusion Bill. Counter-petitions were also forwarded by the **Abhorrers,** expressing their " abhorrence " of the petitions and the Exclusion Bill. Afterwards these names were changed to " Whigs " and " Tories." When Parliament met the Exclusion Bill passed the Commons, *but was thrown out by the Lords*.

1681 Charles's **last Parliament** met at Oxford.

The Whigs, believing that there was a conspiracy to bring back the Roman Catholic religion, brought armed followers with them to the Parliament, wearing ribands on which were the words " No Popery, no slavery," and the kingdom seemed on the verge of a civil war. *This warlike attitude on the part of the Whigs ruined their cause.* .

A third time the Exclusion Bill was brought forward, but Charles at the end of a week's sitting again dissolved Parliament, and did not summon another.

The **Tory Reaction.** The violent conduct of the Whigs produced a great Tory reaction, and the nation began to rally round the King. The Tories followed up their victory by taking vengeance on their opponents.

(1) **Shaftesbury** was prosecuted by the Government for treason, but the Bill was thrown out by the grand jury in London. Subsequently he fled to Holland, where he died.

(2) The **Charters of London** and other towns which had supported the Whigs were examined by a writ of Quo Warranto and taken away.

A.D.

1683   (3) **The Rye House Plot.** The extreme Whigs, in the height of despair, formed a plot *to assassinate the King while returning from Newmarket at a lonely farmhouse called the Rye House.* The plot, however, was disclosed by one of the conspirators. Lord William Russell and Algernon Sydney were executed for a supposed share in the plot. Essex committed suicide in the Tower; Monmouth was pardoned and banished.

1685   **Death of the King**

Memorable Events

1665   The **Great Plague,** which had been raging on the Continent, broke out in London and lasted from May to September, *destroying upwards of 100,000 people.*

1666   The **Great Fire of London** raged for three days and three nights. *Two-thirds of the city were reduced to ashes.*

     NOTE.—This year was called by Dryden, Annus Mirabilis, the " year of wonders," in allusion to the Great Fire and the Dutch War.

1679   The **Rebellion of the Covenanters** in Scotland.

     Cause: The attempts made by Lauderdale and Sharpe, Archbishop of St. Andrews, to introduce Episcopacy into Scotland. Sharpe was murdered by a body of fanatical Covenanters on Magus Moor, near Cupar. This was the signal for a general rising of the Covenanters. The Duke of Monmouth defeated the insurgents at **Bothwell Bridge,** and the rebellion was suppressed.

JAMES II 1685–1689 (4 YEARS)

Title: Son of Charles I.

Married: (1) Anne Hyde; (2) Mary of Modena.

Children: By Anne Hyde: Mary and Anne. By Mary of Modena: James Francis Edward, called the Old Pretender.

Accession

James declared *that he would maintain the Government both in Church and State as established by law,* but the events of his reign are curiously at variance with this declaration.

1685   **Illegal Taxation.** James continued to levy taxes, which had been voted to Charles II only for life, and could not therefore be legally collected until Parliament had renewed the grant.

The Rebellions of Argyle and Monmouth

A two-fold rebellion was planned by the exiled Whigs in Holland *to regain their power, dethrone James, and place the Duke of Monmouth on the throne.*

(*a*) Under **Argyle,** who landed in **Scotland,** but was taken prisoner and executed, and the rebellion was suppressed.

(b) Under **Monmouth,** the "Protestant Duke," as he was called, who landed at Lyme (Dorset). He was joined only by the lower classes, and proclaimed King at Taunton. At **Sedgemoor** he was defeated by the Royal forces, captured, and executed.

Results: A terrible revenge on Monmouth's adherents followed: (1) Colonel Kirke and his soldiers, called "Kirke's lambs," ruthlessly put to death upwards of 100 at Taunton. (2) Judge Jeffreys was sent out on the Western Circuit, known as the **Bloody Assize,** in which 320 persons were hanged, and 840 sold into slavery to the West Indies. Jeffreys was rewarded with the office of Lord Chancellor for his services.

1686   **James's** great aims were to **rule absolutely,** and **restore the Roman Catholic Religion.** To effect this:

(1) He tried to get the Test and Habeas Corpus Acts repealed.

(2) He maintained a large standing army by forming a camp of 13,000 men at Hounslow, to overawe London.

(3) He claimed and used "*the Dispensing Power.*"

NOTE 1.—Sir Edward Hales, a Roman Catholic and Colonel of a regiment, was brought to a "sham" trial under the Test Act. Eleven of the twelve judges declared that the King had a right to use "the dispensing power," and he was acquitted.

NOTE 2.—Dispensing power is the right claimed by the King to "dispense with," or set aside, the penal laws in individual cases.

(4) He established an **Ecclesiastical Commission,** which in 1687 attacked the rights of the Universities of Oxford and Cambridge. (a) At **Oxford** he appointed Dr. Massey, a Roman Catholic, to the Deanery of Christ Church, and expelled the Fellows of Magdalen College, *because they would not elect Dr. Parker, a Roman Catholic, as their President.* (b) At **Cambridge,** he suspended Dr. Pechell, the Vice-Chancellor, *for refusing a degree to a Benedictine monk without the usual oaths.*

1688   James issued on his own authority a **Second Declaration of Indulgence** suspending all penal laws against Nonconformists and Roman Catholics, and ordering the clergy to read it during Divine Service in all churches on the first two Sundays in June. The clergy in general disobeyed.

NOTE.—"Suspending Power" is the right to "suspend," or do away with, the entire operation of any law or laws.

Trial of the Seven Bishops

Seven Bishops (Archbishop Sancroft, Ken, Turner, Lake, Lloyd, White, and Trelawney) petitioned the King in person to be excused from reading the Declaration. James ordered the Seven Bishops to be sent to the Tower, and, although public sympathy was on their side, he was determined to bring them to trial; "*Indulgence,*" said he, "*ruined my father.*" The Bishops were tried for having published "*a false, malicious, and seditious libel,*" but were acquitted to the great joy of the nation.

The Revolution

Summary of Causes: (1) the attempts made by James to overthrow the Church of England and introduce the Roman Catholic Religion; (2) his exercise of arbitrary power in bringing the Seven Bishops to trial; (3) his claim to the right of dispensing with and suspending the laws of the land.

(1) An invitation, signed by seven leaders of the Whigs and Tories, was sent to William of Orange, requesting him *to come over with an army and defend the rights and liberties of the people of England.*

(2) James in alarm adopted conciliatory measures: (*a*) gave back the towns their Charters; (*b*) dissolved the Ecclesiastical Commission; (*c*) reinstated the Fellows of Magdalen College.

(3) William landed at **Torbay** and marched to Exeter. Meanwhile, James, deserted by all his friends, left the country for France, and William arrived in London.

1689 (4) A **Convention** met. After a long discussion, both houses agreed *to settle the throne on William and Mary conjointly, all the executive power being vested in William.* At the same time they drew up the Declaration of Right, which William and Mary accepted, and they were declared King and Queen.

WILLIAM III AND MARY 1689–1702 (13 YEARS)

Title of William: Son of Mary, daughter of Charles I.

Title of Mary: Daughter of James II. William and Mary had no children.

Proceedings of the Convention

The Convention was declared a Parliament. It passed the following important Acts:

1689 (1) All **Holders of Offices** in Church and State were required to take the oath of **allegiance** and **supremacy** to William. Seven Bishops (including Archbishop Sancroft) and about 300 clergy refused, and were deprived of their offices. *They formed the sect called the Non-Jurors.*

(2) The **First Mutiny Bill;** which: (*a*) places the army under martial law; (*b*) enacts that the maintenance of a standing army without consent of Parliament is illegal.

Note.—By this Act, which has to be renewed every year, Parliament maintains a complete control over the army.

(3) The **Toleration Act,** *allowing freedom of worship to all Protestant Dissenters.*

(4) The **Bill of Rights,** *an embodiment of the Declaration of Right.* It declared to be illegal: (1) the pretended power of suspending or dispensing with the laws; (2) the Court of Ecclesiastical Commission; (3) levying money without consent of Parliament; (4) maintaining a standing army in time of peace without consent of Parliament.

The **Bill also declared:** (1) that subjects have a right to petition the King; (2) that Protestants may have arms for their defence; (3) that elections of members of Parliament ought to be free; (4) that speeches and debates in Parliament ought to be free; (5) that excessive bail, fines, and punishments ought not to be inflicted; (6) that Parliament should be held frequently.

Opposition to William in Scotland and Ireland

(1) **In Scotland:** Viscount Dundee raised the standard of rebellion and defeated the Royal forces under General Mackay at **Killiecrankie,** but was killed in the action, and the rebellion failed.

1692   **The Massacre of Glencoe.** William summoned all the Highland Chiefs to take the oath of allegiance before January 1, 1692, but Ian Macdonald of Glencoe neglected to do so. Dalrymple, the Secretary of State for Scotland, misrepresented the matter to William and got a Royal warrant to root out " that set of thieves," the Macdonalds of Glencoe. The Campbells, their hereditary foes, were sent to carry out this sentence. Nearly the whole clan was massacred.

1689   (2) **In Ireland:** Tyrconnel, at the head of the Roman Catholics, rose in favour of James II. The Protestants in the North declared for William, and to the number of 30,000 took refuge in Londonderry, where they were besieged by the Roman Catholic army under Hamilton.

The **Siege of Londonderry.** A blockade of 105 days followed, during which time the town was gallantly defended, in face of famine, by Major Baker and the Rev. George Walker, until relief arrived.

The same day, Colonel Wolseley defeated the Irish army at **Newton Butler.**

Meanwhile James II ruled as King in Dublin, and passed severe laws against the adherents of William.

1690   Threatened **invasion** of England **by France.** The English fleet under Herbert (Lord Torrington) was defeated off **Beachy Head** by the French, who burned Teignmouth and " swept the Channel unopposed."

Battle of the Boyne. William landed at Carrickfergus and defeated James at the battle of the Boyne, where Schomberg, one of William's generals, was slain. James fled to Waterford and thence to France.

1691   William then subdued the South of Ireland, while the rebel Irish retreated beyond the Shannon. Having failed in his attempt to take Limerick, which was bravely defended by a very able Irish general, Patrick Sarsfield, William returned to England, leaving Ginkell to complete the conquest.

Ginkell took **Athlone** and defeated the insurgents at **Aghrim,** where St. Ruth, their leader, was killed.

A.D.

The **Surrender** and **Treaty of Limerick** (the last stronghold of the rebels) closed the war.

This Treaty stated: (1) that all officers and soldiers in the Irish army, who desired it, should be conveyed to France; (2) that Irish Roman Catholics should be allowed the exercise of their religion.

NOTE.—About 10,000 Irish soldiers passed over to France and entered the service of Louis XIV; subsequently they were known as the " Irish Brigade."

War with France. Cause: *The support given by Louis XIV to the exiled King James II.*

1692   Louis XIV, in support of James II, collected a large fleet at **Brest,** and an army of 30,000 men on the coast of Normandy to invade England.

Russell, High Admiral of the fleet, Godolphin, head of the Treasury, and Marlborough were suspected of carrying on treasonable communication with James. The latter was dismissed from office.

Battle of La Hogue. The French were utterly defeated by Lord Russell off Cape La Hogue, and Louis gave up all thought of an invasion.

William was defeated at **Steinkirk,** and again at **Landen** in 1693, but in 1695 he took the strong fortress of **Namur,** said to have been " *the finest thing he ever did in war.*"

1697   The **Peace of Ryswick** was concluded between England, France, Holland, and Spain, *by which William III was acknowledged the rightful King of England and Anne his successor.*

The **Partition Treaties** and the **Grand Alliance**

1698   The **First Partition Treaty.** Charles II of Spain was near death and had no children. His nearest of kin was the Dauphin of France, but the other European States *did not wish to see the whole of his extensive dominions joined to France. (See Table, page 173.)*

Hence the First Partition Treaty for dividing the possessions of Charles II was agreed upon between England, France, and Holland:

(1) Spain, the Indies, and the Netherlands were to go to **Joseph,** electoral Prince of Bavaria.

(2) Naples and Sicily to the **Dauphin.**

(3) Milan to the **Archduke Charles** of Austria.

NOTE.—In the following year Joseph died, and this caused a Second Partition Treaty to be made.

1700   The **Second Partition Treaty** was signed, which gave: (1) Spain, the Indies, and the Netherlands to the Archduke Charles; (2) Milan was added to the Dauphin's share.

NOTE.—Charles II died the same year, and by will left the whole of his dominions to Philip, Duke of Anjou, and second son of the Dauphin.
Louis, utterly disregarding the Second Partition Treaty, which he had signed, accepted the inheritance for his grandson, remarking that " the Pyrenees had ceased to exist." This led to the formation of the Grand Alliance.

1701 The **Grand Alliance** was formed between England, Holland, and Austria, *to place the Archduke Charles on the throne of Spain to the exclusion of Philip, grandson of Louis XIV.*

On the death of James II, **Louis XIV acknowledged James Francis Edward, son of James II, afterwards known as the Old Pretender, as the rightful King of England,** in defiance of the Treaty of Ryswick.

This bold step the English nation considered as a breach of the Treaty of Ryswick and a national insult, and both Whigs and Tories now voted for war.

William dissolved the Tory Parliament, and a new Parliament met with a large majority of Whigs.

War was declared against France, which took the form of the " *War of the Spanish Succession* " in the next reign.

1702 **Death of William.** In the midst of the preparations for war, William died from the effects of a fall from his horse.

Memorable Events

1693 (1) The **National Debt** was commenced. *It originated in a loan raised by Montague, Chancellor of the Exchequer, to defray the expenses of the war with France.* Unlike other debts, the " interest " only is paid. At William's death it had increased to £16,000,000.

1694 (2) The **Bank of England** was established. The plan of a National Bank had been suggested some years previously by **Paterson,** a Scotchman. **Montague** now adopted that plan. *He borrowed upwards of a million and formed the lenders into a banking company, which was to do all the money business of the Government and get interest on their money.* This interest was secured upon the taxes. Previously the Government had banked with private goldsmiths, and the great fault of such a system was its insecurity. This bank has been a great success, and its security has become a proverb, " Safe as the Bank of England."

(3) The **Triennial Bill** was passed, *limiting the duration of Parliament to three years, and providing that three years should not pass without a Parliament.*

1696 (4) The **Second Treason Bill** passed, *for regulating trials for High Treason.* It enacted: (1) that the prisoner should have a copy of the indictment and a list of the jury a few days before his trial; (2) that he should have the aid of counsel; (3) that two witnesses should be required for conviction.

(5) The **Assassination Plot.** A plot formed by Sir George Barclay, Sir John Fenwick, and others to murder William near Turnham Green. The plot was disclosed, and the leaders executed.

Note 1.—An **Association** was formed by the Lords and Commons, and many others, to avenge William's death, if he was murdered, and to place Anne on the throne.

Note 2.—In 1697 **Sir John Fenwick** was tried for high treason. One of the two witnesses required by the Second Treason Bill absconded and the trial could not be proceeded with. A Bill of Attainder was, however, passed against Fenwick, and he was executed.

A.D

1699   (6) The **Darien Scheme,** projected by Paterson, *was an attempt made by the Scottish people to found a colony on the Isthmus of Darien, and carry on a trade with the two Indies.*

Causes of its failure: (*a*) the East India Company, and Dutch merchants petitioned William against the Scheme, as an infringement of their rights, and he was compelled to disown it; (*b*) the want of support from Scotland; (*c*) the unhealthy climate of the locality and the attacks of the Spaniards.

NOTE.—The Scottish people threw all the blame on William and the East India Company, and in 1703 the Scottish Parliament passed an Act of Security by which it was made impossible that the same person who had been chosen to sit on the English throne after the death of Anne should be elected to the Scottish throne also, unless security was given for the " religion, freedom, and trade of Scotland."

1701   (7) The **Act of Settlement** or **Succession Act** was passed. *Its main object was to secure the Protestant Succession to the English Crown.*

It enacted that: (1) the Crown should pass after Anne to Sophia, grand-daughter of James I, and her heirs *being Protestants*; (2) the sovereign should join in communion with the Church of England; (3) the sovereign should not leave England without consent of Parliament; (4) the nation should not go to war in defence of any territories not belonging to England; (5) the judges should hold their offices during good behaviour, and be removed only upon an address of both Houses.

NOTE.—This Act excluded the " Old Pretender " from the succession on the ground that he was a Roman Catholic.

ANNE 1702–1714 (12 YEARS)

Title: Daughter of James II.

Married George of Denmark.   Anne's children all died young.

A **Combined Ministry** of Whigs and Tories, under Marlborough and Godolphin, took the Government.

The **War of the Spanish Succession** (1702–1713) in support of the Grand Alliance of 1701 began.

(1) In the **Netherlands** and **Germany:**

1702   Marlborough, being appointed commander-in-chief of the allied forces, captured Venloo and Liège; Bonn in 1703.

1704   He won a glorious victory over the united forces of the French and Bavarians under Tallard at **Blenheim,** in which two-thirds of the French Army were killed, wounded, or taken prisoners.   Tallard also was captured. *This great victory saved Austria.*   Marlborough was rewarded with a pension for himself and his descendants, as well as with the magnificent estate and palace of Blenheim near Woodstock.

A.D.

1706 He again defeated the French under Villeroi at **Ramillies,** and took possession of nine of the strongest fortresses in the Netherlands.

1708 At **Oudenarde** he gained another battle over the French under Vendôme, and captured Lille, "the key to Northern France," and the following year he again overcame the French under Villars at the bloody battle of **Malplaquet,** and Mons fell into his hands.

(2) In **Spain:**

1704 **Gibraltar** was taken by Sir G. Rooke and Sir Cloudesley Shovel.

1705 Lord Peterborough captured **Barcelona,** and the following year the Earl of Galway and the Allies entered Madrid.

1708 The Allies were defeated by the French under Berwick at **Almanza,** but in 1710 Stanhope won the battles of **Almenara** and **Saragossa** over the French.

NOTE.—The war in Spain was more directly to carry out the purpose of the Allies, viz., to dethrone Philip and set up the Archduke Charles, but most of the Spaniards were in favour of Philip.

1710 **Fall of the Whig Ministry** and consequent **End of the War.**

(1) The Whig Ministry being dismissed by the Queen, a Tory administration was formed under Harley and St. John.

NOTE 1.—This change in the ministry was mainly due to the following causes: (a) Mrs. Masham, a cousin of Harley, had superseded the Duchess of Marlborough as the Queen's favourite; (b) the preaching of Dr. Sacheverell against the Whig Ministry; (c) the fierce writings of Swift against the war, "six millions of supplies and almost fifty millions of debt," he wrote, "the Allies have been the ruin of us"; (d) people generally were becoming weary of the war and the heavy taxation it caused.

NOTE 2.—The French, too, wished for peace, "as much as a sick man wishes to recover," said the French ambassador.

1711 (2) Marlborough was accused of peculation and removed from his command, and the Duke of Ormond, a strong Tory, but an incompetent general, was made commander-in-chief, and carried on the war unsuccessfully.

1713 The **Treaty of Utrecht** was *brought about by the Tories, Harley, and St. John.* It stated: (1) that the French and Spanish Crowns should never be united, but that Philip V, grandson of Louis XIV, should be King of Spain; (2) that England should have Gibraltar, Minorca, Hudson's Bay, Nova Scotia, and Newfoundland; (3) that the English should have the Assiento (i.e., the sole right of importing Negro slaves into America for thirty years), and be allowed to send one ship a year to the South Seas; (4) that France should acknowledge the Protestant Succession in England, and cease to aid the Pretender; (5) that Austria should have Milan, Naples, and the Spanish Netherlands.

1714 **Death of the Queen**

Memorable Events

1703 The **Methuen** or **Port Wine Treaty** was concluded with Portugal. It stated: (1) that English woollen goods should be admitted into Portugal; (2) that the duty on Portuguese wines should be less by one-third than that on French.

D

Queen Anne's Bounty was instituted, *by which the first-fruits of benefices were placed in the hands of governors for the augmentation of small livings.*

1707   The **Act for the Union of England and Scotland.** This Act was passed owing to: (1) *the dissatisfaction in Scotland arising from the failure of the Darien Scheme*; (2) *the heavy duties raised on goods passing between the two countries.*
It enacted: (1) that the two kingdoms should be united under the name of " Great Britain "; (2) that the Succession to the throne of Great Britain should be the same as that settled before for England; (3) that the United Kingdom should be governed by one Parliament; (4) that sixteen Peers and forty-five Commons should represent Scotland in Parliament; (5) that the laws relating to trade, customs, and excise should be the same in both countries; (6) that Scotland should retain her own Church, Laws, and Courts of Justice.

1710   **Dr. Sacheverell,** a rash, hot-tempered Tory clergyman, was impeached by the Whigs for having preached a sermon before the Corporation of London: (1) against the Revolution and the existing Whig Ministry; (2) abusing Godolphin; (3) advocating the doctrines of " *divine right* " and " *non-resistance* "; (4) attacking the Toleration Act and Dissenters, and declaring the Church of England to be in danger. He was found guilty and condemned to abstain from preaching for three years, and his sermon was ordered to be burnt by the common hangman. *Popular feeling, however, was on his side, and the whole affair created a great Tory reaction.*

1711   An Act was passed to prevent " **Occasional Conformity,** " i.e., the practice adopted by many Nonconformists *of taking the Sacrament according to the rites of the Church of England merely to get into office.*

1714   The **Schism Act** was passed. It enacted that no person should keep a school unless he was a member of the Church of England and licensed by the Bishop.

NOTE.—Both these Acts were repealed in 1718.

This reign was remarkable for the fierce contests which took place between the **Whigs** and the **Tories.**

(1) **Origin of the names.** " Whig " was originally a nick-name given to the insurgent Presbyterians of Scotland, and " Tory " to the outlawed Roman Catholics in Ireland.

(2) In **Politics** the Tories upheld the " *divine right of kings* " and the " *doctrine of non-resistance,*" the Whigs were inclined to consider the King only as " an official " who was responsible to the people for what he did and could be dethroned if he ruled unconstitutionally.

(3) **In Religion** the Tories were staunch supporters of the Established Church, while the Whigs, though themselves Churchmen, leaned somewhat towards the Nonconformists.

NOTE.—Both Whigs and Tories were to be found in every class of society.

THE HOUSE OF HANOVER OR BRUNSWICK

GEORGE I 1714–1727 (13 YEARS)

Title: Son of Sophia, grand-daughter of James I.

Married Sophia of Brunswick.

Children: George II.

1714   A **Whig Ministry** was formed under Townsend, Stanhope, and Walpole.

1715   (1) A new **Parliament** with a large **Whig majority** met, and impeached Oxford (formerly Harley), Bolingbroke (St. John), and Ormond for having treacherously sacrificed British interests and honour in bringing about the Treaty of Utrecht. Bolingbroke and Ormond escaped to France, while Oxford was committed to the Tower.

1716   (2) The **Riot Act** was passed *in consequence of serious Jacobite riots in the Midland counties and elsewhere.* It enacted that, if any twelve or more persons are unlawfully assembled to disturb the peace, and if any one justice shall by proclamation order them to disperse, it shall be considered felony if they remain together for one hour afterwards.

(3) The **Jacobite Rebellion of Fifteen**

The **Earl of Mar** raised a rebellion *in favour of James Francis Edward, the " Old Pretender,"* in Scotland, and Forster and the Earl of Derwentwater in England.

At **Sheriffmuir,** near Stirling, the Scottish rebels were defeated by the Duke of Argyle, and on the same day the English Jacobites, who were in arms, surrendered at **Preston.**

About a month later the Pretender landed in Scotland, but was compelled to return to France with the Earl of Mar.

Derwentwater, Kenmure, and others were afterwards executed. Nithsdale escaped from prison in his wife's dress. Forster and Lord Wintoun also escaped.

(4) The **Septennial Act** was passed, *to extend the duration of Parliament to seven years, but not longer.*

NOTE.—The Septennial Act was passed because it was thought unsafe to risk a new election, while the country was so unsettled, owing to the frequent Jacobite riots.

War with Spain

1717   The **Triple Alliance** was formed between England, France, and Holland, *to uphold the Treaty of Utrecht* by securing: (1) the succession of the House of Hanover to the English throne; (2) the succession of the House of Orleans to the French Crown if the young King Louis XV should die.

A.D.

Cardinal Alberoni, the chief minister of Philip, was anxious: (1) to destroy the Treaty of Utrecht; (2) to replace Spain in the list of the great European powers; (3) and recover the dominions which that country had lost.

He espoused the cause of the Pretender and persuaded Charles XII of Sweden to invade Scotland in favour of that Prince.

1718   **The Quadruple Alliance** was formed between England, France, Holland, and Austria **against Spain,** *its object being also to uphold the Treaty of Utrecht and the general peace of Europe.*

Philip took possession of Sardinia, and attacked Sicily.

Admiral Byng was sent by England with a fleet to protect Sicily, and in a naval engagement off **Cape Passaro** he totally destroyed the Spanish fleet.

1720   Peace was made with Spain, the terms of which were: (1) that Philip should dismiss Alberoni from office; (2) and renounce all claims to the French throne and evacuate Sardinia.

The **South Sea Scheme,** called also **the South Sea Bubble.** *By this scheme the Directors of the South Sea Company offered to pay off part of the National Debt, if in return they should have the exclusive right of trading in the South Seas.* The Company's shares rose from £100 to £1,000, but afterwards fell to £170, thereby causing the ruin of thousands. In 1721 Sir Robert Walpole restored public credit.

NOTE.—The Directors were prosecuted, and their estates confiscated and applied to the benefit of the sufferers.

Walpole's Ministry (1721–1742)

1721   Walpole became First Lord of the Treasury. *He was the first man to whom the title of " Prime Minister " has been given.*

1723   **Wood's Halfpence.** Wood, an English ironmaster, obtained a patent from Walpole to issue a copper coinage in Ireland to the value of £108,000. Swift, dean of St. Patrick's, Dublin, in his famous Drapier's letters, wrote against the coinage, stating that it was base, and stirred up popular indignation in Ireland to such a degree that Walpole was obliged to withdraw the coinage.

1727   **Death of George I**

GEORGE II 1727–1760 (33 YEARS)

Title: Son of George I.

Married Caroline of Anspach.

Children: Frederick, Prince of Wales.

Walpole's Administration continued

1733   Walpole brought in his **Excise Bill** *to prevent smuggling and increase the revenue.* By this Bill he proposed that the " *customs* " levied on tobacco and wine, when these goods were brought into the seaports, should be transferred to the " *excise*," which was to be paid on the goods when they were sent throughout the country. Meeting with violent opposition, he withdrew the Bill.

1736   The **Porteous Riots** took place in Edinburgh, *occasioned by Captain Porteous firing on the mob, which had become enraged at the execution of a smuggler named Wilson.*

Porteous was condemned to death, but on being reprieved, the infuriated mob broke open the Tolbooth prison, dragged Porteous out, and hanged him on a barber's pole in the Grassmarket. The magistrates of Edinburgh were reprimanded and the city itself was fined £2,000.

1737   The Opposition Party, supported by the Prince of Wales, took the name of " **Patriots.**"

1739   Unsuccessful **War with Spain**

The **Causes** were: (1) the smuggling of English goods into the Spanish ports of America contrary to treaty (see Treaty of Utrecht, clause 3); (2) the right claimed and used by the Spaniards of searching all English vessels at sea; (3) the consequent acts of violence done by the Spaniards to English sailors.

NOTE.—This war is sometimes called **The War of Jenkins's Ear,** because an English sea-captain named Jenkins stated before Parliament that his ear had been cut off by the Spaniards.

Events in the War: (1) Admiral Vernon took **Portobello** on the Isthmus of Darien. (2) Commodore Anson, in his celebrated voyage round the world, captured several richly laden Spanish treasure ships, and returned in 1744.

1742   Walpole opposed the war and was in consequence compelled to resign his office. He was raised to the peerage as the Earl of Orford.

NOTE.—This fact shows how powerful the House of Commons had become, by being able to remove a minister without impeaching him.

War of the Austrian Succession (1743–1748)

1743   England with Hanover upheld the **Pragmatic Sanction** against France, Prussia, and Bavaria.

NOTE.—Charles VI of Austria wished to leave all his hereditary dominions to his daughter, Maria Theresa, and so he persuaded nearly all the great European powers to accept an arrangement called the " Pragmatic Sanction," binding themselves to uphold her claim.

On his death, however, Frederick II of Prussia seized Silesia, the Elector of Bavaria claimed Austria, and both France and Spain sided with the latter. Only England and Hanover stood loyally by their promises. This led to the war of the Austrian Succession.

Events in the War

Battle of **Dettingen:** George II, commanding an army of English and Hanoverians, defeated the French.

1744   The French retaliated by sending a fleet, with 15,000 men on board, to land in England, under Charles Edward, son of the Old Pretender. A storm scattered the fleet, and the attempt was abandoned.

A.D.

1745   At **Fontenoy** the English and their Allies were defeated by the French under the famous Marshal Saxe.

The **Rebellion of Forty-Five.** *The War with France roused the disheartened Jacobites to renew their attempt to place the young Pretender on the throne.*

Charles Edward, called the Young Pretender and " The Chevalier," made a second attempt to regain the English throne for his father. He landed in Scotland with only seven followers, soon found himself at the head of a large army, entered Edinburgh, and proclaimed his father king.

Battle of **Preston Pans.** Here the royal forces under Sir John Cope were cut to pieces by the Highland troops.

Charles now marched into England, hoping the English would rise in his favour, but he was disappointed. Reaching **Derby,** he lost heart, and, on the advice of his Scottish chiefs, retreated to Glasgow.

1746   At **Falkirk** he defeated the royal troops under General Hawley, who had been sent to relieve Stirling.

At **Culloden** Charles was utterly defeated by the Duke of Cumberland, and, after wandering about in the Highlands for five months, escaped safely to France, although the price of £30,000 had been set on his head.

Results: (1) The most atrocious barbarities were perpetrated by the Duke of Cumberland, surnamed " The Butcher," in quelling this rebellion. (2) The Highlanders were disarmed, and forbidden to wear their national dress. (3) The hereditary jurisdiction of the Highland chiefs over their clans was abolished. (4) The Lords Lovat, Kilmarnock, and others, " the martyrs," as they were called, were beheaded.

1748   The Peace of **Aix-la-Chapelle** stated: (1) that there should be a mutual restitution of conquests (exception was to be made in the case of Prussia, which was allowed to keep Silesia); (2) that Maria Theresa's husband, Francis of Lorraine, should be acknowledged Emperor; (3) that France should acknowledge the Protestant succession in England; (4) that the Pretender should be expelled from France.

NOTE 1.—This Treaty practically put an end to the intrigues of the Stuarts.

NOTE 2.—The War of the Austrian succession cost England fifty-four millions sterling.

1756   The **Seven Years' War** (1756–1763), *carried on under the administration of Pitt, as Secretary of State, although the Duke of Newcastle was Prime Minister.*

The **Causes of the War.** Maria Theresa was anxious to recover Silesia from Frederick II, surnamed " the Great," and France, Russia, and Saxony had banded themselves together to assist her, and crush Frederick's growing power. To strengthen his cause Frederick formed an alliance with England. In addition, France and England were competing for colonies in India and America.

A.D.

Events in the War.   In Europe:

1757 **Byng,** son of Admiral Byng, having failed in an attempt to relieve **Minorca,** which was besieged by the French, *was tried by court martial and shot " pour encourager les autres."*

Cumberland was defeated at **Hastenbeck,** and shortly after capitulated at **Klosterseven.**

Frederick of Prussia routed the French and Austrians at **Rossbach** and **Leuthen.**

1758 Cumberland was recalled, and Duke Ferdinand of Brunswick, an able general, took command of the Allied English and Hanoverian forces.

NOTE.—Highland regiments for the first time served in this war.

1759 This year has been called " *the most glorious in the annals of our History,*" on account of the great victories gained by our troops in various parts of the world.   " One is forced to ask every morning," said Horace Walpole, " what victory there is for fear of missing one."

The **French** were defeated: (1) at **Minden** by Ferdinand; (2) off **Lagos,** in Portugal, by Admiral Boscawen; (3) in **Quiberon Bay** by Admiral Hawke.

The **Colonial War** between England and France in India and North America.

(1) In **India,** where the **Foundation of our Indian Empire** was laid, the French power, under Dupleix, had been for some time predominant.   In 1751 Clive captured and defended Arcot, and shortly after relieved Trichinopoly, which was being besieged by the French. Dupleix was recalled, and a peace favourable to the English made in 1754.

1756 **Tragedy** of the **Black Hole.** Surajah Dowlah, the Nabob of Bengal, seized Calcutta, and confined 146 English prisoners in the narrow guard room of the garrison, called the Black Hole. Next morning only twenty-three were found alive, the rest having died of suffocation.   Clive was sent from Madras to punish the Nabob. He retook Calcutta, and compelled the Nabob to sign a peace.

1757 At **Plassey** Clive, with only 3,000 men, utterly routed the Nabob's army of 60,000.   This was the first great battle fought by the English in India.   *It secured Bengal for England.*

1760 Colonel Eyre Coote defeated the French at **Wandewash,** and secured Madras.   *This completed the downfall of the French power in India.*

(2) In North America

Continual warfare had been going on for some time between the French and English colonists about the boundaries.

The English had thirteen flourishing colonies, extending all along the east coast, from New Brunswick to the Gulf of Mexico, and from the Atlantic westward to the Alleghany mountains.

A.D.

The French also had established colonies in Canada and Louisiana, and in 1749 claimed all the lands west of the Alleghanies, and drove out the English settlers. *To secure these lands for France and to shut the English in, Montcalm, the French general, built a line of forts between Canada and Louisiana.*

1756　　General **Braddock** was sent out by the English Government to assist the colonists, but his army was defeated at **Fort Duquesne,** on the Ohio, and he himself mortally wounded.

1758　　Fort Duquesne was taken from the French by a body of Highlanders and Americans under Generals Forbes and Washington. *It was afterwards named " Pittsburgh," in honour of the great minister.* This Fort secured the valley of the Ohio and the territories of the " Far West " for England.

1759　　General **Wolfe** was appointed by Pitt to the command of the English army in Canada with instructions to drive out the French from that country.

Capture of Quebec. Failing to take the town by bombardment, Wolfe led his little army of about 3,000 men by night, up a steep and narrow path, to the **Heights of Abraham,** where, the next day, he gave battle to Montcalm, but was killed in the moment of victory. Montcalm was also mortally wounded, and died the next day. Five days later Quebec surrendered.

NOTE 1.—The capture of Quebec practically ensured the conquest of Canada, and put an end to the French power in North America.

NOTE 2.—" It is to the grand results of this war that the United States owes its origin."

1760　　**Death of George II**

Memorable Events

1739　　**George Whitefield** and **John Wesley** began their great religious revival, chiefly among the poorer classes, untouched by the Anglican Church. Although the leaders of the movement were Churchmen, their followers formed a new body of Nonconformists, and were called " *Methodists.*" The Anglican Church revived, and there was a general improvement in the tone of the nation.

GEORGE III 1760–1820 (60 YEARS)

Title: Son of Frederick, son of George II.

Married Charlotte-Sophia of Mecklenburg-Strelitz.

Children: George IV, William IV, and Edward, Duke of Kent.

The **Seven Years' War** was continued.

1761　　Pondicherry was taken from the French.

Pitt, fearing the union of France and Spain under the Family Compact, wished to declare war against the latter country, but the rest of the ministry refused and he resigned office.

A.D.

1762   England declared war against Spain and took Havana and Manila.

1763   **First Treaty of Paris** (Fontainebleau), between England, France, Spain, and Portugal, and **end of the Seven Years' War.**

By this Treaty: (1) England kept: (*a*) in Europe, Minorca, but restored Belle Isle; (*b*) in America, Canada and some important islands in the West Indies; (*c*) in India, all her conquests except Pondicherry, which was restored to France unfortified.

(2) Spain gave up Florida for Havana, but kept the Philippines.

(3) France lost all her conquests in Germany.

NOTE.—The Seven Years' War added upwards of seventy-five millions sterling to the National Debt.

1764   **Quarrel** with the **North American Colonists**

The relations between the Colonists and the mother country were not very cordial, owing to the restrictions on colonial trade, on the theory that colonies existed for the benefit of the mother country.

1765   The **American Stamp Act. Grenville,** the Prime Minister, to meet the expenses incurred by the late war, proposed to levy money on the American Colonists by means of a Stamp Act, i.e., *a charge of so much on legal documents such as contracts, wills, etc., as in England.*

The Stamp Act was passed, although six of the thirteen colonies petitioned against the Act, declaring " *that taxation without their consent was illegal.*"

1766   The **Repeal** of the **Stamp Act.** The opposition of the Colonists induced the new Prime Minister, **Lord Rockingham,** to repeal the " American Stamp Act."

Pitt strongly supported Rockingham in this measure, asserting *that England had no right to tax the Colonists because they were unrepresented in the English Parliament, and fearing the growth of absolute power of the monarchy.*

Pitt was invited by the King to join the Ministry, with the **Duke of Grafton** as Prime Minister. Subsequently he was raised to the peerage as " Earl of Chatham."

1767   The **Revenue Act. Charles Townsend,** Chancellor of the Exchequer, during Pitt's absence owing to ill-health, passed a new " Revenue Act," imposing duties on tea and five other articles imported into America, to pay for the defence and government of the colonies.

1770   Resignation of the Duke of Grafton. **Lord North** became Prime Minister.

The **Tea Duty.** To conciliate the Colonists Lord North abolished all the American import duties except that on tea, retained for the purpose of asserting the right of England to tax the Colonists.

A.D.

1773   The **Boston Tea-party.** A number of men, dressed and painted as Red Indians, boarded the India Company's tea-ships in Boston harbour and emptied all the tea-chests into the sea.

To punish this act of violence and contempt of authority the English Government declared the port of Boston closed, and took away the Charter of the colony.

1774   The **Declaration of Rights** was put forth. The **First Congress** of fifty-five delegates from all the colonies except Georgia met at Philadelphia and issued a " Declaration of Rights," prohibiting the importation of any goods from England till the rights of Boston were restored.

The **American War of Independence** (1775–1783)

1775   **Skirmish at Lexington.** The first fighting occurred at Lexington, 10 miles from Boston, where the Royal troops engaged the colonists *with indecisive results.*

At the battle of **Bunker's Hill,** a height on the peninsula which commands Boston, the English dislodged the colonists after some desperate fighting.

George Washington, a gentleman of Virginia, was appointed commander-in-chief of the colonial forces.

1776   The English, under **General Howe,** were compelled to evacuate **Boston.** After this the English had never again any real hold on the Northern States.

The **Declaration of Independence.** On the **Fourth of July** Congress drew up and passed the " Declaration of Independence," which was signed by delegates from all the thirteen States. It declared " *that the United Colonies of America are, and ought to be, free and independent States.*"

1777   Battle of **Brandywine.** Here the English defeated Washington and took Philadelphia, but did not follow up this success.

The **Convention of Saratoga.** General Burgoyne, in an attempt to cut off the Northern States from the rest, marched from Canada down the valley of the Hudson to join a force under Clinton, from New York. At Saratoga he was, however, hemmed in by the American troops, and forced to surrender.

NOTE.—This surrender was a great disaster to the English cause, and the turning-point of the war in favour of the Colonists.

1778   **France,** being eager to avenge the humiliation of the Seven Years' War, formed an alliance with the United States and recognized their independence. In consequence of this England declared war with France.

Lord North brought in and passed his **Reconciliation Bill,** granting the Colonists all their demands except independence, *but the interference of France turned popular feeling in England against the Colonists.*

NOTE.—The death of Chatham put an end to all hope of peace and reconciliation with the Colonists. In his last speech he had protested against the severance of the Colonies from England and pleaded reconciliation, but not at the sacrifice of England's honour to France.

A.D.

1779 **Spain joined France** in the war against England, and their combined fleets besieged **Gibraltar** from 1779 to 1782. The fortress was gallantly defended by **General Elliot,** who *destroyed the enemy's fleet with red-hot shot,* and was ultimately relieved by the fleet under Lord Howe.

1780 **England was alone against all Europe.** Russia, Sweden, and Denmark entered into an alliance called the **Armed Neutrality,** *to prevent the English from exercising the right of searching their vessels for " contraband of war," i.e., for goods belonging to an enemy.* Afterwards Prussia, Holland, France, and Spain joined the League.

Rodney defeated the Spanish fleet off **Cape St. Vincent.**

1781 Lord Cornwallis defeated the Colonists at the battle of **Guildford,** but being cut off from supplies by Washington on land and the French fleet by sea, he was compelled to **surrender at Yorktown,** and the American war of independence was at an end.

1782 Rodney won a great victory off **St. Lucia,** in the **West Indies,** over the French, under Count de Grasse, who was threatening Jamaica. *This battle lasted eleven hours, and was, as Rodney himself said, " one of the most severe ever fought at sea."*

1783 The **Treaty of Versailles** was signed between England, France, Spain, and the United States, by which: (1) England formally recognized the independence of the United States; (2) Pondicherry, with other small possessions in India, was given back to France; (3) Spain recovered Florida and Minorca.

NOTE 1.—The glorious victory of Rodney in the West Indies, and the successful defence of Gibraltar, brought about this Treaty, which was on the whole honourable to England.

NOTE 2.—It is estimated that by the American War of Independence 100 millions sterling were added to the National Debt.

Indian Affairs (1773–1803)

1773 English misrule in India induced the Ministry, under Lord North, to pass an Act for the **Regulation of India,** by which: (1) Warren Hastings, the Governor of Bengal, became Governor-General of the three Presidencies of Bengal, Bombay, and Madras; (2) a Supreme Court of Justice, like that in England, was established at Calcutta, and in this way English law was introduced into India.

1781 **Hyder Ali,** an adventurer, having made himself master of Mysore, invaded the Carnatic, but was defeated by Sir Eyre Coote at **Porto Novo.**

1783 **Fox** introduced his **India Bill.** *It passed the Commons, but by the express orders of the King was thrown out by the Lords.* It enacted that the authority of the East India Company should be transferred to seven commissioners nominated by Parliament, and capable of holding office for four years, after which the vacancies were to be filled up by the Crown.

A.D.

1784   **Pitt,** "*the younger*," the second son of Chatham, being Prime
Minister, brought in and passed his **India Bill,** establishing a "*Board
of Control,*" consisting of six members of the Privy Council, with
supreme authority over the administration of the Company, both
civil and military. All patronage and business was to be left in the
hands of the Company.

1788   **Impeachment of Warren Hastings** *on a charge of robbery, cruelty, and
oppression towards the native princes of India.*

The impeachment, containing twenty-two charges, was entrusted to
Burke, Fox, and Sheridan. The trial lasted more than seven years,
during which time the Court sat altogether 145 days. Finally, in
1795, Hastings was acquitted.

1799   War with **Tippoo Sahib,** son of Hyder Ali.

Tippoo, having made an alliance with the French, prepared to invade
the English territory. His capital, **Seringapatam,** was taken after a
desperate struggle, and he himself slain. *His dominions, called
Mysore, were ceded to England.*

1803   War with the **Mahrattas.** Sir Arthur Wellesley utterly defeated the
Mahrattas at **Assaye.**

Shortly after, General Lake won the great battle of **Laswaree,** *and in
1805 the power of the Mahrattas was completely crushed.*

1789   The **French Revolution,** said to be "*the greatest event in the eighteenth
century,*" took place. The **causes,** briefly, were: (1) the extravagance
and despotism of the French Monarchy; (2) the oppression of the
lower classes by the nobles, higher clergy, and upper middle classes;
(3) the political writings of Voltaire and Rousseau advocating the
need of a revolution.

Louis XVI, being desirous of reforming the Government, *called
together, after an interval of 175 years, the Great Assembly, known as
the "States-General."*

The Commons, or "*Third Estate,*" having assumed the power of
the other two estates, declared itself a **National Assembly** and overthrew the Government.

Riots broke out in Paris and the **Bastille,** the great French State
prison, was demolished.

All feudal rights and exclusive privileges of the nobles, clergy, and
all other classes were abolished.

Louis, in trying to escape from France, was captured and detained a
prisoner in Paris.

1792   **Austria and Prussia invaded France** to *suppress this revolutionary
movement and restore Louis to his throne, but were driven back.*
This interference on the part of foreign powers led to: (1) the
horrible September massacre of Royalists by the enraged mob of
Paris; (2) the meeting of the National Convention which took the
place of the National Assembly, and declared France a Republic;
(3) the execution of Louis in 1793.

A.D.

NOTE.—The " Reign of Terror." The period of the tyrannical and bloodthirsty Government which Robespierre, St. Just, and the Jacobins carried on for fourteen months, during which many thousands (including the Queen, Marie Antoinette), were put to death in Paris and in other places.

War with the **French Republic** (1793–1797). The younger Pitt was Prime Minister (1784–1801).

1793   The **Causes** were: (1) the " Decree of November the 19th," 1792, published by the French Convention, *offering help to all those nations who desired to overthrow their kings*; (2) the opening of the navigation of the Scheldt by the French contrary to treaty; (3) the threatened invasion of Holland, which was protected by a treaty with England.

1794   The Battle off **Brest**, called " *the glorious first of June*," where Lord Howe gained a great victory over the French fleet.

1795   War was declared by England against the **Dutch,** who had joined France. The Cape of Good Hope, Ceylon, and Malacca were taken from them.

Spain declared war against England

NOTE.—Pitt, alarmed at the sympathy shown by clubs and societies for the Revolution, and believing the Monarchy to be in danger, suspended the Habeas Corpus Act, and suppressed the freedom of the Press. Great distress prevailed, caused by the heavy taxation and stagnation of trade consequent on the war.

1796   The French expedition to Ireland, under General Hoche, was dispersed by a terrific storm, and failed.

Pitt's negotiations for peace with the French Directory (as the French Government was now called) were broken off.

1797   The battle of **Cape St. Vincent.** The Spanish fleet was defeated by Admiral Sir John Jervis and Commodore Nelson, and driven back to Cadiz.

Mutiny among the fleet at **Spithead** took place. It was suppressed mainly through the efforts of Lord Howe. The Mutiny at the **Nore** followed. This was also suppressed, and a few of the ringleaders executed.

The battle off **Camperdown.** The Dutch were defeated by Admiral Duncan. *This victory put an end to all danger of an immediate invasion of England by France and Holland.*

The **First War** with **Napoleon Bonaparte** (1798–1802)

1798   (1) In **Egypt** and **Syria.** Napoleon, aiming at the conquest of Egypt, Syria, and possibly India, invaded Egypt.

The **Battle of the Nile.** Nelson annihilated the French fleet, which had conveyed the French Army to Egypt, at the famous Battle of the Nile or Aboukir Bay, and Napoleon's attempt to conquer Egypt failed.

NOTE 1.—By this defeat Napoleon and his army were left stranded on the sands of Egypt. Crossing the desert, he stormed Jaffa and laid siege to **Acre,** where he was gallantly repulsed by the British and Turkish troops under **Sir Sidney Smith.** On hearing that the French forces were defeated in Europe, Napoleon slipped away from Egypt, returned to France, and was made First-Consul.

A.D.

NOTE 2.—**Battle of Alexandria.** In 1801 **Sir Ralph Abercrombie** defeated the French at Alexandria, but was mortally wounded in the action. The capitulation of the whole of the French army in Alexandria ended the war in Egypt. The French army was allowed to return to France, but the fleet fell into the hands of the English.

(2) In **Europe**

1800   The **Armed Neutrality** of 1780 was revived between Russia, Sweden, Denmark, and Prussia (called the Northern League) to resist the claim made by England of searching vessels.

1801   Sir Hyde Parker, with Nelson second in command, destroyed the Danish fleet off **Copenhagen.**

NOTE.—This victory and the assassination of Paul, Emperor of Russia, broke up the Northern League.

1802   The **Peace of Amiens** was signed—" A peace which all men are glad of, but no man can be proud of " (Sheridan).

The disastrous campaign in Egypt and the breaking-up of the Northern League led France to seek this temporary peace. By its terms (1) England gave up all her conquests except Trinidad and Ceylon; (2) Malta was to be restored to the Knights of St. John; (3) the French were to withdraw from Naples and the Roman States; (4) Egypt was to be restored to the Porte; (5) the King of England gave up the title of King of France.

Irish Affairs (1782–1800)

1782   Grattan's Bill, called the **Declaration of Right,** was passed *repealing the laws which gave the English Parliament power over the Parliament of Ireland.*

1791   Formation of the **Society of United Irishmen,** consisting of Roman Catholics and Republican Protestants. Its object was *to get the French to invade Ireland, and with their assistance to set up an independent Republic.* The chief leaders were Lord Edward Fitzgerald, Wolfe Tone, and Hamilton Rowan. The Party opposed to this society consisted of loyal Protestants, known as " Orangemen."

NOTE.—The French invasion in 1796, under General Hoche, failed.

1798   The **Irish Rebellion. Cause:** The unsettled state of the country owing to the spread of Republican principles.

At **Vinegar Hill,** near Wexford, the rebels were defeated by General Lake, and the rebellion was crushed.

1800   Pitt passed his Bill for the **Union of Great Britain and Ireland.** It enacted: (1) that there should be one Parliament for the United Kingdom; (2) that four Bishops, twenty-eight temporal peers, and 100 commoners should sit for Ireland in that Parliament; (3) that free trade should be established between the two countries.

Second War with Napoleon, now Emperor (1805–1815)

The younger Pitt was again Prime Minister from 1804 to 1806.

The **Causes** of this second outbreak of war were: (1) Napoleon had annexed to France Parma, Placentia, and Piedmont, States in

A.D.

Italy, and now invaded Switzerland; (2) England had not left Malta according to treaty; (3) England had given refuge to many French refugees.

1805 The **Battle of Trafalgar.** Napoleon made great preparations for invading England. *He had at Boulogne a flotilla of gun-boats ready to pour 150,000 men into England.*

Nelson, having been decoyed to the West Indies in pursuit of the French and Spanish fleets, now returned, *and won the memorable Battle of Trafalgar, but was himself mortally wounded in the action.*

A coalition between England, Russia, and Austria was formed by Pitt against France.

NOTE.—In this year Napoleon crushed the allied armies of Austria and Russia at **Austerlitz.** The news of this defeat and the failure of his plans for a coalition are said to have killed Pitt in 1806.

1806 The **Berlin Decrees.** Napoleon, *knowing that the strength of England lay in her commerce,* issued the " Berlin Decrees " to destroy her foreign trade. They: (1) declared the British Isles to be in a state of blockade; (2) forbade France or any of her allies to trade with them.

The **Peninsular War** (1808–1814)

The **Causes** were: (1) Portugal had refused to obey the Berlin Decrees, and the French had, in consequence, invaded the country; (2) Napoleon had conferred the Crown of Spain on his brother Joseph contrary to the wishes of the Spaniards.

The people of the Peninsula rose to a man against the French, and appealed to England for assistance. Sir Arthur Wellesley and Sir John Moore went into Portugal to assist them.

1808 (1) The **First Campaign** (1808–1809).

(*a*) Under **Wellesley.** The French forces under General Junot were defeated at **Roliça** and **Vimiero.**

Wellesley was superseded by Sir Hugh Dalrymple, who, by a treaty called the " **Convention of Cintra,**" allowed the French to evacuate Portugal. Napoleon invaded Spain.

NOTE.—This leniency provoked much dissatisfaction in England, and ultimately Dalrymple was deprived of his command and replaced by Sir John Moore.

1809 (*b*) Under **Sir John Moore.** To gain time for the Spaniards to rally, Moore struck at the French line of communication. As he expected, he was then forced to retreat, closely pursued by Napoleon and Soult. *His retreat is said to have been the most masterly on record.* At **Corunna** he defeated the French and so enabled the army to be embarked, but was killed in the action.

NOTE.—In this year a great expedition under Lord Chatham, the eldest son of the Earl of Chatham, was sent to Walcheren, but owing to mismanagement and sickness, it proved a miserable failure.

(2) The **Second Campaign** (1809–1814) under **Wellesley,** who again took command.

He defeated the French under Marshal Victor at **Talavera,** *for which victory he was created Viscount Wellington.*

A.D.

1810   Wellington constructed on the heights of **Torres Vedras,** some distance north of Lisbon, *three strong lines of fortified works, known as the "lines of Torres Vedras,"* extending fifty miles in length, from the Tagus to the sea. At **Bussaco** he defeated the French general Masséna and then retired behind the "Lines." Masséna, failing to dislodge him, retreated.

1811   At **Albuera** Beresford defeated Soult.

1812   Wellington stormed **Ciudad Rodrigo** and **Badajoz,** *fortresses which guarded the western frontier of Spain.*

At **Salamanca** Wellington defeated the French under Marmot and entered Madrid, but had to retreat before a French concentration of superior strength.

1813   At **Vittoria** he defeated Joseph, stormed **St. Sebastian,** after a brave defence of sixty-three days, *and swept the French entirely out of the Peninsula.*

NOTE.—Meanwhile Napoleon had invaded Russia, but the Russians burnt Moscow, their capital, and the French were compelled to retreat in the depth of winter, losing upwards of 400,000 men, many thousands of whom perished in the snow. At Leipzig, 1813, his enemies closed in upon him, and after three days' desperate fighting he was utterly defeated.

1814   Wellington invaded France, won the battle of **Orthez,** and defeated Soult at **Toulouse,** *the last battle in the Peninsular War.*

The victorious allies now entered Paris, and Napoleon abdicated and retired to Elba.

The **First Treaty of Paris** was signed between England, France, Russia, Austria, and Prussia, by which: (1) England was to keep Malta, Tobago, St. Lucia and Mauritius; (2) she was to restore all the Dutch colonies she held except Ceylon, Cape Colony, and part of Guiana; (3) the boundaries of France were limited to those of 1792.

NOTE 1.—The brother of Louis XVI, under the title of Louis XVIII, was placed on the French throne, as the Dauphin, who was called Louis XVII, had died in prison during the Revolution.

NOTE 2.—A general Congress of European Powers met at Vienna to carry out this treaty. England was represented at first by Lord Castlereagh, afterwards by the Duke of Wellington.

The Fall of Napoleon and End of the War

1815   After a feverish peace of eleven months Napoleon escaped from Elba and gained the Army's support. Marching on Paris, he was Emperor again in three weeks, and Louis XVIII fled the country. At **Ligny** Napoleon defeated the Prussians, but, on the same day, Wellington successfully opposed Marshal Ney at **Quatre Bras.**

At **Waterloo,** nine miles from Brussels, Napoleon and Wellington met for the first time face to face in battle. The English withstood repeated attacks until 8 p.m. As previously arranged, the Prussians began to attack the French right wing, about 4.30 p.m. After defeating a final attack and breaking the French Guard, Wellington's forces advanced, sweeping the French away.

Napoleon fled to Paris, where he abdicated in favour of his son.

Finding his escape from France impossible, he gave himself up to the captain of an English man-of-war, the *Bellerophon, and was condemned to exile in the island of St. Helena,* where he stayed till his death in 1821.

NOTE 1.—The " Hundred Days " is the name given to the period from Napoleon's escape from Elba to the Battle of Waterloo.

NOTE 2.—The National Debt had now increased to 860 millions sterling.

The **Second Treaty of Paris:** (1) It stated the amount (£28,000,000) to be paid by France to the Allies for the expenses of the war. (2) It restricted the boundaries of France to what they were in 1790. (3) It stipulated that the fortresses of the Northern French Frontier should be held by the Allies for five years.

The **Holy Alliance** or **Convention of September**

Its **Object.** Since the French Revolution, the sovereigns of Europe had been afraid that their subjects would rebel and compel them to establish free governments. Accordingly, the Holy Alliance was formed between the Emperors of Russia and Austria, and the Kings of Prussia, France, and Spain binding themselves to promote peace and goodwill among nations upon the basis of Christianity; but their real object was to help each other in crushing any attempts at liberal movements.

England refused to join this Alliance.

1816   The **Bombardment of Algiers**

Cause: For centuries the small Mahommedan States of Tunis, Tripoli, and Algiers had swept the Mediterranean as pirates, captured the vessels of all nations, and sold the Christians into slavery. They had even extended their ravages to the English Channel, and it was a common thing for charitable persons in England to leave money in their wills, " *for the ransom of Christian slaves from the Moors.*"

Lord Exmouth, with an English fleet, assisted by a small Dutch squadron, set sail to the Mediterranean, and compelled the rulers of **Tunis** and **Tripoli** to give up their Christian slaves, numbering 1,800. The **Bey of Algiers**, a stronger power, refused, and so the town of Algiers was bombarded for nine hours, the forts reduced to ruins, and the Christian slaves to the number of 1,083 released.

Home Affairs

1763   **John Wilkes,** member for Aylesbury, was imprisoned under a general warrant (i.e., a warrant in which no name is inserted) *for violently attacking the King and the Grenville Ministry in a paper called the* North Briton.

Subsequently he was released under the Habeas Corpus Act, but in 1764, having fled to France, he was outlawed.

1769   *General warrants were declared illegal.*

Although Wilkes was elected four times in succession for Middlesex, he was not allowed by the House of Commons to take his seat, but on re-election in 1774 he was allowed to do so.

NOTE.—This is important as showing that the House of Commons has no power over its own elections.

A.D.

The **Letters of Junius.** These letters were commenced in the *Public Advertiser, and contained vigorous attacks upon the King and the Grafton Ministry.* The writer was probably Sir Philip Francis.

1772   **The Royal Marriage Act** was passed, *forbidding any of the Royal Family under 25 years of age to marry without the Sovereign's consent.*

1778   Sir George Savile's **Roman Catholic Relief Bill** was passed, *repealing some of the more oppressive laws against Roman Catholics.*

The laws repealed were: (1) that which punished priests for celebrating Roman Catholic Mass; (2) that which forfeited the estates of Roman Catholic heirs educated abroad to the next Protestant heir; (3) that which prohibited Roman Catholics from acquiring property by purchase. Popular feeling was much against the Roman Catholics after this, and the cry " No Popery " was raised everywhere.

1780   The **Great Yorkshire Petition** was sent to Parliament by twenty-three counties and many large towns, asking for **Economical Reforms.**

NOTE.—This Petition was the beginning of the system of " Petitioning Parliament."

The **Gordon Riots** took place in London. They were led by Lord George Gordon, a half-crazy fanatic and President of the Protestant Association, against the Roman Catholics in consequence of the concessions granted to them by the Roman Catholic Relief Bill. A mob of 60,000 held London for a week, hustled and ill-used the members of both Houses, and failing in their endeavours to burst into the House of Commons, broke open Newgate and other prisons, burnt and sacked Roman Catholic Chapels, and burnt the house of Sir George Savile. Parliament rejected their petition, and order was restored only by the aid of 10,000 troops.

NOTE.—Upwards of 500 of the mob were killed and wounded, twenty-five captured, tried, and executed. Gordon himself was tried for high treason, but acquitted.

1797   **Suspension of Cash Payments** by the Bank of England. The cause of this was that the Bank of England had run short of gold, owing to:

(1) The great naval and military expenses incurred in the War with the French Republic.

(2) The enormous subsidies granted to England's allies, and paid for the most part in specie. In 1796 no less than £4 million had been sent to Austria.

(3) The compensation made to foreign states for the cargoes of neutral ships which England had seized.

(4) The threatened invasion of England by France, which had induced people to withdraw their deposits from the country banks, and this had in turn caused a run upon the Bank of England.

In the crisis, the Bank applied to the Government, and a proclamation was issued forbidding payments in cash. For twenty-four years bank-notes were accepted in lieu of cash, but in 1821 a Bill introduced by Peel, recommending that the Bank of England should resume its cash payments, was carried.

1807   An Act was passed for the **Abolition of the Slave Trade.**

Since the foundation of the American and West Indian Colonies, Negro slaves had been regularly captured in Africa and taken to work in the American plantations. The horrible sufferings of the poor wretches on their passage roused the sympathy of the people of England, and after the question of the slave trade had been agitated for upwards of twenty years, an Act was passed for its abolition. This was effected mainly by the efforts of Wilberforce and Thurlow in Parliament, and Granville Sharp, Clarkson, and Zachary Macaulay (the father of the historian) outside; and these men were nobly assisted by the great statesmen Pitt and Fox, who, though opposed on most questions, were united in this.

NOTE.—The Act for the Abolition of Slavery in all the British Dominions was passed in 1833.

1812   **Percival** the Prime Minister was assassinated while entering the House of Commons by a lunatic named Bellingham.

1816   **General distress** and **discontent.** The Twenty-two Years' War (1793–1815) with France was followed by a period of peace, which lasted 40 years, but that peace was marred by home troubles, riots, and internal distress and discontent, affecting both the agricultural and manufacturing interests of the country.

The **Causes** of this were, briefly stated:

(1) The heavy taxation, which seemed to be more oppressive in peace than it had been in war.

(2) The stagnation of trade owing to the exhausted condition of the continental nations after the war.

(3) Foreign nations had also begun to produce their own goods, and so the demand for English manufactured goods was becoming less.

(4) The bad harvests, especially that of 1816.

(5) In 1815 Parliament, almost entirely consisting of land owners, passed a Corn Law, *forbidding the importation of foreign corn, unless the price of wheat should rise to 80s. a quarter.* This law, while it benefited farmers and landowners, fell heavily on the poor.

(6) The substitution of machinery for hand labour, which for a time caused much distress in some districts.
The **chief riots** in this period were: (1) those of 1816; (2) Spa Fields Riots; (3) March of the Blanketeers; (4) Derbyshire Insurrection; (5) Manchester Massacre.

The **Riots of 1816** occurred in many places, particularly in the agricultural parts of the East of England, and were only put down by the soldiery. The violence of the rioters (who were called Luddites) was mainly directed against machinery, to the existence of which they ignorantly attributed their misery.

The **Spa Fields Riots** took place in London, where the mob attempted to procure arms from gunsmiths' shops, but the riots were easily suppressed.

NOTE.—Cobbett's *Weekly Political Register,* now reduced in price to 2*d.*, was at this time the organ of the Reform Party. It exercised a powerful influence over the working classes.

1817   A Bill was passed **suspending the Habeas Corpus Act.** This was owing to: (1) the outrage done to the Prince Regent by breaking the windows of his carriage as he was returning from the House; (2) the frequent riots and disturbances; (3) the existence of secret republican societies and clubs, formed under the pretence of bringing about " Parliamentary Reforms," which were said to be " stirring up the minds of the people with disaffection and contempt of law, religion, and morality."

The **March of the Blanketeers** from Manchester. This was a movement set on foot by the distressed operatives of Manchester, who " *clad in blankets in which they intended to sleep,*" marched towards London to petition the Regent, but, being stopped on the way, dispersed.

The **Derbyshire Insurrection** headed by a man named Brandreth, known as " the Captain," was soon quelled.

Lord Sidmouth's Circular was sent to the lord-lieutenants of the counties, authorizing them to apprehend any person accused of publishing blasphemous or seditious libels.

NOTE.—Under this Act Mr. Hone was tried for publishing certain political parodies on the Church Catechism and Book of Common Prayer, one of which was *The Litany, or General Supplication,* and notwithstanding the strenuous efforts of Lord Ellenborough, the Chief Justice, to obtain his conviction, he was acquitted.

1819   The **Manchester Massacre,** called the " *Peterloo Massacre,*" took place. A crowd of some 50,000 met for the purpose of petitioning Parliament for reform, in St. Peter's Field at Manchester, where they were addressed by a popular agitator, known as " Orator Hunt." A force of mounted yeomanry, supported by the 15th Hussars, was sent by the magistrates to effect his capture, and in the terrible charge of the soldiers several persons were crushed to death and a considerable number wounded. Hunt was apprehended, tried for misdemeanour, and sentenced to imprisonment.

The celebrated **Six Acts** passed. **Object:** Parliament thought that the only effectual way to put down these riots and " radical " meetings was by passing strong repressive measures.

NOTE.—" Every meeting for Radical Reform," said a distinguished lawyer, " was not merely a seditious attempt to undermine the existing constitution and government, but an overt act of treasonable conspiracy against the King and the Government."

These Acts were:

(1) To prevent delay in the administration of justice in the case of misdemeanour.

(2) To prevent the training of persons in the use of arms, and the practice of " military evolutions."

(3) To prevent and punish blasphemous and seditious libels.

(4) To authorize the justices of the peace in certain disturbed counties to seize and detain arms collected and kept for purposes dangerous to public peace.

(5) To subject certain publications to the same stamp duties as those required for newspapers, and to make other regulations for restraining the abuses arising from the publication of blasphemous and seditious libels.

(6) To prevent the assembling of seditious meetings.

The Demand for Reform

The general cry of the nation was " Reform," but the Parliament, recollecting the terrible results which followed the French Revolution, was slow to adopt any changes whatever, and thought that all " reforms " were revolutionary.

Upwards of 600 petitions for Reforms poured into Parliament in the year 1817 alone, and no less than **Ten Bills** for Parliamentary Reform had been introduced between 1776 and 1819, but had failed to pass. Of these Bills the following may be noticed:

(1) 1780. Burke's Bill, demanding the abolition of " sinecures," the only use of which was the purchase of votes. " *The King's turnspit*," he said, " *was a peer of Parliament*."

(2) 1785. Pitt's second Bill for Parliamentary Reform. In this Bill he proposed to buy up 72 seats belonging to private persons (*rotten boroughs* they were called) for £1 million, and give the seats to different counties and to London.

(3) 1818. Sir Francis Burdett's motion for annual Parliaments and universal suffrage.

(4) 1819. Lord John Russell's resolutions for reform.

NOTE.—In 1819 the term " Radicals " was for the first time used, and applied to the demagogue Hunt and his followers. They were so called because they thought that by going to the " root " of things and making " radical " and extreme changes the country would be relieved from the general distress which then prevailed.

Memorable Events

1812   The first steam vessel, the *Comet*, the work of Henry Bell, plied on the Clyde.

1813   Westminster Bridge was first lighted with gas.

GEORGE IV 1820–1830 (10 YEARS)

Title: Son of George III.

Married Caroline of Brunswick.

Children: Charlotte (d. 1817).

Three great events mark the period from 1820 to 1887 as one of great social progress:

(1) The Emancipation of the Catholics (1829).

(2) The Great Reform Bills of 1832, 1867, and 1884.

(3) The Repeal of the Corn Laws (1846).

NOTE.—In connection with this period, the following facts should also be noticed: (1) the expansion of our Colonial Dominions: (2) the Great Exhibition of 1851; (3) the application of steam power to navigation and railways; (4) the invention and perfection of the electric telegraph.

Lord Liverpool's Ministry is continued (1812–1827).

1820

The **Cato Street Conspiracy.** A plot was formed under the leadership of a man named Thistlewood, to murder all the Cabinet Ministers while at dinner at Lord Harrowby's. The plot having been revealed by an informer, the police found the conspirators arming themselves in a loft over a stable in Cato Street, Edgware Road. The greater number of the conspirators, including Thistlewood, escaped, but the next day the leader was captured, tried, and executed with four others.

NOTE.—This conspiracy caused the greatest alarm throughout the country; people said that the atrocity of the attempt equalled that of the Gunpowder Plot. The blame fell on the " Radical Reformers," and, after this, the word " Radical " became a bye-word and a disgrace.

The **Trial of the Queen.** George IV had in 1795 married Caroline of Brunswick, but the marriage was far from being happy, and during the Regency, Caroline had lived in Italy. On the accession of George IV she hastened to England to claim the honours due to herself as Queen; but Lord Liverpool, then Prime Minister, at the King's request, introduced in the House of Lords a Bill of " Pains and Penalties " to deprive her of her rank and dissolve the marriage. After a long trial the Bill was abandoned, to the great joy of the people, who were all on her side and pitied her for her misfortunes.

NOTE.—Parliament afterwards granted her an annuity of £50,000. At the King's coronation she tried to force her way into Westminster Abbey, but was refused admittance, and nineteen days after she died broken-hearted.

1822

Lord Sidmouth retired from the office of Home Secretary and was succeeded by **Sir Robert Peel.**

Lord Londonderry (formerly Castlereagh) committed suicide, and **Canning,** who had been made Governor-General of India, resigned his appointment and became **Foreign Secretary.**

1823

William Huskisson was made President of the Board of Trade.

NOTE.—These three men, **Peel, Canning,** and **Huskisson,** belonged rather to the middle class than to the landed aristocracy, and understood, better than their colleagues, what reforms were most needed in the Government and in the social conditions of the people at that time.

Reciprocity of Duties Bill was passed by Huskisson. The Navigation Laws of Cromwell (see page 82) were still in force, and if goods were brought into English ports by foreign vessels they were subject to very heavy duties.

The results of this were: (1) that the carrying trade (i.e., *the carrying of foreign goods*) had been taken from the Dutch and given to the

English; (2) that other countries retaliated, and greatly injured our trade by imposing heavy duties on goods brought into their countries by English ships. The Reciprocity of Duties Bill tended in a great measure to remedy this evil, and at the same time to increase our trade.

The **Bill enacted** that both English and foreign ships should have equal advantages in the way of duties on coming into English ports, whenever foreign nations would grant the same to English ships trading to their ports.

1824 This year was marked by three important **Labour Acts.**

(1) An Act repealing the law which allowed magistrates to fix the wages of workmen.

(2) An Act repealing the law which prevented workmen who were seeking employment, from travelling about to different parts of the country.

(3) An Act passed called the Combination Laws, *making " Combinations " both of masters and men* **legal** *if joined solely for the purpose of fixing wages, but* **illegal** *if joined for any other purposes.*

Import Duties on raw silk and wool were greatly reduced by Huskisson.

NOTE.—The heavy duties on raw silk had caused French silks to be everywhere preferred to English, and led to extensive smuggling. It is said that it even paid an English manufacturer to get his manufactured silk goods smuggled into England under the name of French goods.

1825 **The Great Money Panic** in England took place.

Causes: (1) People had indulged in the most reckless speculations and started the wildest of joint-stock companies, such as extracting gold from the Andes, constructing a canal across the Isthmus of Darien, etc. (2) Loans in bullion had been made to almost half the states in the world, and paper money had been issued by many banks to an extent far beyond what was prudent. It was, in fact, *a revival of the great speculating mania of 1720.*

Results: In 1825 a reaction took place, between sixty and seventy banks stopped payment, and more than 200 merchants became insolvent. The greatest distress prevailed among the poor, and riots followed.

Action of the Government. The panic was checked, and the commercial credit of England only restored by the Government: (1) coining sovereigns at the rate of 150,000 a day; (2) inducing the Bank of England to lend money to the amount of £3 million to merchants upon the security of their goods.

The distress among the poor was relieved by sending into the market the corn which was " in bond " in the warehouses (to remain there till the prices should rise to the level which allowed the importation of foreign corn).

NOTE.—In 1828 Huskisson passed a law called the " **Sliding Scale of Duties,**" enacting that the duty on corn should fall as the price rose, and should rise as the price fell. This was the first step towards the repeal of the obnoxious Corn Laws.

Lord Liverpool resigned through illness.

1827   **Canning** became **Prime Minister,** but died four months after.

Lord Goderich (formerly Robinson) became **Prime Minister,** but being unable to form a Cabinet, resigned.

1828   **The Duke of Wellington** became **Prime Minister,** with Sir Robert Peel as Home Secretary.

The **Repeal of the Test and Corporation Acts.** Lord John Russell's motion was passed after bitter resistance of Lord Eldon and the extreme Tories.

NOTE.—These Acts (see pages 86 and 88) had prevented Roman Catholics and Nonconformists from holding any important civil or military office, except by a special Act of Indemnity, which was passed in the first year of the reign of George I, and had to be renewed annually.

The **Struggle** for the **Roman Catholic Relief Bill** (Catholic Emancipation Bill) (1821–1829).

NOTE 1.—Since the Popish Plot of 1678 no Roman Catholic had been allowed to sit in either House (see page 88).

NOTE 2.—The Military and Naval Officers' Bill, passed in 1817, had opened all ranks in the army and navy to Roman Catholics. This Bill, together with the repeal of the Test and Corporation Acts, paved the way for the passing of the Catholic Emancipation Bill.

NOTE 3.—No less than four Roman Catholic Relief Bills had been brought forward since 1821, and all had been thrown out by the Lords.

1825   The agitation in Ireland was most intense. The Catholic Association was formed in 1823 under the leadership of Daniel O'Connell, to support Catholic Emancipation. So powerful had this association become that it had almost superseded the Government of Ireland, and in 1825 *the English Parliament passed an Act to suppress it.*

1828   The **Clare Election.** O'Connell was elected member for Clare. Being a Roman Catholic, he could not take his seat; but it was certain that, in spite of his inability to sit in Parliament, he would be re-elected, and that, when Parliament was dissolved, almost every county in Ireland would elect a Roman Catholic.

1829   The **Bill passed.** The situation was so threatening that a civil war seemed inevitable, and the Duke of Wellington said " *he would lay down his life if civil war could be avoided.*" Subsequently the Lords gave way and the Bill passed. It enacted: (1) that all Roman Catholics should be admitted to Parliament after taking a new form of oath; (2) that they should be eligible for all offices, civil, military, or municipal, except those of Regent, Lord-Chancellor, and Lord-Lieutenant of Ireland.

NOTE 1.—O'Connell was re-elected for Clare, and took his seat.

NOTE 2.—Wellington and Peel were denounced as traitors to their Church and King by the Protestant party. Peel, to show his sincerity, resigned his seat for the University of Oxford, and Wellington, to maintain his honour, was compelled to fight a duel with the Earl of Winchelsea, one of his warmest supporters.

Memorable Events

Criminal Law Reforms. In this and the latter part of the previous reign many improvements were made in the criminal law. No less than 200 crimes, such as theft, forgery, shop-lifting, picking pockets, etc., were punishable by death. **Sir Samuel Romilly** and **Sir James Mackintosh** had already done much to alter these unjust laws, and in 1823 Sir Robert Peel brought in Bills for the abolition of the penalty of death for more than a hundred crimes.

NOTE.—It is computed that between 1810 and 1845 upwards of 1,400 persons suffered death for crimes which have since ceased to be capital.

Foreign Affairs

The **National Rising in Greece** (1821–1827).

Its **Object** was: *To free the country from the oppressive rule of the Turks, and gain national independence.*

The French Revolution had given a great impulse to the ideas of constitutional freedom in most of the countries of Europe.

1822   The Greeks threw off their allegiance, and the Turkish Government sent two great armies to subdue the insurgents. One of these armies was repulsed, the other perished miserably in the mountains.

1824   The Sultan Mahmoud appealed for assistance to Mahomet Ali, the Pasha of Egypt, who sent an Egyptian army under his adopted son, Ibrahim Pasha. Crete was subdued and the Morea ravaged.

1826   The Turks captured **Missolonghi.**

1827   A treaty was signed known as the **Treaty of London,** between England, France, and Russia, *binding the three powers to offer mediation with a view to establish peace between Turkey and Greece, and in the event of either party refusing to accept the mediation, to put an end to the struggle by force.* Sir Edward Codrington was despatched with the English fleet to the Mediterranean to cut off the Turkish supplies, and was joined by the French and Russian squadrons. As the Sultan continued obstinate, and the Egyptian army under Ibrahim Pasha continued to devastate the Morea, the combined fleets completely annihilated the Turkish and Egyptian fleet in **Navarino Bay.** This put an end to the war, and by the **Treaty of Adrianople** (1828) Greece became an independent kingdom.

1823   The **freedom of the South American Republics** was recognized by England.

Canning's Foreign Policy was " *to leave each country free to settle its own internal affairs.*"

(1) He refused to join the Holy Alliance. (2) He recognized Peru, Chile, and the other South American Spanish colonies as independent states, sent English Consuls to them, and said " *that he had called a New World into existence to redress the balance of the Old.*"

NOTE.—These colonies had succeeded in throwing off their allegiance to Spain during the French occupation of that country.

(3) He sympathized with the Greeks, although he did not assist them in their attempt to throw off the Turkish yoke.

(4) When a Liberal Government had been established in Portugal, **Spain** and **France,** acting in accordance with the Holy Alliance, invaded that country, and Canning promptly sent English troops into Portugal and averted the danger.

1824   The **Ashanti War.** This was a brief war with the Ashantis, a tribe of Western Africa bordering on the Gulf of Guinea. The British force which was sent against them was cut to pieces, but ultimately the Ashantis were subdued.

The **First Burmese War. Cause:** The repeated aggressions made by the Burmese on the East India Company's territory in Bengal. An expedition under Sir Archibald Campbell captured the town of Rangoon. In 1825 General Morrison seized the whole province of Aracan, and in the following year the war was terminated by the treaty of **Yandabor,** by which **Assam, Aracan, and Tenasserim** were ceded to England.

Memorable Events

1819   The use of broken stones in making roads was first introduced by Macadam, a blind Scotsman, and the roads so made were called " macadamized roads " after his name.

1829   The old watchmen were abolished in London, and " policemen " introduced by Sir Robert Peel.

WILLIAM IV 1830–1837 (7 YEARS)

Title: Son of George III.

Married Adelaide of Saxe-Meiningen. No children.

The **Duke of Wellington's** ministry was continued.

1830   The **first great railway** between **Liverpool and Manchester** was opened. Huskisson was accidentally killed.

The Duke of Wellington excited a storm of indignation by declaring " that the House of Commons needed no reform and that the present system of representation and legislature enjoyed the full confidence of the country." On the defeat of the Government on a motion connected with the Civil List, the Duke resigned. **Lord Grey became Prime Minister.**

The Second French Revolution

On the death of Louis XVIII, who, after the fall of Napoleon, had been restored to the throne, his brother Charles X became King. His attempt to rule despotically led to the overthrow of the monarchy a second time, and a revolution broke out in Paris on July 27. Charles X abdicated and fled to England, and the Duke of Orleans was placed on the throne as " King of the French."

The **Belgians** also at this time threw off the yoke of allegiance to Holland, and formed themselves into a separate kingdom.

NOTE.—This second revolution in France exercised a powerful influence over the English people, and strengthened the demand for " Reform " throughout England.

The **Struggle for the Reform Bill** (1831–1832).

1831   The **First Reform Bill** was introduced by **Lord John Russell.** The greatest excitement prevailed everywhere, both in the House and outside.

NOTE.—The evils it sought to remedy were: (1) The existence of " rotten boroughs," i.e., places with few electors and sometimes no inhabitants, and yet returning two members to Parliament; e.g., Old Sarum, " only a green mound without a single dwelling-place in it," and Gatton, " only a ruined wall," both of which returned two members. (2) Large towns, such as Birmingham and Manchester, which had greatly increased owing to trade and manufactures, were totally unrepresented. (3) The unequal distribution of the franchise itself, as only a small portion of the population had the right of voting in parliamentary elections.

The **Bill was rejected.** On its introduction the Bill was fiercely opposed by the members of both Houses. After a debate which lasted seven nights, eighty-one members having spoken, *it was carried by one vote only*, but in Committee, i.e., when each separate clause is discussed, it was rejected.

Dissolution of Parliament. The King dissolved Parliament. The election cry throughout the country was, " *The Bill, the whole Bill, and nothing but the Bill*," and in the new Parliament there was a large majority for Reform.

A **Second Reform Bill** was introduced, and was carried by the Commons, but rejected by the Lords. The results were: (1) A tremendous outburst of indignation all over the country, and meetings in support of the Bill were held everywhere. (2) A cry was raised for the abolition of the House of Lords. (3) Fierce riots took place at Derby and Nottingham, where the castle was burned; the Political Union held a meeting, at which speakers declared that they would pay no taxes till the Bill was passed. (4) At Bristol the rioters got possession of the city and broke open the prisons.

1832   A **Third Reform Bill,** called the " **Great Charter of 1832,**" was introduced; it passed the Commons by the large majority of 162, but was thrown out by the Lords.

Lord Grey pressed the King to create new peers to outvote the opposition, but the King refused, and the ministry resigned.

The **Bill passed.** The Duke of Wellington was asked to form a new ministry, but was unable to do so, and Lord Grey's Ministry was reinstated, the King promising to create new peers if necessary. Wellington withdrew his opposition and abstained, with 100 supporters, from voting, and so the *Bill was passed by a majority of 84*.

The **King gave his consent** and the **Bill became Law.**

Its **chief Provisions** were: (1) The **Disfranchisement** of certain Boroughs.

(a) 56 nomination or rotten boroughs with less than 2,000 inhabitants, and returning 111 members in all, were swept away, leaving	111	seats vacant
(b) 30 boroughs with less than 4,000 inhabitants were each deprived of 1 member, leaving	30	,,
(c) Weymouth and Melcombe Regis gave up 2 members, leaving	2	,,

Total number of seats to be disposed of 143

(2) The **Redistribution** of Seats.

(a) To the counties	65 seats were given
(b) To 22 large towns, including Birmingham, Manchester, Leeds, and Sheffield, and the metropolitan districts (all of which had been previously unrepresented), 2 members each, in all	44	,,
(c) To 21 smaller towns, previously unrepresented, 1 member each ... ...' ...	21	,,
(d) To Scotland	8	,,
(e) To Ireland	5	,,
	143

(3) The **Franchise**, or right of voting:

(a) In the boroughs the right of voting was for the first time made uniform, and given to all householders paying a yearly rental of £10.

(b) In the counties the right was given to **freeholders** to the value of 40s., to **copyholders** (i.e., those holding property perpetually, but subject to certain payments) to the value of £10 a year, to **leaseholders** for twenty years paying an annual rent of £50 and over, and to **tenants at will** paying £50 rental.
This last clause (called the " Chandos clause " from its mover the Marquess of Chandos) was carried in opposition to the Ministry, and like 2 (a) above shows the landowners' influence.

NOTE.—" No law since the Bill of Rights is to be compared with this Act in importance." Despite the continued influence of the landed gentry, the period 1832–1868 is marked by the political supremacy of the middle class, due to this Bill. It also gave increased political influence to the industrial Midlands and North. The electorate was increased by about 500,000.

1833 The **First Parliament under the Reform Bill** met. The Whigs were greatly in the majority, and the small Tory party, who now assumed the name of " Conservatives," were organized under Sir Robert Peel.

The following important Acts were passed:

(1) An **Act for the Abolition of Slavery** in all the British Dominions. The English nation had to pay £20 million as compensation to the owners who had thus lost their slaves.

(2) **First Factory Act,** introduced by Lord Ashley, afterwards the Earl of Shaftesbury. It enacted: (a) that children under nine years should not be employed in factories; (b) that children under thirteen years should not labour in factories more than eight hours a day; (c) that women and young persons under eighteen should not be employed more than twelve hours a day.

(3) The **Educational Grant Act,** under which Parliament for the first time granted £20,000 annually for the purposes of elementary education.

NOTE.—In 1839 this grant was increased to £30,000, and its distribution was entrusted to the Committee of the Privy Council on education. The schools, assisted by the grant, were to be subject to Government inspection.

1834 (4) The **New Poor Law Act.** It enacted: (a) that Parishes should be united into Unions, and that Union workhouses should be substituted for Parish workhouses; (b) that those who were unable to keep themselves and their families should live in the Union workhouses; (c) that outdoor relief should not be given to the able-bodied.

The **Break-up of the Grey Ministry.** An open rupture occurred among the ministers on Lord John Russell declaring that " Parlia-

A.D.

ment had a right to appropriate the misused revenues of the Irish Church to other purposes." " *Johnny had*," said Stanley, " *upset the coach*."

Grey resigned and the Melbourne Ministry formed, but in a few months was dismissed by the King.

NOTE.—This is the last time that a Ministry has been dismissed by the sovereign.

Sir Robert Peel's First Ministry

Parliament was dissolved. A new Parliament met in which the Conservatives were in the majority.

Lord John Russell's motion *relating to the appropriation of the surplus revenues of the Irish Church to the purposes of education* was carried, in opposition to the Ministry, by the Liberals, who formed a coalition with the Irish members under an agreement known as the " *Lichfield House Compact*."

Sir Robert resigned.

1835 ### Lord Melbourne's Second Ministry (1835–1841)

Three important Acts marked this Ministry.

(*a*) The **Municipal Reform Act** providing: (1) that all members of Town Councils should be elected by the ratepayers instead of being self-chosen as they frequently were (the city of London was to be exempt from this law); (2) that Town Councils should publish their accounts and show how they had spent the public money.

1836 (*b*) The **Marriage Act,** allowing Nonconformists to celebrate their marriages in their own chapels, or before the registrar of the district.

(*c*) The **Tithe Commutation Bill.** It enacted that tithes should be paid in money, and that the amount should vary according to the average price of corn during the seven preceding years.

The Stamp Duty on newspapers was reduced from 4*d*. to 1*d*.

VICTORIA 1837–1901 (64 YEARS)

Title: Daughter of Edward, Duke of Kent, son of George III.

Married Albert of Saxe-Coburg.

Children: Victoria, Edward VII, Alice, Alfred, Helena, Louise, Arthur, Leopold, and Beatrice.

Lord Melbourne's Ministry was continued.

1837 ### Insurrection broke out in the Canadas

There were frequent disputes between the English and French settlers, and also conflicts between the nominated Councils and the elected Assemblies. Largely owing to these latter conflicts, there were risings in Upper and Lower Canada, which were suppressed without difficulty. Lord Durham was sent as High Commissioner, and though recalled because of arbitrary action, his

Report was adopted: in 1840 the Union Act united the two provinces, gave financial control to the Assemblies, and laid the foundations for self-government.

1838 **Rise of the Chartists.** To achieve economic and social reform by extending political power to the working classes, the Chartists, in the "*People's Charter*," demanded **six sweeping reforms** in the constitution: (1) universal suffrage, i.e., that every man should have a vote; (2) that a fresh Parliament should be elected every year; (3) that voting should be by ballot; (4) that every man, whether he owned property or not, should be eligible for a seat in Parliament; (5) that Members of Parliament should be paid; (6) that the country should be divided into equal electoral districts.

NOTE 1.—Of these demands, Nos. (3), (4), and (5), and in some degree No. (1), have since become law.

NOTE 2.—In 1839 a petition signed by Chartist delegates from all the large towns was rejected by Parliament, and Chartist riots occurred in Birmingham, Sheffield, and other places. At Newport an open rebellion took place, led by a magistrate named Frost, but was easily suppressed. The agitation, however, continued until the great Chartist Demonstration in 1848.

1839 The **New Postage Scheme** was adopted.

The charge for postage was at this time from 6*d.* to 1*s.* 6*d.*, according to the distance. Mr. Hill, afterwards **Sir Rowland Hill,** an officer in the Post Office, advised the Government *to reduce the postage to a penny on letters between all places in the United Kingdom.* He showed: (1) that the actual cost of carrying each letter was very small; (2) that instead of diminishing the revenue, " penny postage " would increase it, owing to the greater number of letters which would be sent.

Results: (1) A postage of 4*d.* for every ½ oz. was at first introduced, but in 1840 " penny postage " was adopted. (2) Postage stamps were used, and the privilege of " franking " letters, i.e., *of sending them free of charge, reserved to the Members of Parliament and their friends,* was abolished. (3) The system of postage stamps and low rate of postage have since been adopted by every civilized country in the world.

NOTE.—Hill was afterwards knighted, and received a pension of £2,000 a year.

1840 **Marriage of the Queen** to Prince Albert of Saxe-Coburg, her cousin.

Irish Affairs (1840–1843)

The **Irish Municipal Act** was passed. It abolished 58 corporations, established 10 new ones, and reformed several municipal abuses.

1843 In this year the agitation for the Repeal of the Union which had been begun under O'Connell in 1829, reached its height. It received the support of the Roman Catholic priesthood to such an extent *that the collections made at chapel doors, called " Repeal Rent," amounted in one year to £48,000.*

A monster " Repeal " meeting was summoned by **O'Connell** at **Clontarf,** near Dublin, but the Government poured 35,000 troops into Ireland and forbade it by proclamation, and no attempt was

A.D.

made to hold it. O'Connell was arrested, tried for sedition and conspiracy, and sentenced to a year's imprisonment and a heavy fine, but the judgment was reversed by the House of Lords and he was released. The demand for " Repeal " once more subsided.

The First War with China (1839–1841)

Cause: The Chinese Government, alarmed at the increase of the use of opium among the Chinese, forbade its importation, but the British merchants, who had made large profits by the trade, still smuggled it into the country. Cargoes of the poisonous drug were destroyed by royal authority, and Captain Elliot, the British Commissioner, imprisoned.

The Events in the War. In 1840 war was declared against China; the British troops captured the town and island of Chusan, reduced the Bogue Forts at the mouth of the Canton River, and took Amoy and Ningpo.

Peace was concluded. In 1841 peace was concluded; the Chinese Government agreed to open five ports (including Canton) to British trade, and Hong Kong was ceded to Britain.

1841   Following a Government defeat, the Conservatives gained a majority in the new Parliament.

Sir Robert Peel's Second Ministry (1841–1846)

The First Afghan War (1839–1842)

Cause: The danger to India from Russian expansion in Central Asia made it seem important that a prince friendly to the English cause should sit on the throne of Afghanistan.

1839   **The Invasion of Afghanistan.** The Afghan ruler Dost Mahommed refused an alliance with England. He was deposed, and the exiled Shah Sajah restored.

1841   **Akbar Khan,** son of Dost Mahommed, led a rising against the British. The Resident and the Envoy were murdered, and the British forces annihilated as they withdrew through the passes: only Dr. Brydon survived.

1842   **General Pollock** forced the Khyber Pass and captured Kabul. Dost Mahommed was restored. British troops were withdrawn from a position which it was difficult and expensive to maintain.

The Income Tax was established. To supply a constantly deficient revenue, Sir Robert Peel carried an Income Tax Bill, *imposing a tax of 7d. in the pound on all those who had incomes of more than £150 a year.*

NOTE.—This tax was to last for three years only, in the hope that it might then be dispensed with, but no pledge was given to that effect, and so in 1845 it was renewed, and has been in existence ever since.

1843   ### The Conquest of Sindh

Cause: A dispute with the Amirs of Sindh about the territory round the Indus, which during the Afghan War had been occupied by British troops.

Sir Charles Napier defeated the Amir at **Meanee,** and the territory was annexed to the British Empire.

The establishment of the **Free Church of Scotland**

Cause: *Numbers of the Scottish clergy and people objected to the system by which lay patrons held the appointment of ministers to Church livings.* In this year 470 ministers (one-third of the whole clergy) threw up their livings, seceded from the Church, and, followed by their numerous congregations, formed themselves into a separate communion, which they called the " Free Church of Scotland."

NOTE.—The rapid formation and organization of the Free Church was largely owing to the indefatigable exertions of **Thomas Chalmers.**

1845 The **First Sikh War**

Cause: On the death of Runjeet Singh, the " lion of the Punjab," who had been a firm ally to the British, the power fell into the hands of the army, and the Sikhs invaded British India.

The **Events in the War.** Sir Hugh Gough drove back the Sikhs, and defeated them at **Ferozeshah** and **Moodkee,** but they again crossed the Sutlej, and were completely routed by Sir Harry Smith at **Aliwal,** and their strongly fortified camp at **Sobraon** taken.

Results: The Sikhs submitted, and by the Treaty of Lahore (1846) gave up the " Doab " (the territory between the Beas and Sutlej) to the British power.

Free Trade and **the repeal of the Corn Laws** (1838–1846).

The **Corn Laws** were heavy duties levied on corn imported into England. The landowners and agriculturists wished to keep foreign corn out of the country, by imposing high duties on imported corn so that the price of home-grown corn would be kept up. The Corn Laws, however, not only caused much suffering among the poorer classes but also crippled our trade.

1838 (*a*) An association was formed in Manchester to urge the Government to abolish the duties on corn. This was the beginning of the **Anti-Corn-Law League,** and its chief leaders were **Richard Cobden** and **John Bright.**

(*b*) For eight years the agitation for the repeal continued, and the Anti-Corn-Law League became more and more powerful. To improve finances and remedy the impoverishment of the working classes Peel determined on a free trade policy. His Budget of 1842 embodied this principle, and its success encouraged him to carry it further, by removing or reducing still more duties on trade, in his Budget of 1845.

1845 Famine in Ireland, owing to failure of the potato crop, led Peel to accept the necessity to repeal the Corn Laws.

1846 Peel's Corn Bill was passed, fixing a sliding scale of duties varying with price, until 1849, and a small nominal duty thereafter. The repeal of the Corn Laws split the Conservative Party. The

A.D.

" Peelites," supporting Free Trade, formed a new middle party and ultimately contributed to the forming of the Liberal Party. A combination of anti-Peelites, Whigs, and Irish members, defeated Peel on an Irish Coercion Bill.

Lord John Russell's Ministry (1846–1852) with Lord Palmerston as Foreign Secretary.

1848   The **Year of Revolutions.** In this year the Third French Revolution broke out in Paris. King Louis Philippe was driven from his throne and fled to England, and a Republic was established in France based on universal suffrage. The shock of this revolution caused the throne of nearly every monarch in Europe to totter; insurrections took place in Italy, Spain, Germany, and Austria, and a demand for a " popular government " was put forward everywhere.

(1) In **Ireland** the more violent members of the Repeal Society (i.e., *for the Repeal of the " Union "*) formed themselves into the " Young Ireland Party," and headed by Smith O'Brien, who had taken the place of O'Connell, made preparations for an armed resistance against the Government. Several newspapers had excited the people to open rebellion, the most violent being the *United Irishman*, edited by John Mitchell, who was arrested, tried, and transported. This disconcerted the conspirators, and a feeble rising under O'Brien in Tipperary was easily suppressed; the leaders were captured and four condemned to death, but the sentence was afterwards commuted to transportation. No other attempt was made after this to subvert the Government.

(2) In **England** a great Chartist demonstration took place. Several circumstances encouraged the Chartists to put forth all their strength: (*a*) the successes gained by their party in parliamentary elections, especially in the election of Feargus O'Connor for Nottingham; (*b*) the recent revolution in Paris, the overthrow of Louis Philippe, and the establishment of a Republic; (*c*) the rebellion of the " Young Ireland Party."

Failure of the Great Chartist Rising. Feargus O'Connor, having summoned a monster meeting on Kennington Common, proposed to march towards the House of Commons and present a petition said to be signed by more than 5 million persons. The Government forbade the procession, and 200,000 citizens were sworn in as special constables. In case of emergency the Duke of Wellington had secretly posted soldiers in all parts of London. The whole affair proved a miserable failure; the march was given up, the petition was found to contain only one-third of the stated number of signatures and many of these were fictitious, and no more was heard of the Chartists as an organized body.

Note.—The failure of the Chartist rising made it clear that any great changes in the government of the country could not be brought about by " physical force."

1849   The **Second Sikh War** (1848–1849)

Cause: A revolt broke out at Moultan, and some English residents were murdered.

E

The **Events in the War.** Lord Gough won the battle of **Chillian-walla,** but the loss on the part of the British forces was so great that Gough was blamed for his indiscretion in risking a battle and superseded by Sir Charles Napier. Before Napier arrived, however, Gough had retrieved his reputation by the total overthrow of the enemy at **Gujerat.**

Result. The whole country submitted, and the **Punjab** was annexed to our Indian Empire.

NOTE.—The Sikh soldiers, who had hitherto been the most formidable antagonists of the British army, now became, under the just rule and kind treatment of the two brothers, Henry and John Lawrence, our most unwavering supporters.

1851

The **Great Exhibition** of the Industries of All Nations, *the first of all the great exhibitions,* was held in London, in the Crystal Palace. The idea originated with the Prince Consort. Its **object** was: (1) " to teach English manufacturers that they might improve their own work by comparing it with and studying the work of foreign nations "; (2) to show what stage the industries of the different nations of the world had reached.

French Coup d'État of December 2, 1851

Prince Louis Napoleon, who had been President of the French Republic for three years, overthrew the Republic, procured his election as President for ten years, and ultimately became Emperor as Napoleon III.

Lord Palmerston was dismissed. Although the Ministry was supposed to be strictly neutral, Palmerston, as Foreign Secretary, without consulting his colleagues or his Sovereign, *wrote to Napoleon and expressed his approval of the coup d'état.* This led to his dismissal from office.

NOTE.—The following year (1852), however, Palmerston had his revenge by carrying against the Ministry an amendment to the Bill for the organization of the Militia, and Lord John Russell resigned.

1852

Lord Derby became Prime Minister, but resigned the same year, and **Lord Aberdeen formed a Coalition Ministry** of " Whigs and Peelites."

The **Russian** or **Crimean War** (1853–1856)

Its **origin:** (1) A dispute had arisen between Russia and Turkey about the guardianship of the Holy Places at Jerusalem. (2) Nicholas, the Czar of Russia, claimed the right to protect all Christian subjects in those countries bordering on the Danube, which were under Turkish rule. (3) The Czar had aggressive designs on Turkey, and wished to extend his power to the Dardanelles and secure Constantinople. (4) In 1853, England, France, Austria, and Prussia held a conference at Vienna, and, in what is called the " Vienna Note," forwarded a proposal to the Sultan *that he should accede to the claim made by the Czar.* The Sultan, however, refused, and the Czar declared war against Turkey.

NOTE.—In 1853 the Czar, anxious to secure the neutrality of England in the quarrel, proposed to the English ambassador, Sir Hamilton Seymour, that if the " sick man died." i.e., if the Turkish Empire was dismembered, England should have as her share Crete and Egypt, and that the Sultan's European provinces should be formed into independent states and placed under Russian protection. The English ministry rejected these proposals.

Events in the War

1853 **In Turkey.** (1) The Russians began the war by attacking the Turkish provinces bordering on the Danube, but were defeated at **Oltenitza.** The Russian fleet destroyed the Turkish fleet at **Sinope.** Meanwhile the English fleet was sent to the Black Sea.

1854 (2) The Russians laid siege to **Silistria,** but the appearance of the English and French army at **Varna** caused them to withdraw their troops.

In the **Crimea.** The English and French troops were transported from Varna to the Crimea to destroy the great Russian naval arsenal of **Sebastopol.**

(1) The **Battle of the Alma** was fought six days after the Allies under Lord Raglan had landed. The Russians were totally defeated.

NOTE.—If the Allies had followed up this victory they might have taken Sebastopol, but the French General refused, and the delay gave General Todleben, the Russian engineer, time to close the harbour against the Allies, and improve the fortifications.

After the battle the Allies encamped on the South side of the town, and the Siege of Sebastopol began.

(2) The **Battle of Balaclava,** rendered memorable by the charge of the Light Brigade.

NOTE.—The Russian army had attempted to cut off the communication between the English army and the little port of Balaclava. Lord Cardigan received an order, from Lord Raglan, by which his Light Brigade was meant to retake some guns captured by the Russians, but by a series of misunderstandings charged at enemy batteries along a valley lined with Russian troops. Of the 600 who rode into " the jaws of death " only a handful returned.
" It is magnificent, it is heroic," said a French general, " but it is not war."

(3) The **Battle of Inkerman.** In this battle an attempt was made by the Russians under cover of a mist to surprise the British army. This was frustrated by a few regiments of British soldiers, who kept the whole Russian line in check until the French troops came up to their assistance, and compelled the Russians to retreat. It was, strictly speaking, a *soldiers' battle.*

(4) The **Winter of 1854.** During the severe winter of 1854 the troops suffered greatly from want of food and shelter, owing to the miserable management of the commissariat. The hospital services were extremely bad until the improvements carried out by Florence Nightingale.

The indignation of the people at home was roused against the Government, and a motion, brought forward by Mr. Roebuck, to inquire into the cause of the mismanagement, passed the Commons, and Lord Aberdeen resigned.

1855 Lord Palmerston became Prime Minister

(5) The **Fall of Sebastopol.** The war was now pushed on vigorously, a railroad was constructed from Balaclava to the camp to supply the troops with provisions, and in September 1855, after a month's incessant bombardment, the **Malakof** and the **Redan,** two strong fortresses, were taken by assault and Sebastopol fell. The Russians evacuated the town, blew up the forts, and left their sick and wounded behind them.

In the **Baltic, Bomarsund** and **Sweaborg** were bombarded by the English fleet with only partial success. In **Asia Minor, Kars,** whose garrison was under the command of General Williams, surrendered to the Russians, after a gallant defence of six months.

1856 Peace was concluded and the Third Treaty of Paris signed. By this treaty Russia promised: (1) not to re-fortify Sebastopol; (2) not to keep a fleet in the Black Sea.

The Second War with China

Cause: The capture of a vessel called the *Arrow*, sailing under the British flag. War followed and Canton was seized by the combined French and British troops, but the **Treaty of Tientsin** brought the war to a close. By this treaty: (1) additional ports were opened to our trade; (2) British subjects were allowed to travel into the interior of China; (3) a British ambassador was received at Pekin.

NOTE.—Cobden's motion condemning the action of the Government in the affair of the *Arrow* was carried, and Palmerston appealed to the country. The result was he was returned to power in a stronger position than ever. Cobden lost his seat.

1857 The Indian Mutiny (1857–1858)

Causes: (1) The annexation of Oudh in 1856 (a state from which many Sepoys, i.e., native troops, were raised) caused much irritation among the natives. (2) A widely spread report among the natives that the British intended to introduce Christianity by force, and compel them to give up their religion. (3) The Sepoys refused to bite the cartridges before loading, because they thought that they had been greased with cow's fat and hog's lard, and their religion taught them that if their lips came into contact with these substances they would lose caste.

The Events in the Mutiny

(1) The **Capture of Delhi** by the rebels. The discontent first showed itself in an outbreak of Sepoys at Meerut. English officers were murdered, Delhi was seized, and a descendant of the great Mogul set up as Emperor of India.

(2) The **Massacre of Cawnpore.** This place was taken by the rebels, and the garrison, consisting of about 500 soldiers, decoyed to their destruction by Nana Sahib, a native prince. Their wives and children, upwards of 500 in number, were then barbarously slaughtered and their bodies flung into a well.

A.D.

(3) The **Recapture of Delhi.** Delhi was stormed by Generals Wilson and Nicholson, the latter losing his life in the assault.

(4) The **Siege and Relief of Lucknow.** Lucknow held out until it was relieved by General Havelock and Sir James Outram, who, being besieged by the rebels, were in turn relieved by Sir Colin Campbell. *The Relief of Lucknow terminated the war.*

1858   **Results:** (1) The Government at home put an end to the authority of the East India Company by *transferring its power to the Crown.* (2) The Governor-General or Viceroy in India was brought directly under the control of the Queen, and acted through a British Secretary of State for India residing in England. (3) A council of fifteen persons, experienced in Indian affairs, was appointed in England to give advice to the Secretary of State for India. (4) The Queen was proclaimed Sovereign of India.

NOTE.—Lord Canning, the son of George Canning, became the First Viceroy, as well as Governor-General.

1855   The **Conspiracy to Murder Bill,** brought in by Lord Palmerston. Its **object** was: *To punish those who contrived or plotted the assassination of foreign princes in England.*

A plot had been formed in England by Orsini, an Italian refugee, to murder the French Emperor, and the French Government demanded that England should no longer offer facilities for such conspiracies.

The Bill was defeated owing: (1) to the unpopularity of the French Emperor in England; (2) to the boastful and abusive language used by some French officers, who even called on the Emperor to invade England. Palmerston resigned.

Lord Derby became Prime Minister

A Bill was carried admitting Jews to Parliament.

1859   The **Volunteer Movement.** The fear of a French invasion led to the formation of large bodies of volunteers as a permanent part of our regular army, who took for their motto " *Defence, not Defiance.*"

Disraeli's Reform Bill. Disraeli introduced his Parliamentary Reform Bill: (1) lodgers at £20 per annum were entitled to vote; (2) also graduates, schoolmasters, and holders of savings in banks and public funds; " *fancy franchises,*" as Mr. Bright called them. The Bill was defeated and the dissolution of Parliament followed.

NOTE.—The new Parliament had a Liberal majority.

Lord Palmerston became Prime Minister a second time.

During the ministry the **Italian War of Liberation** took place. Events in the War: (1) In the North the combined forces of France and Sardinia defeated the Austrians at the battles of **Montebello, Magenta,** and **Solferino,** and expelled them from Lombardy. (2) In the South, **Garibaldi,** an enthusiastic patriot and distinguished soldier, liberated Sicily and Naples, whereupon these countries joined Sardinia. Victor Emmanuel, King of Sardinia, was proclaimed " King of Italy."

1861   The **American Civil War** began. This was a terrible contest between the Northern or " Federal " States and the Southern or " Confederate " States, and lasted four years.

The Northern manufacturing states had a Protectionist trade policy which was resented in the agricultural South. The latter depended on slave labour for tobacco, cotton, and sugar plantations. Northern opponents of slavery secured a majority in Congress and abolition of slavery seemed near. The South claimed the right to secede from the Union. This affected the very existence of the United States, and war resulted.

NOTE.—England remained neutral during the struggle, but the upper classes generally sympathized with the South, the working men, in spite of hardship caused by the cotton famine, with the North.

Three important events connected with this war affected England.

(1) The **Trent Affair.** Two Confederate envoys, while sailing to Europe under the protection of the English flag to seek for the friendship of England and France, were captured by a Federal man-of-war. The British protested, and the Federal States immediately surrendered the men, and acknowledged that their officers had acted wrongly.

(2) The **Alabama Claims.** The *Alabama* was a swift war-cruiser, built at Birkenhead for the Confederates, notwithstanding the protest of the American ambassador. The English Government, however, allowed the ship to leave harbour, and she sailed away to America, where she did an immense amount of damage to the commerce of the Northern States. The conduct of the English in this matter was considered a breach of neutrality, and roused the greatest indignation in America against England. The Northern States claimed compensation, and it was not till 1872 that the matter was settled, when, during Gladstone's Government, a Court of Arbitration held at Geneva *awarded to the United States the sum of £3,000,000 as damages.*

(3) The **Cotton Famine in Lancashire.** The Civil War had cut off our supplies of cotton from the United States, and great distress occurred in consequence among the operatives in Lancashire, known as the Cotton Famine. The nation contributed more than £2 million to a Relief Fund, and although the operatives suffered terribly before cotton could be obtained from Egypt and India, they bore their misfortunes with fortitude and patience.

NOTE 1.—In 1865 the North completely overcame the South, slavery was abolished in the whole country, and the integrity of the Union preserved. This was accomplished mainly by the " indomitable perseverance of Abraham Lincoln, the president, and the military skill of General Grant, the Federal commander."

NOTE 2.—The same year Lincoln was shot by an assassin named Booth in a theatre in Washington.

1860   **Cobden's Treaty with France.** This was a commercial Treaty, based on free trade principles, and negotiated by Cobden with France. (See page 231.)

1861   **Death of the Prince Consort**

1863   **The Ionian Islands** separated from England and joined Greece.

1865 **Death of Lord Palmerston**

Lord John Russell (now Earl Russell) **became Prime Minister** a second time, and Gladstone, as Chancellor of the Exchequer, leader of the House of Commons.

The cruel suppression of a rebellion in Jamaica by Governor Eyre was condemned by Parliament, and Eyre was superseded.

1866 **Gladstone's Reform Bill** was introduced, making the county franchise £14 rental, the borough franchise £7 rental, and lodgers' franchise £10 per annum.

A section of the Liberals, called by Bright the **Adullamites,** and led by Robert Lowe, seceded from the Ministry, and so the Bill was defeated, and the Ministry resigned.

Lord Derby became Prime Minister, and Disraeli, Chancellor of the Exchequer, leader of the House of Commons.

1867 A new **Parliamentary Reform Bill** (sometimes called the *Second Great Reform Bill*) was brought forward by Disraeli and passed. The great principle of this Bill was that the franchise was based upon the **rating** and not on the **rental.**

It enacted that: (1) in **boroughs** the franchise should be given to all householders paying rates, and to lodgers paying a rental of £10; (2) in **counties** to occupiers of property rated at £12 a year.

NOTE 1.—In boroughs which returned three members each voter was allowed to give two votes only.

NOTE 2.—Lord Derby characterized this Bill as " a leap in the dark," but added " that he had the greatest confidence in the sound sense of his countrymen."

NOTE 3.—The Bill added 1 million to the electorate, and gave a share of political power to the working classes.

The **Fenian Conspiracy** (1866–1867). The Fenians were a " secret " society of Irishmen, who formed themselves into the Republican Brotherhood under the leadership of James Stephens, the " Head Centre."

Their aims were: (1) to bring about a separation of Ireland from England; (2) to set up a republic in Ireland.

They were supported by an immense number of Irish in the United States, many of whom had served in the American Civil War, and they had the sympathy of many Irishmen who resided in Ireland and England.

In 1866 the situation in Ireland was so threatening owing to Fenianism, that the Government passed a Bill " in a single day," *suspending the Habeas Corpus Act* in that country. More than 100 Fenians were arrested.

Fenian Risings and Outrages

(1) In **Ireland.** Many of the Irish soldiers, who had been engaged in the Civil War, having returned from America to Ireland, a general rising was attempted in 1867, but was suppressed by the Irish Constabulary force with little bloodshed.

A.D.

(2) In **England.** (*a*) A plot was formed to seize the arms in Chester Castle, but was frustrated by the treachery of one of the conspirators.

(*b*) In **Manchester** several Fenians rescued some Fenian prisoners from a prison van, and in the struggle which ensued a police sergeant was killed.

(*c*) An outrage was committed in London by some Irishmen, who blew down with gunpowder the walls of **Clerkenwell prison,** in which two Fenians were confined. The explosion shattered the adjacent houses and injured the inhabitants.

1850

Extension and Consolidation of our Colonial Empire

(1) The **Australian Colonies**

Lord John Russell passed a Bill giving a representative Government to each of the four Australian Colonies, New South Wales, Victoria, South Australia, and Van Diemen's Land, and in 1852 a Constitution was given to each of the six colonies in New Zealand.

NOTE.—In 1851 the English Government put an end to the system of " Transportation of Criminals " to New South Wales. In the same year the discovery of gold in Victoria led to an enormous emigration from England to that colony.

1867

(2) The North American Colonies

In this year a Bill was passed for the Confederation of the North American Colonies, which were united under the name of the " Dominion of Canada." The Bill provided that there should be: (*a*) a Governor-General of the Dominion appointed by the Crown; (*b*) a Parliament consisting of a Senate and a House of Commons, for legislating matters of common interest.

The **Abyssinian Expedition**

Cause: Theodore, King of Abyssinia, had seized and imprisoned all the British subjects he could lay hands on in his country.
Sir Robert Napier led a British army through an almost impassable region to the fortress of Magdala. Although the prisoners were released, Magdala was stormed, and dismantled. Theodore himself committed suicide. Sir Robert became Lord Napier of Magdala.

1868

Disraeli became Prime Minister on the resignation of Lord Derby. Gladstone brought in and carried against the Government his resolution concerning the Disestablishment of the Protestant Church in Ireland, *as being the Church of the minority.* Disraeli appealed to the country.

The New Parliament was strongly Liberal—Disraeli resigned and Gladstone became Prime Minister.

1869

Gladstone's Ministry (1869–1874)

The Bill for the **Disestablishment and Disendowment of the Irish Church was passed.**

1870

Gladstone's first Irish Land Act was passed. It provided: (1) for the compensation of outgoing tenants for improvements made by them; (2) for loans to landlords to be spent in improvements, and to tenants wishing to purchase their holdings; (3) for means of putting a restraint upon hasty and unjust evictions; (4) for the establishment of courts of arbitration to settle disputes between landlords and tenants.

Forster's Elementary Education Act. It enacted that: (1) wherever the school accommodation for the education of children of the poorer classes was insufficient, a School Board should be elected by the ratepayers of that district, with authority to build and maintain Board Schools at the expense of the ratepayers; (2) that the School Board should have power to enforce the attendance of children at the Board School or some other efficient school; (3) that all sectarian religious teaching should be excluded from Schools supported by the School rate.

The **Franco-Prussian War** (1870–1871)

Cause: A strong feeling of jealousy had existed between France and Prussia since the defeat of Austria in 1866, and in 1870 the Emperor Napoleon picked a quarrel with the King of Prussia. War suddenly broke out, and all Germany joined Prussia. The German army was well prepared, and chiefly under the command of a consummate strategist, Count Moltke, while the French were in a state of hopeless confusion.

Events in the War

(1) The Germans invaded France, defeated the French at the battles of **Wörth** and **Forbach,** and drove Marshal Bazaine into **Metz.**

(2) Napoleon, marching to his relief, was defeated at **Sedan,** and he himself and his whole army taken prisoners. A revolution at Paris followed, the Empire was overthrown, and a Republic established.

(3) The German army invested Paris. Meanwhile Bazaine capitulated at Metz with 170,000 men.

Paris was taken in 1871, and a peace was signed by which: (1) the provinces of Alsace and Lorraine were ceded to Germany; (2) France had to pay £200 million to Germany for the expenses of the war.

King William was proclaimed German Emperor.

1871   **Russia** refused any longer to be bound by the clauses in the Treaty of Paris (1856), which forbade her keeping ships of war in the Black Sea. A conference of the representatives of the Great Powers held at London released her from the engagement. A Bill was passed abolishing all **Religious tests in the Universities** of Oxford and Cambridge.

The successes of the Prussian army strengthened the need for reform in the British army. Viscount Cardwell introduced great improvements, including the establishment of a Secretary of State for War (responsible to Parliament), the adoption of short service enlistment and the organization of a proper reserve, and the abolition of the purchase of commissions (rejected by the Lords but achieved by Royal warrant).

1871   **Trades Union Act** recognizing the legality of Trades Unions and protecting union funds against misuse by officials.

1872   **The Ballot Act** was passed, "*to secure secret voting by means of the ballot.*" It was intended to prevent intimidation.

1873   The **Second Ashanti War.** Koffee, King of the Ashantis, invaded British territory in the Gulf of Guinea, but was defeated by Sir Garnet Wolseley, and his capital, Coomassie, taken and burnt. The war was concluded in 1874.

The **Supreme Court of Judicature** Act was passed, constituting a High Court of Justice (in which the Court of Queen's Bench, Common Pleas, and Chancery were united) and a Supreme Court of Appeal.

1874   On the resignation of Gladstone, **Disraeli became Prime Minister.**

The **Public Worship Regulation Act** was passed, giving parishioners the power (subject to the sanction of the bishop) to prosecute a clergyman for ritualistic practices.

1875   The **Fiji Islands** were annexed to England by the desire of the inhabitants.

The **Unseaworthy Ships Bill** was introduced by Mr. Plimsoll and passed. By this Act the Board of Trade was empowered to detain from sailing any vessels deemed unsafe, "*coffin ships,*" as they were called.

Disraeli's Proposal to buy the Khedive's **share of the Suez Cana** at the price of £4 million was unanimously sanctioned by the House of Commons.

The **Prince of Wales visited India,** where he met with a most enthusiastic reception from the Indian princes and people. To commemorate his visit the **Additional Titles Bill** was passed by Disraeli in 1876, *which gave the Queen authority to assume the title of Empress of India.*

The **Russo-Turkish War** (1877–1878)

Cause: Roused by the misdeeds of Turkish officials, the states of Servia and Montenegro made war on Turkey. A revolt also occurred in **Bulgaria,** but was crushed by the Turks with the most frightful barbarities.

"*The embarrassment of Turkey was the opportunity of Russia,*" who now interfered on behalf of the Christian subjects living under the Sultan's rule.

The **Rejection** of the **mediation of the Great Powers.** A conference of the Great Powers sat at Constantinople, but its proposals were rejected by the Porte. Shortly after the Great Powers signed a Protocol at London, demanding certain reforms in the Turkish Government and the mutual disarmament of the contending parties. The Porte resented their interference, and in consequence *Russia declared war against Turkey.*

1877   **Events in the War**

(1) The Russians were defeated by the Turks under **Osman Pasha** with great loss at the battle of **Plevna** Shortly after, however, he was surrounded by the Russians and compelled to capitulate with 40,000 men.

(2) **Kars,** a town in Asia Minor, was taken by assault by the Russians, the loss on the side of the Turks being very great.

(3) The Turkish army was captured at the **Shipka Pass,** and the Russians advanced to within 30 miles of Constantinople. *To prevent the Russians from occupying Constantinople the British fleet was ordered to sail to the Sea of Marmora, and 7,000 Sepoys, the " Indian Contingent," were brought from India to be in readiness at Malta.*

(4) The Treaty of **San Stephano.** A preliminary treaty was signed between Russia and Turkey at San Stephano, which Lord Beaconsfield afterwards insisted should be submitted to all the European Powers. The **Berlin Congress** was the result.

1878   **The Treaty of Berlin.** By this Treaty: (1) Roumania, Servia, and Montenegro gained their independence; (2) Bosnia and Herzegovina were handed over to Austria; (3) Bulgaria was erected into a principality, paying tribute to the Sultan; (4) Eastern Roumelia was to be ruled over by a Christian Governor nominated by the Sultan; (5) Thessaly was ceded to Greece; (6) Russia received a piece of territory near the mouth of the Danube, and another piece round Kars; (7) Cyprus was ceded to England on condition that England should pay tribute to the Sultan for the island and protect Asia Minor.

NOTE.—The British representatives at the Congress were Lords Beaconsfield and Salisbury, who, on their return to England, were welcomed as bringing back " peace with honour."

The Second War with Afghanistan (1878–1879)

Russia, having been checked in her aggressive policy at Constantinople, began to press forward towards the north-west frontier of India. A Russian embassy had been received at Cabul, whereupon a British envoy was also despatched to Shere Ali, the Afghan ruler, but was stopped at the frontier. War immediately followed, and Cabul was taken. In the following year the English Envoy, **Sir Louis Cavagnari,** together with the whole of his Indian guard, was murdered by the Afghans. This led to the second invasion of the country under **Sir Frederick Roberts** and recapture of Cabul, but in 1881 the English Government decided to withdraw their troops from the country altogether.

1879   **The Zulu War**

The Zulus, a powerful and warlike tribe of Kaffirs, made war on the English settlers in the South of Africa. At **Isandula** the British troops were surrounded and cut to pieces, but shortly after the English gained a victory over the enemy at **Ulundi,** and the country was brought into subjection.

NOTE.—The Prince Imperial, son of Napoleon III, volunteered to serve in the English Army during this war, but was killed, while reconnoitring, by a party of Zulus in ambush.

Irish Affairs (1881–1882)

(1) The **Land League.** Owing to the numerous evictions of tenants for the non-payment of rents, great agitation existed in Ireland, accompanied by many murders and agrarian outrages. The Land League was formed by Michael Davitt to *oppose the landlords*. A Parliamentary party was also formed, among the Irish members, under the leadership of Parnell, demanding **Home Rule** for Ireland.

1881

(2) **Gladstone's Second Irish Land Act** was passed. It appointed a " Land Court " with power: (*a*) to fix rents for fifteen years; (*b*) to reduce rents where necessary.

(3) The **First Coercion Act** was passed for the protection of life and property. Parnell and others were imprisoned for opposing the Government, but shortly after released.

Mr. Forster, the Irish Secretary, resigned in consequence.

A proclamation was issued by Parliament to the effect *that the Land League was a criminal and illegal association.*

1882

(4) The **Murder of Lord Frederick Cavendish** and **Mr. Burke.** Lord Frederick Cavendish, Mr. Forster's successor, and Mr. Burke, the Irish Under-Secretary, were murdered in the Phœnix Park, Dublin, by the " Invincibles." *This led to the passing of a second and much more severe Coercion Act*, called " The Prevention of Crimes Bill."

The **Closure Bill** was brought forward by Gladstone and passed. This was the name " given to a power vested in the Speaker of the House of Commons, or Chairman of Committees, to close a debate, when it seemed to him that the subject had been fully discussed, or when he was authorized to do so by a motion duly supported."

NOTE.—It was passed because the Irish members, under Parnell, began the annoyance of " obstruction," and prevented the passing of many useful bills. The followers of Parnell had declared themselves to be the opponents of any English Government, either Whig or Tory.

Affairs in Egypt and the Sudan (1879–1885)

1879

Egypt was declared a bankrupt state, and placed under the dual control of England and France.

1882

(1) **Arabi Pasha's Rebellion.** An insurrection was set on foot against the Khedive of Egypt by an officer named Arabi Pasha, *to liberate Egypt from European influence.*

The **Forts of Alexandria**, which were in Arabi's power, were destroyed by the English fleet, and Arabi himself defeated by Sir Garnet Wolseley at **Tel-el-Kebir,** and taken prisoner. England assumed the protectorate of Egypt.

A.D.

1883 (2) The **Mahdi:** In the Sudan the Mahdi, a Mohammedan fanatic, roused his followers against the Egyptian Government and *defeated and destroyed almost to a man an Egyptian army of 11,000 men who had been sent against him under an Englishman named Hicks Pasha.* Khartoum held out against him.

1884 (3) **General Gordon** (called also " Chinese Gordon " from his brilliant exploits in China) volunteered to go to the Sudan and negotiate for the withdrawal of the Egyptian troops. Reaching **Khartoum,** he was there besieged by the Mahdi's troops, and Lord Wolseley was sent out to relieve him, but arrived too late, for Khartoum was betrayed into the hands of the Mahdi, and Gordon himself murdered (1885).

The **Third Great Parliamentary Reform Bill** was introduced by Gladstone and passed. It may be considered as a continuation of the Great Reform Bills of 1832 and 1867.

Its most important provisions were:

(1) It extended the " household " franchise of the boroughs to the counties.

(2) It split up the county and large town constituencies into several separate constituencies, each of which had the right of returning a single member.

NOTE 1.—The details of this Re-distribution Bill were settled by a mutual arrangement between the leaders of both Liberals and Conservatives.

NOTE 2.—The Bill added 2 millions to the electorate (1867, 1 million; 1832, 500,000) and enfranchised the agricultural labourer.

1885 On the resignation of the Gladstone Ministry, **Lord Salisbury became Prime Minister,** but in the general election which followed, the Liberals secured a large majority. Lord Salisbury in consequence resigned, and **Gladstone became Prime Minister** a third time.

1886 **Gladstone's Home Rule Bill for Ireland**   It proposed:

(1) That a Parliament should sit in Dublin to settle all Irish matters not purely imperial.

(2) That the executive government of Ireland should be vested in the Irish Parliament.

(3) That Ireland should still pay her share of the Imperial expenses.

(4) That the Imperial Parliament at Westminster should have control over foreign affairs, the Army and Navy, Customs and Excise.

The Bill was defeated on the second reading, and the Queen, acting on Gladstone's advice, dissolved Parliament and made an appeal to the country.

In the new Parliament the Conservatives and Liberal Unionists had a powerful majority, and so Gladstone resigned, and **Lord Salisbury again became Prime Minister.** The Home Rule issue split the Liberal Party.

The **Plan of Campaign.** Parnell's Tenants' Relief Bill for Ireland having been rejected, the Home Rulers retaliated by devising the " *Plan of Campaign*." It stated that all tenants on certain estates should league together and hand over a half-year's rent to a managing committee, to be used in maintaining a struggle against the landlords. In consequence of this, much ill-feeling arose between landlords and tenants, and evictions and outrages became common.

The **Crofters' Holdings Act** (Scotland) was passed " giving crofters more secure tenure, compensation for improvements, and appointing commissioners to revise rents."

1887 **The Celebration of the Queen's Jubilee** took place.

The **Criminal Law Amendment Act** (Ireland) was passed. The disturbed state of Ireland which followed the Plan of Campaign led the Government to pass the " *New Crimes Act*," empowering:

(1) Resident magistrates to try and punish persons accused of certain crimes *without a jury.*

(2) The Lord-Lieutenant to prohibit or suppress any dangerous associations, and to stop the holding of public meetings.

The **New Rules of House of Commons Procedure** were introduced, enacting *that on a motion of any member, a debate might be closed if the consent of the Chair was obtained, and at least 200 members were in favour of it.*

The **Third Irish Land Bill** was passed.

(1) It revised the " *judicial rents* " fixed before 1886, in accordance with a change in the price of agricultural produce.

(2) It introduced provisions for facilitating purchase.

(3) It laid down certain rules with regard to evictions.

Note.—In 1888 the sum of £10 million was voted by the Government for Irish Land Purchase, and in the following year large sums were granted " to develop the drainage of Ireland, and to facilitate trade by the introduction of light railways."

A **Great Nationalist Meeting at Mitchelstown** (Ireland) took place. The police, in trying to clear away the mob were repulsed, and fired upon the people, killing one man and mortally wounding two others.

Shortly after, Sullivan, Lord Mayor of Dublin, and several Irish Members of Parliament were imprisoned under the Crimes Act.

The **Allotments Act** was passed, allowing the compulsory purchase of land for the purpose of allotments.

1888 Under the direction of **Mr. A. J. Balfour,** Chief Secretary for Ireland, the New Crimes Act was rigidly enforced, and the number of outrages and agrarian crimes greatly diminished.

Goschen's scheme ᾽ or reducing the interest on certain portions of the **National Debt** from 3 to $2\frac{1}{2}\%$ was introduced and afterwards passed.

A.D.

Parnellism and Crime. *The Times* newspaper had published a number of articles headed "Parnellism and Crime," in which Parnell and his colleagues were charged with complicity in the many outrages which had taken place in Ireland. Parnell himself was said to have written a letter in reference to the Phœnix Park murders, in which he said, "*Though I regret the accident of Lord F. Cavendish's death, I cannot refuse to admit that Burke got no more than his deserts.*" A Special Commission was appointed by Government to try the case.

NOTE.—In 1890 the Special Commission delivered its report, stating:

(1) That the "letters"—the publication of which originated the charges—were declared to be forgeries.
(2) Irish members incited to intimidation but not to other crimes, and conspired against rent payments.
Parnell was cited as co-respondent in a divorce case. Influenced by Nonconformist pressure, Gladstone withdrew his co-operation. The Irish Nationalist Party split. Parnell died in October 1891.

A Bill was passed for the **Establishment of County Councils.** "The levying of County rates, the maintenance of roads, bridges and asylums, the conduct of registrations, and nearly all the duties hitherto reposed in country gentlemen in the capacity as members of Quarter Sessions, were transferred to purely elective councils chosen by the ratepayers."—(*Maxwell.*)

1890 Treaties were made between the **British, French, German, Portuguese, and Italian Governments,** defining the bounds of their respective "*spheres of influence*" in Africa. **Heligoland** was ceded to Germany.

The payment of Government grants to schools was now to be based on their general condition and not on examination results of each pupil.

1891 The **Assisted Education Act** established free elementary education. A **General Election** took place, in which the Conservatives and Liberal Unionists were in the minority. Lord Salisbury resigned, and **Gladstone became Prime Minister for the fourth time.**

The **Newcastle Programme.** Meanwhile the Gladstonian Liberals had embodied their political views in what is known as the "*Newcastle Programme,*' including Irish Home Rule, Welsh and Scottish disestablishment, and the limitation of hours of work.

Keir Hardie, John Burns, and two other members of the Independent Labour Party were elected to Parliament.

Gladstone's Second Home Rule Bill for Ireland was passed by the Commons. In February Gladstone again brought forward his famous Home Rule Bill, substantially the same as the First, with this exception, that the *Irish members*, instead of being excluded from all share in Imperial affairs as in the Bill of 1886, *were to sit in the Imperial Parliament, but only vote on Imperial questions.* After 82 days' discussion the Bill was carried through the House of Commons, but when it reached the House of Lords *it was thrown out by 419 to 41 votes.*

A.D.

1894 The **Parish Councils Bill.** The Ministry, however, still kept office, and proceeded to pass the Parish Councils Bill. It enacted that Parish Councils should be established in parishes with powers: (1) to carry out the Burial Acts, Public Improvement Acts, and many others; (2) to deal with parish property; (3) to raise certain rates; (4) to acquire and manage land for allotments. It completed the process of local self-government which had begun in the Reform Act of 1832, the Corporation Act of 1835, and the County Council Act of 1888.

Gladstone resigned, after having sat in Parliament almost uninterruptedly for a period of 62 years (1832–1894), and **Lord Rosebery became Prime Minister.**

Sir William Harcourt's Budget was passed, in which he largely increased the " *Death Duties* " on large properties as a substitute for the graduated income-tax, and for the first time the taxation of *land* was placed on the same footing as other kinds of property.

NOTE 1.—The war between **China and Japan.** The cause of this war was the claim which China made to the suzerainty of Korea. The Chinese were defeated by the Japanese both by sea and land, and sued for peace. This was granted on condition that: (a) China should acknowledge the independence of Korea; (b) and should pay 28 millions sterling as a war indemnity.

NOTE 2.—This year was remarkable for " Anarchist " outbreaks, culminating in the assassination of **President Carnot** by an Italian Anarchist.

1895 The **Factory and Workshops Bill** was passed, dealing with the sanitary conditions and safety of factories and workshops, abolishing overtime for young persons, providing for certain fixed holidays, and making further regulations with regard to dangerous trades.

The **Armenian Massacres** took place. The oppressive cruelty exercised by the Turkish officials in Armenia caused the Armenians to rise against the Turkish Government. In the suppression of these risings the Turks perpetrated atrocities of the most revolting character. 100,000 Christian Armenians perished during the years 1894, 1895, and 1896. Indignation ran high throughout Great Britain. Mr. Gladstone, although retired from politics, wrote a number of letters urging England to take vengeance, single-handed, if need be, on the " *Assassin of Europe*," but no active steps were taken in the matter.

The **Resignation of Lord Rosebery. Lord Salisbury became Prime Minister.**

1896 The **Jameson Raid**

The **Origin of the Transvaal or South African Republic**

(a) 1840. Some Dutch Boers emigrated from the Cape Colony and settled in Natal. Shortly after they wished to make the country into an independent state, but British troops were sent out and Natal declared to be a British colony. The majority of the Boers, however, refused to submit, and crossed the **Vaal River** and established the " South African Republic."

(b) 1854. The British Government acknowledged the Transvaal as a free and independent state.

(c) 1877. Owing to the troubles between the Boers and the Native States, the British Government interfered and annexed the country.

(d) 1880. The annexation of their country was violently resented by the Boers. They had by this time greatly increased in numbers, and were determined not to submit to British rule, and so war was declared. British troops were sent to Natal, but they were defeated at **Laing's Nek** and subsequently at **Majuba Hill,** where **Sir George Colley** was slain (1881). In the same year peace was made and treaty signed: (a) *giving the Boers their independence*; (b) *and placing their country under the suzerainty of the British Crown.*

(e) 1884. The British suzerainty was much modified; the British Resident was removed and replaced by a British Agent. But England still reserved the right *of controlling the foreign relations of the country*, except as regards the Orange Free State.

The **discovery of gold and diamonds** led to a great influx of English and other nationalities, but the refusal of the Boers to grant these " Uitlanders " (i.e., *outlanders or foreigners*) electoral rights and privileges excited the greatest discontent. The Uitlanders invoked the aid of the British South African Company, and an armed force under **Dr. Jameson** advanced to Johannesburg, under the impression that the Uitlanders, their wives and children were in a most critical position. **President Kruger** intercepted the expedition and compelled Dr. Jameson and his men to surrender at Krugersdorp.

The interference of the **Emperor of Germany** aggravated the situation, but the firm attitude of **Joseph Chamberlain,** the Colonial Secretary, who disclaimed all sympathy with Jameson, and reminded President Kruger of the rights of England as suzerain over the Transvaal, averted what might have led to the most serious results.

Dr. Jameson and his officers were handed over to the British Government, tried under the Foreign Enlistment Act, and sentenced to various terms of imprisonment. *The control of the Armed Forces was taken from the African Company and vested in the British Government.*

The **Expedition to Coomassie.** The King of Coomassie had violated the treaty by which he had promised to stop human sacrifices and to preserve freedom of trade; a British expedition enforced compliance with the treaty.

The **Venezuelan Dispute.** This was a dispute between Great Britain and Venezuela *about the boundary-line between Venezuela and our South American possession of British Guiana.*

Supported by the " Monroe Doctrine," which prohibited any European Power from occupying new territory in America, the United States took up the question, " *resenting England's policy as an act of unjustifiable aggrandizement.*" So great was the friction between this country and the United States that war seemed imminent.

Subsequently, however, the " Boundary question " was amicably settled by arbitration.

1897 The **Cretan Question.** The Cretans rose against their Turkish rulers, and being assisted by Grecian troops, wished to throw off their allegiance to the Sultan and join Greece. The Great Powers at once intervened, and by means of a " *Collective Note* " informed the Greek Government that the Island of Crete would be made " *autonomous*," though still remaining under the Sultan's rule. Warships were sent by the Great Powers, and a strict blockade maintained.

Greece declared war against Turkey. After having been defeated at Velistino and Domoko, the Greeks submitted, and a treaty was signed, by which Greece had to pay a large war indemnity, and Turkey had to evacuate Thessaly. Under pressure from the Great Powers, the Turks withdrew from Crete.

The Queen's Diamond Jubilee was celebrated.

1898 The **War between the United States and Spain**

In consequence of the unsettled state of Cuba, the Government of the United States sent a battleship, the *Maine*, to Havana to protect the American residents in the island, but the ship was sunk by an explosion.

Subsequently the United States determined to recognize the independence of Cuba, and sent an ultimatum to Spain to that effect. War was declared between the United States and Spain.

Commodore Dewey destroyed the Spanish fleet at Manila. A **Treaty of Peace** was afterwards signed at Paris, by which *Cuba was released from Spanish control, and the Philippine Islands ceded to the United States.*

The **Sudan War** (1896–1899)

(1) The unsettled state of the Sudan and the danger of an attack on Egypt compelled the British Government to undertake its conquest. The Sirdar or Commander of the Egyptian army, **Sir Herbert Kitchener,** succeeded in organizing an efficient army, and in 1896 advanced up the Nile and took **Dongola.**

(2) The **Battle of Omdurman.** On September 1, Sir H. Kitchener, with an Anglo-Egyptian army of 25,000 men, annihilated the Khalifa's forces, amounting to 50,000, at the **Battle of Omdurman.**

The **Fashoda Incident.** Almost immediately after the victory of Omdurman, a brave and enterprising French officer, **Major Marchand,** having penetrated the African Continent from the French territories on the West, appeared with a small band of men at **Fashoda** (a place situated on the Nile above Khartoum), and claimed it for France. The British Government regarded this act as a distinct invasion of their rights, and ordered the French Government to withdraw Major Marchand. War seemed inevitable, but France, probably recognizing the weakness of her army, and being doubtful of the support of the Czar of Russia as an ally, very reluctantly gave way.

In 1899 a Treaty was signed, by which *the whole of the Valley of the Nile was placed under the " Sphere of British influence."*

September 10. Assassination of the **Empress of Austria** at Geneva by an Italian Anarchist.

December 25. The **Imperial Penny Postage** came into operation through the efforts of **Mr. Henniker-Heaton,** Member for Canterbury. Under this arrangement the charge for letters to all the Colonies, except the Australian Colonies, Tasmania, and New Zealand, was reduced to one penny the half-ounce.

The **Niger Territories Bill** passed the House of Commons, by which *all the lands claimed by the Niger Company were placed under the administration of the British Government.*

On July 29 the **Peace Conference** at The Hague was brought to a close. The following proposals were approved of: (1) the establishment of a permanent Court of Arbitration; (2) the modification of certain rules of warfare. No definite decision was arrived at on the main object of the Conference, viz. " *the disarmament of nations."*

1899   September 20. **Dreyfus,** a captain in the French army, having been previously convicted of communicating military information to a foreign power, was sentenced to ten years' imprisonment. This verdict, generally acknowledged to be most unjust, produced universal indignation, and shortly after the French Government revoked the verdict, pardoned Dreyfus, and released him from prison.

Establishment of the Board of Education, a central authority to deal with technical, secondary, and elementary education.

The **Boer War** (1899–1900)

Causes: As a result of the Jameson raid the Outlanders suffered further restrictions. The Boers demanded the abolition of British suzerainty, in return for the grant of the franchise to the Outlanders. Britain refused, and war broke out.

The Boers underestimated the strength which Britain could eventually bring to bear. The British underestimated the Boers' skill in irregular warfare, and initial preparations were inadequate. Imperial contingents were sent to assist Britain.

Events in the War

(1) **In the North-west of Natal.** Immediately after the declaration of war the Transvaal Boers invaded Natal, but were driven back at **Glencoe** by General Symons.

The Boers invested Ladysmith, which was being held by General White. The defence of Ladysmith disrupted the Boer plan for an advance to the coast.

The Boers also besieged Kimberley and Mafeking.

December 10–15 " The Black Week." Gatacre was defeated at Stormberg; Methuen at Magersfontein while trying to relieve Kimberley; and Buller at Colenso while attempting to relieve Ladysmith.

A.D.

1900 Meanwhile an enormous number of reinforcements were sent to the Cape, and the supreme command entrusted to **Lord Roberts,** with **Lord Kitchener** as Chief of Staff. On February 15 **Kimberley** was relieved by General French, and the investing army of Boers fled eastwards to Bloemfontein.

Shortly after Lord Roberts defeated **Cronje** at **Magersfontein.** At **Paardeburg,** Cronje surrendered. This battle secured the Orange Free State. Lord Roberts occupied **Bloemfontein.** Subsequently the Orange Free State was annexed to the British Empire, under the name of the " *Orange River Colony.*"

On May 17 Colonel Mahon relieved **Mafeking,** which had been successfully defended by **Colonel Baden-Powell** since October 15, 1899, a period of 215 days.

On June 5 Lord Roberts entered **Pretoria,** and three months later published a proclamation annexing the Transvaal.

Afterwards, for nearly two years the Boers carried on skilful guerilla warfare.

The Government appealed for confirmation of their South African policy by a General Election, in which they received a majority.

The **Chinese Question.** The weakness of China had been shown by its defeat by the Japanese in 1894. Germany, France, and Russia had acquired footholds in China which they wished to extend. Britain, who had 80% of China's trade, prevented further occupations by dividing China into " spheres of influence " for purposes of commerce.

National opposition to the foreigners culminated in a rising by the " Boxers," who murdered native Christians and foreigners and besieged the Legations. In August 1900 an international European army raised the siege and the Boxers were suppressed.

1900 First underground electric railway opened in London

1901 The **Commonwealth of Australia** was inaugurated at Sydney (January 1). The Act of 1900 had vested legislative power in a Federal Parliament.

Death of Queen Victoria, on January 22.

In the **Taff Vale** case the House of Lords decision made Trades Unions liable for claims of damages as a result of a strike.

EDWARD VII 1901–1910 (9 YEARS)

Title: Eldest Son of Queen Victoria.

Married Alexandra, daughter of Christian IX of Denmark.

Children: Albert Victor (died 1892), George, Louise, Victoria, and Maud.

President McKinley of the United States assassinated.

Marconi sent messages from Cornwall to Newfoundland by wireless telegraphy.

1902   An **Alliance** was concluded between Great Britain and Japan (January 30, 1902). The chief terms were: (1) that if either Power should become involved in war with another nation the other Power should remain neutral; (2) that if either Power should be attacked by more than one foreign nation the other Power should assist that Power and make peace in mutual agreement with it.

A **Peace Conference** was held with the Boer leaders at Vereeniging. At Pretoria **peace was signed** by Lord Milner, Lord Kitchener, and all the Boer leaders (May 31).

NOTE.—The loss of men on the side of the British in the Boer War is estimated at 23,000, and the cost of the war upwards of 220 millions sterling. The war had lasted two years and seven months.

Lord Salisbury resigned and **A. J. Balfour became Prime Minister.**

A **New Education Bill** was passed. It provided, among other things:

(1) That **Rate Aid** should be given to all Voluntary Schools.

(2) That **no denominational form of religious instruction** should be given in State-aided schools.

(3) That School Boards should be abolished, and elementary education placed under the control of Town and County Councils, through an Education Committee.

NOTE.—Subsequently the clause referring to the support of denominational schools out of the rates occasioned much violent opposition on the part of the Noncon-formists, and gave rise to a widespread movement known as " **Passive Resistance.**" Many Nonconformists preferred to have their goods distrained, rather than pay rates which would be devoted to the maintenance of denominational schools.

1903   **The Great Coronation Durbar** took place at Delhi (January 1).

Joseph Chamberlain proposed changes in the **Fiscal Policy** of the country, whereby *small duties would be imposed on corn, meat, dairy produce, and manufactured goods imported from foreign countries, and preference given in our markets to Colonial produce.* The aim would be to develop Colonial resources and reduce England's dependence on foreign supplies. The supporters of Free Trade resigned from the Government and the Unionist Party was split.

Alexander, King of Servia, and his **Queen, Draga,** were brutally murdered by a troop of soldiers and their officers, at Belgrade (June 11).

Death of Lord Salisbury (August 22).

The **Irish Land Purchase Bill** was passed (August 13). By this Bill: (1) Estate Commissioners were appointed with powers to buy and re-sell estates to tenants or promote voluntary sales of land between landlords and tenants; (2) the actual payments made by the tenants in lieu of rent would be reduced, and the landlords would receive aid-grants from the Treasury to the extent of £12 million.

The Wright brothers in America flew a biplane 852 feet.

The first motor-bus was put into use.

1904   An **Agreement** was signed between **Great Britain** and **France** by which a great number of international questions were settled between the two countries, especially with regard to *Egypt, Morocco, West Africa, Madagascar, and Newfoundland.* This agreement is known as the " *Entente Cordiale* " (April 8).

War broke out between **Russia** and **Japan,** owing to disputes over Manchuria and Korea. The Japanese were generally successful on land and sea, and by the Treaty of Portsmouth **1905** Russia withdrew from Manchuria and acknowledged Japanese predominance in Korea.

" **Empire Day** " was inaugurated in London and the Colonies (May 24).

A **Crown Colony Government** was introduced into the **Transvaal** and the **Orange River Colony,** to replace the military administration.

A British Mission to Tibet under Colonel Younghusband reached Lhasa after some fighting, and a treaty establishing British influence was signed. Fear of Russian penetration had caused this move.

1905   A Bill was passed in France for the *complete separation of Church and State* (July 3).

Treaties were signed between **Sweden** and **Norway,** in virtue of which, **Oscar, King of Sweden,** renounced the Crown of Norway (October 27).

The Aliens Bill controlled the immigration and residence of aliens. A **General Election** was held and the **Liberal Party returned to power** with a large majority. **Sir Henry Campbell-Bannerman became Prime Minister.** A Labour Party in Parliament was formed for the first time.

The **Russian National Duma** was opened in person by the Czar at St. Petersburg (May 10).

1906   Self-government was granted to the **Transvaal.**

Trades Disputes Act. This improved the position of Trade Unions by: (1) making legal for a combination all acts which were legal for individuals, e.g., peaceful picketing; (2) making Trade Union funds not liable to actions for damages.

Workmen's Compensation Act. By this Act employers had to make compensation to a worker for injury arising out of and in the course of employment.

The first " **Dreadnought** " battleship was launched.

1907   Reorganization of the army under **Haldane's scheme,** the chief feature being the establishment of the Territorial Army by combining the former Militia, Yeomanry, and Volunteers.

The **Suffragette** movement continued its agitation for votes for women, and many numbers of the movement were imprisoned for riotous conduct.

An agreement was signed with Russia, paving the way to the Triple Entente.

Establishment of **Court of Criminal Appeal.**

New Zealand became a Dominion.

1908   The Act establishing the office of Public Trustee came into operation. The Public Trustee has power to administer estates of small value and to act as an ordinary trustee or executor.

The **Housing and Town Planning Act** empowered municipal corporations to buy land for future building.

The **Childrens Act** protected children against several evils, e.g., forbade the taking of children into the bars of public-houses.

The **Coal Mines Act** limited work in coal mines to eight hours a day.

An earthquake in Sicily and Southern Italy destroyed Messina and many other towns.

The **King** and Crown Prince of Portugal were assassinated in Lisbon.

Campbell-Bannerman resigned in April 5, 1908, and died on April 22. **Asquith became Prime Minister.**

1909   The **Old Age Pensions Act** came into operation, giving 5s. per week pension to people over 70 years old with an income less than £31 10s. a year.

Labour Exchanges were set up to register vacant jobs and facilitate contact between employers and employed.

A step towards Indian self-government was taken by the admission of native members to the Councils of the Viceroy, Secretary of State, and Provincial Governors.

Lloyd George introduced his **" People's Budget,"** increasing taxation of large incomes, levying a tax on unearned increment in land values, taxing mineral royalties, etc., to pay for social reforms and for increased naval expenditure. The Lords rejected the Budget, contrary to constitutional practice, an action condemned by the Commons, on a resolution by Asquith. The Unionists supported the Lords. (A General Election in January 1910 returned Asquith, but with a smaller majority. The Budget was re-introduced and carried in the Commons, and in April was accepted by the Lords.)

December. By the **Osborne judgment** of the House of Lords, Trade Unions were legally prevented from using their funds for political purposes.

Blériot flew the English Channel in an aeroplane.

1910   May 6. Death of King Edward VII.

GEORGE V 1910–1936 (26 YEARS)

Title: Second son of King Edward VII.

Married Princess Victoria Mary of Teck.

Children: Edward, Albert, Mary, Henry, George, John.

1911   **Parliament Act.** Ensuring the sovereignty of the House of Commons, the Act: (1) deprived the Lords of the power of rejecting " Money Bills"; (2) laid down that a Bill passed three times by the Commons in a single Parliament became law without the assent of the Lords, after two years; (3) reduced the life of a Parliament from seven to five years.

By the Payment of Members Bill, M.P.s were granted an annual salary of £400.

Insurance Act. Provided insurance against sickness and unemployment, by contributions from the State, the employer, and the employed. Maternity grants were established.

The Railway Strike. A national railway strike and a strike of the Port of London transport workers were settled, but heralded growing labour unrest until 1914.

1912   Captain Scott's Expedition reached the South Pole, but perished on the return journey.

Joint Boards to fix district minimum wages were set up after a national miners' strike.

1913   Opening of the Panama Canal.

Trade Union Act allowed Trade Unions to establish a special voluntary fund for political purposes.

1914   **Home Rule Bill** passed, setting up an Irish Parliament with limited powers.

Welsh Disestablishment Bill passed, disestablishing and partly disendowing the Anglican Church in Wales.

Plural Voting Bill passed, preventing an elector voting in more than one constituency.

June 28. Murder of the Archduke Franz Ferdinand of Austria and his wife at **Sarajevo** in Bosnia. This was made the excuse for an Austrian declaration of war on Serbia (July 28); Russia supported Serbia; Germany declared war on France (August 3) and violated Belgian neutrality; in support of the latter **Great Britain declared war on Germany** (August 4). Austria declared war on Russia and France (August 6).

THE FIRST WORLD WAR 1914–1918

Causes: (1) the aggressive spirit of Germany, and her rivalry with Britain for naval and commercial supremacy; (2) the deep-rooted hostility between France and Germany; (3) the rivalry between Austria and Prussia for influence in the Balkans. Europe was divided into two hostile groups, the Triple Alliance of Germany, Austria, and Italy, and the Triple Entente of Russia, France, and England. (Italy broke with the Alliance, however, and declared war on Austria in 1915.)

COURSE OF THE WAR

1914 The British Expeditionary Force took the left of the French line. The Allies were driven back to the Marne, but rallied. Trench warfare soon developed along a continuous line from the Channel to Switzerland.

The Russians were defeated at **Tannenberg.** Turkey joined Germany in November.

1915 The development of the trench system caused large casualties for small gains in a succession of limited advances and retreats. The Allies tried to defeat Turkey by a landing at **Gallipoli** which ultimately failed. An attack on Mesopotamia also failed. A German counter-attack drove the Russians out of Austria.

1916 After an indecisive battle off **Jutland** the German High Seas Fleet never again left port. In the **first Battle of the Somme** and accompanying attacks the Allies advanced nine miles: British losses alone were over 400,000.

1917 The German attempt to starve Britain by submarine warfare caused a dangerous situation, but this was improved by the autumn. The indiscriminate attacks on shipping brought the **United States** into the war on the Allied side.

The **Russian Revolution** destroyed the Czar's rule, and the **Bolsheviks** signed an armistice with Germany.

On the Western Front there were more fruitless offensives. French losses on the Aisne caused mutinies among the troops. The British advanced at Arras and Messines. Small gains were made at Ypres at the cost of appalling casualties in a sea of mud. The success of **tanks** at Cambrai was a pointer to the future, though most of the ground gained was lost to counter-attacks.

Allenby captured **Palestine** from the Turks.

1918 Allied naval supremacy and consequent economic blockade was slowly reducing the Central Powers' material resources. The American army was beginning to grow on the Western Front. It was necessary for the Central Powers to try to force an immediate victory, utilizing the troops from the former eastern front. The expected German attack had considerable success at first, but failed to break up the Allied line. **Marshal Foch,** appointed to supreme command, held the German advances on the Marne, and on July 18 began a counter-offensive. French, British, and American armies drove the enemy steadily back during the following months. Elsewhere, Bulgaria, Turkey, and Austria were collapsing, and inside Germany military defeat and economic privation destroyed the nation's morale. The Kaiser fled. The German armies were saved from final destruction by the **armistice of November 11.**

Fisher's Education Act of 1918 raised the school-leaving age to 14 (15 if local authorities so wished), provided compulsory part-time education to 18, and empowered the provision of nursery schools.

The **Parliamentary Reform Act** of 1918 gave votes to men of 21, and women of 30, increasing the electorate from 8,357,000 to 16 millions.

Ministries of Health, Labour, and Transport were established.

Cost of the First World War: The estimated expenditure of the British Empire was over £13,000 million; over 1 million men were killed. France lost over 1,300,000; Russia 1,700,000; Germany over 2 millions; Austria 1,200,000.

After a General Election a **mainly Conservative coalition** under **Lloyd George** took office. The Liberals were divided, and the Labour Party was the chief opposition group.

1919 **Peace Treaties** were signed. Germany lost Alsace-Lorraine to France, and territory to the new Polish Republic. The Austro-Hungarian Empire was dismembered, and independence given to Hungary, Jugoslavia, and Czechoslovakia. Turkish provinces were mandated and Iraq and Arabia soon achieved independence. The Baltic republics of Finland, Latvia, and Lithuania were set up. The German colonies were mandated, the German navy given up, their future Armed Forces limited, and a large indemnity imposed.

Establishment of the **League of Nations,** the project of President Wilson.

Sex Disqualification (Removal) Act opened to women nearly all public offices and professions.

Sankey Report. A threatened miners' strike was averted by the setting up of the Sankey Commission, which recommended nationalization of the coal mines.

A Railway Strike occurred, and achieved a minimum wage.

1920 In Ireland the militant Sinn Fein group increased its power, and armed clashes with the Government police and soldiers increased. The **Government of Ireland Act** partitioned Ireland, setting up an Ulster Parliament. This did not satisfy some elements of Sinn Fein, and violence continued.

A.D.

1921 Establishment of the **Irish Free State** with Dominion status. For several years the resistance to partition among some elements caused trouble to the Dublin Government.

The **Government of India Act** came into force, setting up a " dyarchy " which gave to Indians responsibility for matters such as education and public health. This measure of self-government did not satisfy the Indian National Congress under Ghandi's leadership.

Miners strike for higher wages.

1922 After a short-lived prosperity a slump set in and unemployment became a continuous problem of growing magnitude, especially in coal-mining and exporting industries.

The Conservative Party broke with Lloyd George, and a General Election established a **Conservative Government** under **Bonar Law.** The Opposition comprised the Labour Party, the National Liberals under Lloyd George, and the Independent Liberals under Asquith.

Egyptian sovereignty was established.

In Italy the Fascist Party seized power, and **Mussolini** became Premier.

The **Washington Naval Conference** laid down the proportion of capital ships for Britain, the United States, and Japan as $5 : 5 : 3$.

1923 **Stanley Baldwin** succeeded to the premiership on Bonar Law's resignation owing to illness. Baldwin appealed to the country on a trade-protection policy, and his majority was much reduced.

By the **Treaty of Lausanne** Turkey, now a republic under Mustapha Kemal, retained the whole of Asia Minor, revising the provisions of the Treaty of Sèvres (1920).

France occupied the Ruhr in an attempt to compel German payment of war debts.

1924 After a **General Election** the **Labour Party** for the first time took office under **Ramsay MacDonald,** but was dependent on Liberal support.and could do little to improve the worsening conditions of employment and wages.

The **Dawes Plan** for German reparations restored the German currency, which had been inflated to a fantastic extent, and arranged a scale of reparation payments.

At a **General Election** the **Conservatives** were returned under **Baldwin.** Suspicion of dealings with Russian Communists helped defeat the Labour Party.

1925 Britain returned to the **Gold Standard.** The resulting fall in exports led to attempts to reduce costs, including the lowering of wages. Unemployment and discontent increased.

Imperial Preference against foreign imports was strengthened. **Widows Pension Act** provided contributory pensions for widows, orphans, and old people.

By the **Treaty of Locarno** France and Germany agreed to submit future disputes to arbitration. Germany became a member of the League of Nations.

1926   **The General Strike.** Conditions in mining areas caused especial hardship. A Government subsidy of wages had been obtained by the threats of strikes, and its renewal was demanded. The miners were supported by other unions, a reflection of general unrest. Some 2,500,000 men struck, but the unions were completely defeated.

The **Electricity Act** set up a Central Electricity Board to develop and organize supply.

1927   The **Trade Union Act** made " sympathetic " strikes illegal, and obliged Trade Unions to have specific contracts by their members for contributions to political funds. (Repealed in 1946.)

1928   **Equal Franchise Act** gave the vote to all women over 21, for parliamentary and municipal elections.

Winston Churchill's **De-Rating Scheme** granted rating relief to depressed areas.

A measure for voluntary Prayer Book revision was rejected.

Sound films were first introduced.

The **British Broadcasting Corporation** came under Government supervision.

By the **Kellogg Pact** war was renounced by the signatories, which included the United States and Russia, who were not members of the League of Nations.

1929   **Local Government Act.** This ended the Old Poor Law and established Public Assistance committees, and Public Health committees, of County and County Borough councils.

At the **General Election** the **Labour Party** was returned to office under **Ramsay MacDonald,** but with fewer seats than the Liberals and Conservatives combined.

The **Young Plan** for reparations superseded the Dawes Plan, and provided for fixed payments and German financial autonomy: the plan proved unworkable.

1930   The Simon report on India recommended the extension of responsible government, but agreement could not be reached with Indian representatives.

1931   **Financial Crisis and the beginning of the great depression.**

Unemployment had risen to nearly 3 millions, and the unemployment benefits, recently increased, were a growing financial strain. Repayment of war debts to the United States increased the difficulties. Finally, the New York Exchange panic, with its effects throughout Europe, brought matters to a head, and bankruptcy seemed imminent. MacDonald's proposals to reduce Service pay and unemployment payments were rejected by most of his colleagues, and he therefore formed a " National Government " of the three parties. Benefits and pay were cut, and taxes increased. The Gold Standard was abandoned.

There was a naval disturbance at Invergordon.

At the **General Election** in October the **Conservatives** gained a decisive majority; the " National " Government was continued, in effect Conservative.

Japan invaded Manchuria, and withdrew from the League of Nations when the aggression was condemned.

The **Statute of Westminster** recognized the autonomy of the British Dominions, and the essential link of allegiance to the Crown.

1932   The Import Duties Act of Neville Chamberlain established a protectionist trade policy.

The **Means Test** for unemployment benefits was introduced, and an Unemployment Assistance Board set up for those who had outrun their claim to benefits.

The **Ottawa Conference** attempted to reduce import duties within the Empire; some individual agreements were made.

The **Lausanne Conference** cancelled German reparations.

A **Disarmament Conference** met at Geneva, but without result.

1933   In Germany **Adolf Hitler** established the totalitarian dictatorship of his National Socialist (Nazi) Party.

1934   Germany withdrew from the League of Nations.

1935   Military conscription was established in Germany. Russia joined the League of Nations and concluded a pact of mutual support with France.

Italy invaded Abyssinia; the League applied economic sanctions, under British lead.

At a **General Election Baldwin** was returned to power with the **National Government,** now almost entirely Conservative.

The Hoare–Laval pact, giving Italy a substantial part of Abyssinia, was repudiated by the Cabinet in face of public disapproval.

Britain embarked on a re-armament programme.

King George V celebrated his Silver Jubilee.

Government of India Act set up responsible government n the provinces with a central Federal Assembly. Full implementation was not achieved before war broke out in 1939, halting further progress.

1936   **Death of King George V.**

Accession of Edward VIII, his eldest son. Following a crisis over the King's wish to marry Mrs. Warfield Simpson, he abdicated the throne in December, and later became **Duke of Windsor.**

GEORGE VI 1936–1952 (16 YEARS)

Accession of George VI, second son of George V.

Married: Lady Elizabeth Bowes-Lyon.

Children: Elizabeth, Margaret Rose.

Germany occupied the Rhineland in defiance of the Versailles Treaty.

Britain began increasing the Armed Forces.

Spanish Civil War. A revolt against the Republican Government was led by General Franco, who, with German and Italian help, was successful and established a dictatorship (1939).

The **Italian conquest of Abyssinia was completed.** Sanctions had never been effectively applied, but Italian resentment, and Hitler's support of Mussolini, caused the establishment of the " **Rome–Berlin** " Axis, an alliance joined later by Japan by the **Anti-Comintern Pact.**

1937 A **Factory Act** extended the provisions of the 1901 Act. New industries were established in " depressed areas."

Japan invaded China.

Baldwin resigned and **Neville Chamberlain** became Prime Minister.

1938 By an agreement with Eire, Britain handed back the Irish ports hitherto used by the British navy, and ended the special duties.

In April Germany annexed Austria.

The Chamberlain Government hoped to avert the growing German menace by a policy of appeasement and concessions, a policy condemned by Winston Churchill and others as being useless and dangerous.

Air Raid Precautions began to be organized.

In September German demands on Czechoslovakia were met by the **Munich Agreement** negotiated by Chamberlain, which gave the Czech Sudetenland to Germany and included a German–British peace pact.

1939 Visit of the King and Queen to Canada and the United States.

Germany invaded and occupied Czechoslovakia (March).

A British Alliance with Poland was concluded.

Britain established **conscription** for military service.

April: **Italy invaded and occupied Albania.**

August: While Britain was negotiating with Russia, the latter concluded a pact with Germany.

THE SECOND WORLD WAR 1939–1945

COURSE OF THE WAR

On September 1 Germany invaded Poland, and on September 3 Britain and France, in support of Poland, declared war on Germany.

The **German conquest of Poland** was rapid: on September 17 Russia invaded Poland from the East and divided the country with Germany.

A British Expeditionary Force went to France. There was no major action for the rest of the year on the Western Front.

1940   **German troops invaded and conquered Denmark, Norway, Holland, and Belgium.** The British army, advancing into Belgium, was cut off by a German attack into France, and was finally, in May, withdrawn over the **Dunkirk** beaches, with the loss of most of its equipment.

France was rapidly overrun by the Germans and an armistice was signed on June 21: the country was divided, Unoccupied France (South and South-West) being governed from Vichy, under Marshal Pétain.

Italy joined Germany, and attacked Greece, but without success. British troops went to Greece; German forces reinforced the Italians, and **Greece** was conquered. British forces withdrew to **Crete,** which was lost to a German airborne invasion in June 1941.

Britain. Standing alone, and with her army greatly weakened, Britain prepared to meet a German invasion.

A **Coalition Government under Winston Churchill** was formed.

A "**Home Guard**" of part-time soldiers was formed to resist invasion.

As a preparation for invasion, Germany tried to destroy the R.A.F. in daylight raids, but the attempt failed in the **Battle of Britain,** and the German air force turned to night bombing raids on London and other cities.

German submarine warfare constituted a grave threat.

1941   Under the leadership of President Roosevelt, the United States gradually abandoned its strictly neutral position. In March the **Lend-Lease Bill** permitted defence materials to be transferred.

Germany invaded Jugoslavia (Rumania, Bulgaria, and Hungary were allied to Germany).

On June 22 **German forces invaded Russia.** The Crimea was lost, and the Russian armies driven back; but they were not broken up, and the Germans were held before Moscow.

On December 7 **Japan** launched sudden attacks on **Pearl Harbour** and other American and British bases, and the **United States joined the Allies** against the Axis powers.

1942 In the **South Pacific** Japan advanced swiftly. Hong Kong, the Philippines, the South Pacific islands, Malaya, and Burma were occupied. India was held, and Allied resources had to be diverted to the Pacific. The Japanese advance, with its threat to Australia, was stemmed by Allied victories in the battles of the Coral Sea (May) and Midway (June).

North Africa. Abyssinia was liberated and Italian Somaliland captured. In spite of Britain's danger, the forces in Egypt were reinforced, and advanced into Libya, but were twice forced to withdraw, German troops reinforcing the Italians, who had earlier been severely defeated by General Wavell.

Russia. The German summer offensive towards the River Don reached Stalingrad.

THE TURN OF THE TIDE

North Africa. In October the British Eighth Army under Montgomery attacked at El Alamein in Egypt, and drove the Axis forces under Rommel back into Tunisia. In November Anglo-American forces landed in North-West Africa, occupied Algeria, and linked up with the Eighth Army.

Russia. The Russian winter offensive relieved Stalingrad and destroyed the German army which was besieging it.

Madagascar was occupied by Allied forces.

1943 Axis resistance in North Africa ended in May. The Allies invaded Sicily (July); Mussolini fell from power, and an **armistice with Italy** was concluded as Allied forces landed on the mainland. German forces established strong defences and the Allied advance was slowed down.

Russia. After defeating a German offensive, the Russians turned to the attack, on a broad front.

Naval. By the end of 1943 the submarine menace was countered, the invention of **radar** being of great help.

Air. The weight of Allied air attacks on Germany, especially on the Rhineland and Ruhr, gradually increased, both by night and day.

Pacific. The Japanese were put on the defensive in New Guinea, and the Allied " island-hopping " counter-offensive began.

1944 **Pacific.** In January American forces landed in the Marshall Islands, and in October on the Marianas and Philippines.

Burma. An Allied offensive began, and by December the British Fourteenth Army reached the Chindwin River.

Eastern Front. The Russians continued to advance: Rumania capitulated in August, as did Finland; the Baltic states were liberated, and an advance into Poland began.

Italy. Rome was captured in June.

Western Front. On June 6 Allied forces landed in **Normandy.** German armoured strength was worn down by British forces around Caen, and then American forces broke out of the Cherbourg peninsula and swept South, then East. German forces were trapped at Falaise and suffered heavy losses. The Allies advanced rapidly eastward from a landing in the South of France. **Paris** was liberated in August, and the Germans were expelled from France. An attempt to make a swift crossing of the Lower Rhine, using airborne forces, failed at **Arnhem.**

(In July German opponents of Hitler tried to assassinate him, but failed.)

In December a German counter-attack was launched in the **Ardennes,** but was eventually defeated.

Two German " **secret weapons** " were launched against England: (1) flying bombs (V1); (2) rockets (V2).

1945   **Pacific.** Against fanatical resistance the Allied advance continued. Okinawa was captured in June, and air attacks on Japan itself were developed.

Burma. The Japanese forces in Central Burma were destroyed, and Rangoon was entered in May.

Eastern Front. The Russian advance continued, driving deep into Poland, Prussia, and Austria.

Western Front. The Allied forces closed up to the Rhine, crossed it an Remagen (by an intact bridge) and later at other points, and advanced into Germany.

The German forces began to disintegrate before the advance of the Allies from East and West; Russian and American troops met on the **Elbe** on April 25. Hitler committed suicide in Berlin as the Russians attacked the city. German armies began to surrender in Italy and Germany, and the final **unconditional surrender of Germany to the Allies** took place on **May 7.**

Japan. Allied air attacks on Japan increased. On August 6 the first atomic bomb destroyed most of Hiroshima. On August 8 Russia declared war on Japan. On August 9 a second atomic bomb ruined Nagasaki. The official surrender of Japan took place on September 12.

Social Measures

1942   The **Beveridge Report** was published in favour of a far-reaching scheme of social insurance to cover the whole community; it was the basis of post-war legislation.

1943   To avoid undesirable and haphazard building and development after the war a **Ministry of Town and Country Planning** was set up. The Ministry and local authorities were given necessary powers by Town and Country Planning Acts of 1943 and 1944.

F

A.D.

1944   **Butler's Education Act:** (1) raised the school-leaving age to 15
(eventually to be 16); (2) provided for secondary education for
all children according to ability and aptitude in Secondary
Grammar, Technical, or Modern Schools; (3) provided for the
eventual establishment of County Colleges for compulsory part-
time education to 18; (4) abolished school fees in schools assisted
by local-authority grants; (5) established a Ministry of Education.

General Results of the Second World War

1. Casualties. Military casualties in battle were less than those
in the First World War, with the possible exception of the
Eastern Front. Instead of static trench warfare, this was a war
of movement, with large-scale use of armoured vehicles. The
war was, however, a "total war" in which there was little
distinction between actual battle-fronts and the rest of the
country, or between soldier and civilian. Invasion and
occupation, and especially air-raids on cities, caused very
severe casualties among civilians. A particular element of
horror was introduced by the German use of concentration camps
with their appalling record of suffering and death. The culmina-
tion was the extermination of some 6 million Jews by the
Germans.

2. Effect upon Britain. Britain, having devoted her entire strength
to the war, was left gravely impoverished, one-quarter of the national
wealth having been lost, and entered upon a period of economic
and financial stringency.

3. The United States of America was left as the universal creditor
nation, in a position of unparalleled economic predominance.
In 1945 a U.S. loan of £1,000 million was made to Britain;
conditions included the abolition of tariff preference to the
Empire.

1945   **General Election.** The Labour Party, on a policy of Socialism,
were returned to power with a large majority over the Conservatives.
Labour 393; Conservatives 189; Liberal 12. **Clement Attlee** became
Prime Minister.

Nationalization of Bank of England.

Death of President Franklin D. Roosevelt (United States); Harry S.
Truman succeeded him.

Establishment of **United Nations Organization** as a permanent
organization for collective security.

Nuremberg Trials of chief Nazis for initiating aggressive war: a
number were executed in 1946. Many lesser war criminals were also
brought to justice.

Germany and Austria were divided into zones of occupation.

Russia annexed part of Eastern Poland, and gave part of Germany
to Poland by moving the frontier to the Oder.

1946　　The **National Insurance Act** established a comprehensive insurance system on the lines of the Beveridge report.

The **National Health Service** was established as a service free to all.

Repeal of Trades Disputes Act of 1927.

Nationalization of the coal mines, the road and rail transport services, and Cable and Wireless Ltd.

First meeting of United Nations Assembly. Several agencies were set up, including the United Nations Economic, Social, and Cultural Organization: the Trusteeship Council to oversee the interests of less-advanced peoples: the Food and Agriculture Organization: the World Health Organization.

The Security Council became paralysed by Russian use of the power of veto. This was symptomatic of the deep cleavage in political thought between East and West; Europe, and Germany, were ever more sharply divided by an " **Iron Curtain** " of differences.

British troops were withdrawn from Egypt.

Peace Treaties with Italy, Bulgaria, Rumania, Hungary, and Finland were signed by the former Allied powers.

A British jet-propelled aircraft created a record of 616 m.p.h. (raised to $617\frac{1}{2}$ m.p.h. in 1947).

1947　　**Nationalization of Electricity industry.**

An **Overseas Resources Bill** established the Colonial Development Corporation and the Overseas Food Corporation.

November 20. H.R.H. Princess Elizabeth married Philip Mountbatten (formerly Prince Philip of Greece and Denmark, son of Prince Andrew of Greece) created Duke of Edinburgh.

Great Britain faced an economic and financial crisis, and the chief task was to combat inflation. Severe import restrictions were imposed. Bread was rationed (until July 1948).

In Eastern Europe Russian influence was consolidated and Communist one-party régimes were established. The **Cominform** was set up, believed to be a revival of the Comintern. Russia and the Western powers again failed to agree upon the future of Germany.

To help avert bankruptcy and starvation in Europe, the United States offered financial help on a gigantic scale; the scheme was known as **Marshall Aid.** (Russia induced her satellites to refuse this help.) Credits of 17,000 million dollars were voted in the U.S. Congress.

Great Britain and France signed the **Dunkirk Treaty of Alliance.**

India. The Indian sub-continent was granted independence; two separate states were set up, India (predominantly Hindu) and Pakistan (predominantly Moslem).

Ceylon achieved Dominion status of responsible self-government

Burma was granted independence, and seceded from the Empire.

In **Palestine** conflict developed between Jews and Arabs. Britain surrendered the mandate for Palestine to the United Nations, who decided that the territory should be partitioned.

1948   The **Representation of the People Bill** provided for the redistribution of Parliamentary seats, and the abolition of separate representation of the universities and the City of London and of the business premises vote.

The **Monopolies Bill** aimed to check monopolies and restrictive arrangements in industry and trade which were detrimental to the public interest.

A **Childrens Bill** made new provision for the welfare of children deprived of a normal home life.

Legal Aid and advice were made free (or partly free) to people of limited means.

The **Gas Industry was nationalized.**

A **Colonial Development and Welfare Act** was passed.

The United Kingdom balance of payments showed a marked improvement, due to increased exports and greater income from " invisible exports " such as shipping and insurance. The remaining gap between income and expenditure was closed by Marshall Aid.

November 14.   Birth of Prince Charles Philip Arthur George.

By a *coup d'état* the Communist Party seized power in Czechoslovakia. Jugoslavia, under **Marshal Tito,** broke away from Russian influence.

Ernest Bevin, British Foreign Secretary, put forward the idea of a **Western Union** between Britain, France, Holland, Belgium, and Luxemburg. This lead to the **Treaty of Brussels** for close co-operation in economic matters and mutual support against attack.

Sixteen Western European countries established the **Organization for European Economic Co-operation** (O.E.E.C.).

The closer unity of the Western powers, and the beginning of re-armament, resulted from the increasingly sharp division between East and West, and Communist actions throughout the world. Russia blockaded Berlin, trying to force the Western powers from the city, and prevent the establishment of an independent Western Germany. An " air lift " defeated the blockade. The final division of Berlin came about.

In **Malaya** the Communists began a campaign of terrorism and murder.

The first meeting of the new **Central Legislative Assembly of East Africa** was held in April.

The State of Israel was established, and enlarged by military action.

1949   Great Britain devalued the £ under the stress of economic adversity.

A Bill for the **nationalization of the iron and steel industry** was passed, to take effect after the next general election.

The **Parliamentary Act** reduced the period for which the House of Lords may delay the enactment of a Bill from three sessions to two and from two years to one.

Eire seceded from the Empire, but without being regarded as a foreign country.

The **North Atlantic Treaty** was signed by the United States, Canada, Great Britain, France, Italy, Portugal, Iceland, Norway, Denmark, and the Benelux Countries (Belgium, Holland, and Luxemburg) for mutual assistance against armed attack and peacetime co-operation in plans for supplies and strategy.

The **Council of Europe** was set up with a Committee of Ministers and a Consultative Assembly.

Civil war in **China** ended with the collapse of the Kuomintang régime and the establishment of a Communist Government.

1950   In Britain a **General Election** in February returned the **Labour** Party to power, but with a decreased majority: Labour 315, Conservative 298, others 12.

Iron and steel nationalization took effect.

Britain began to increase expenditure on re-armaments.

August 15.   Birth of Princess Anne Elizabeth Alice Louise.

June 25.   **Invasion of South Korea** by the Armed Forces of Communist North Korea.   The United States sent immediate assistance to South Korea, and the United Nations called upon its members for aid to South Korea.   After initial success the North Koreans were driven back, but in November Chinese forces entered the war and drove back the United Nations forces.   The latter then advanced to the Yalu River, but were compelled to withdraw, and retired to the 38th parallel (the original frontier).   British troops were in action by September 6.

The military side of Western Union was merged in N.A.T.O.

To by-pass the use of the veto the General Assembly of U.N.O. took over the Security Council's responsibility for keeping world peace.

The **Schuman Plan** was put forward, for pooling Europe's coal and steel resources.

The **European Payments Union** was established.

The **Colombo Plan** was adopted for co-operative economic development in South and South-East Asia, and came into operation in 1951.

A.D.

1951 In the autumn a new balance of payments crisis developed in the United Kingdom, with a fall in the gold and dollar reserves. This sharpened the question of the extent of re-armament which could be afforded. Within the Labour Party, a group headed by Aneurin Bevan held the existing scale to be unnecessary, and other internal dissensions developed.

On May 3 the **Festival of Britain 1951** was opened, centred on the South Bank Exhibition in London, visited by nearly $8\frac{1}{2}$ million people.

In the **General Election** of October 25 the **Conservatives** gained a small majority; Conservatives and associates 321, Labour 295, Liberal 6, others 3. **Winston Churchill** became Prime Minister. The Government raised the bank rate, introduced cuts in imports, and imposed an excess profits tax.

In Europe no progress was made towards agreement with Russia. The emphasis lay rather on increased defence preparations, including efforts to find a way of incorporating Germany in Western Defence.

Progress was made with the Schuman and Pleven plans. The **European Coal and Steel Community** was set up by a treaty of March 18.

The N.A.T.O. was extended to include Greece and Turkey.

In Korea, after a United Nations advance and a Communist counter-offensive, the front was established on the 38th parallel. Armistice talks were opened on July 10.

On September 8 a **Peace Treaty with Japan** was signed.

The Anglo-Iranian Oil Company was expropriated by Persia.

Egypt abrogated treaties with Great Britain. A new Arab state, the **Kingdom of Libya,** was established.

In November heat generated by **nuclear fission** was used in heating a building at the Harwell research establishment; this was the first industrial utilization of atomic energy in Great Britain.

1952 February 6. **Death of King George VI.**

ELIZABETH II

Title: Eldest daughter of George VI.

Married Philip Mountbatten (formerly Prince Philip of Greece and Denmark) created Duke of Edinburgh.

Children: Charles, Anne, Andrew, Edward.

De-nationalization of the iron and steel and road transport industries was planned.

The need for economic stability led to reductions in the re-armament programme. In discussion with the Commonwealth, measures were taken to improve Britain's import–export balance.

Britain's position as Commonwealth centre, Atlantic power, and European power prevented her joining the **European Coal and Steel Community**, which decided to work for a political community in Europe.

Africa. A London conference was held on a plan for a Central African Federation of Northern and Southern Rhodesia and Nyasaland, to which African objections were strong. In Kenya, Mau Mau, a secret society of the Kikuyu tribe, began a campaign of terrorism.

1953   **June 2.** Coronation of Queen Elizabeth II. Television enabled the ceremony to be seen by millions of the Queen's subjects.

On the morning of the Coronation it was announced that **Mount Everest** had been climbed; Sir Edmund Hillary and Sherpa Tenzing reached the summit on May 29.

Plans were announced for an atomic power station to be built at Calder Hall in Cumberland.

Egypt became a republic.

J. V. Stalin died March 5. Russia seemed disposed towards a better relationship with the West. Churchill proposed a high-level conference confined to " the smallest number of powers and persons possible." At a meeting of foreign ministers of Britain, America, and France a proposal was put to Russia for a four-power conference, which eventually was agreed upon for 1954.

Korea. Armistice agreed July 27.

1954   On July 3 **food-rationing** ended after $14\frac{1}{2}$ years.

An **Independent Television Authority** was set up to control commercial television programmes financed by advertising.

A foreign ministers' conference broke down, Russia resisting the West's proposals for **free elections in Germany.**

French opposition caused the collapse of the project for a **European Defence Community.** An alternative agreement was reached whereby a re-armed German Federal Republic should enter the Western alliance. Great Britain undertook to keep military forces in Europe and become a full partner in the new Western European union.

Eden took a leading part in arranging a cease-fire in **Indo-China.**

A **South-East Asia Defence Treaty** for common defence was signed by Britain, the United States, France, Australia, New Zealand, Pakistan, Thailand, and the Philippines.

An agreement was reached with Egypt for the evacuation of British troops from the **Suez Canal zone** within 20 months. Both countries pledged support for freedom of navigation in the Canal.

1955   On March 1 Sir Winston Churchill announced that the **hydrogen bomb** would be manufactured in Britain, saying "There is no defence, no absolute defence, against the hydrogen bomb " and putting forward the policy of defence by the **deterrent** power of the bomb.

April 5. Sir Winston Churchill resigned and was succeeded by Sir Anthony Eden as Prime Minister. **A General Election** on May 26 resulted in a House of Commons of Conservatives and associates with an overall majority of 84.

A **Supplementary Budget** after the election increased purchase tax, profits tax, and postal and telephone charges, and there were cuts in, and later abolition of, the housing subsidy to local authorities.

Economic strain, and **inflation** reflected in rising prices, was accompanied by industrial disputes, including strikes in the docks and on the railways.

In February plans were announced to build 12 **nuclear power stations** in the succeeding ten years. Agreement was reached with America for co-operation in nuclear science, and Britain attended an international conference, under U.N. auspices, on the peaceful uses of atomic energy.

Increasing strain on Britain's **roads** led to a four-year plan for improvements. A **railway modernization** scheme was announced, to include a change from steam to diesel and electric power.

A " **summit conference** " of Russia, the United States, France, and Britain was held in July. Tension was eased, but no fundamental agreement was made. A later meeting of foreign ministers failed to make progress on the **German problem** or on **disarmament.**

In **Cyprus** demands for union with Greece led to violence.

Inflation continued, and budgetary measures were taken. A scheme of **premium bonds** with monthly prizes was introduced.

On October 17 the Queen opened the Calder Hall **nuclear power station,** the first in the world.

Suez. After withdrawal of British and American financial aid for the Aswan Dam scheme in Egypt the latter nationalized the Suez Canal Company. Tension rose, conferences were held and the U.N. Security Council was called on to take account of the Egyptian and Anglo-French attitudes. Israel attacked Egypt, with French connivance. Britain and France issued a 12-hour ultimatum to both sides to cease fire; Egypt rejected this, and on October 31 British and French aircraft attacked. This Anglo-French action was widely condemned in the Commonwealth and abroad, and opinion in Britain was sharply divided. The U.N. General Assembly called for a cease-fire. On November 5–6 Anglo-French forces invaded Egypt, but a cease-fire was agreed and the United Nations set up an international force to police the area. On December 3 the immediate withdrawal of Anglo-French forces from Egypt was announced, being completed on December 22.

Russian troops put down a **Hungarian rising** for independence; sympathy for the Hungarians was widespread in Britain.

In **Cyprus** terrorist violence increased and Archbishop Makarios was deported, charged with encouraging the terrorists.

1957   **Sir Anthony Eden,** on grounds of ill-health, resigned the office of Prime Minister and retired from political life. **Harold Macmillan** became Premier.

Britain's first **hydrogen bomb** was exploded on May 15.

Defence was imposing great demands on Britain's resources, and in April a new policy was announced. The chief purpose was to rely on **nuclear and rocket weapons** for deterrence and to reduce " conventional " forces; conscription was to be ended by 1960.

A new **Homicide Act** limited the death penalty to five categories of " capital murder."

The **Civic Trust** was established to arouse public interest in standards of architecture and town and country planning.

A **Commonwealth Antarctic Expedition** was mounted as part of the International Geophysical Year, and subsequently made the first overland crossing of the Continent. The first Russian satellite was tracked by the newly completed radio-telescope at Jodrell Bank.

Negotiations for a **European free trade area** were entered upon.

1958   In March the **Liberal Party** candidate won the by-election at Torrington, the party's first success for 29 years.

Life peerages were inaugurated: on November 4 Baroness Elliot of Harwood became the first peeress to speak in a House of Lords debate.

In September the R.A.F. took delivery of the first American **ballistic missile,** the Thor.

The **Clean Air Act** was passed, to control smoke in prescribed areas.

Coal rationing and price control was ended after nearly 20 years.

On October 4 a Comet IV airliner inaugurated the first transatlantic jet service.

Prince Charles was created **Prince of Wales.**

The **Restrictive Practices Court,** set up in 1956, gave its first decision.

A dispute arose with **Iceland** over fishing rights.

The situation in **Cyprus** continued to worsen.

January 3. Establishment of the **West Indies** federation.

The negotiations for a European Free Trade Area resulted in disagreement; Britain and others were excluded from the **Common Market** planned by France, German Federal Republic, Italy, Belgium, Holland, and Luxemburg, " the Six."

October 31. A conference opened between the United States, Britain, and Russia on the **suspension of nuclear tests.**

1959   **October 8. General Election** was won by the Conservatives with an overall majority of 102.

Concern mounted over the heavy and increasing rate of death and injury on the roads. Motor traffic was rising substantially. On November 2 Britain's **first motorway** was opened.

A **hovercraft** was demonstrated for the first time.

Skirmishes continued to occur between British trawlers, assisted by naval vessels, and Icelandic gunboats.

Britain signed a treaty for peaceful scientific co-operation in **Antarctica,** and the demilitarization of the Continent.

An agreement was signed in February whereby **Cyprus** was to become an independent republic in 1960.

A state of emergency was declared in **Nyasaland** after disturbances, and a commission of inquiry was later set up. In **Kenya**, the seven-year state of emergency was ended.

Singapore came into existence as a state.

Diplomatic relations with **Egypt** were resumed on December 1.

1960   **February 19. Birth of Prince Andrew Albert Christian Edward. May 6. H.R.H. Princess Margaret married Mr. Anthony Charles Robert Armstrong-Jones.**

On November 1 the Government announced that a base would be established in Holy Loch for American submarines equipped with the **Polaris** missile.

From January 1 the **farthing** ceased to be legal tender; the modern farthing dated from 1672.

The Wolfenden committee on **sport** recommended the establishment of a Sports Development Council with a Government grant of £5 million and the authorization of local authorities to spend a further £5 million on sports facilities.

Disquiet over the increasing concentration of **press ownership** was heightened by the last appearance on October 17 of the *News Chronicle* and *Star*.

In **Tanganyika** the Tanganyika African National Uunion won a sweeping victory in the elections to the Legislative Council, and Julius Nyere became Chief Minister in September.

At midnight on September 30 **Nigeria** became an independent state and a full member of the Commonwealth.

In August **Cyprus** became an independent republic and subsequently joined the Commonwealth. **Somaliland** became independent.

In **South Africa** a referendum of white voters resulted in a majority for the country becoming a republic in May 1961.

A commission was set up to work out a new constitution for **Malta.**

The European Free Trade Association (the " **Outer Seven** ") was established on May 3, comprising Britain, Austria, Denmark, Norway, Portugal, Sweden, and Switzerland.

The Queen launched first British **nuclear submarine,** H.M.S. *Dreadnought* (October 21).

Last **National Service** men called up (November 18).

1961   **Dr. Verwoerd** announced that **South Africa** would withdraw from the **Commonwealth.**

Dr. R. Beeching appointed to reorganize British Railways.
General Assembly of U.N. condemned **South African** Government's policy of " **apartheid** ".

Sierra Leone proclaimed an independent state (April 26).

Mr. Nyerere sworn in as first Prime Minister of **Tanganyika** (May 1).

Mr. C. R. Swart sworn in as first President of **South African Republic** (May 31).

Cyprus applied for admission to the Commonwealth (August 29).

Electrical Trades Union expelled from the **Trades Union Congress.**

Volcano erupted on **Tristan da Cunha.** Population evacuated to Britain.

Negotiations started (November 8) in Brussels for Britain's entry into the **Common Market.**

Tanganyika became an independent state (December 9).

1962   **Uganda** received internal self-government. Mr. Kiwanuka elected Prime Minister. Became fully independent on October 9 with Mr. Obote as Prime Minister.

Liberal Party won **Orpington** by-election from the Conservative Party.

Labour Party Executive opposed Britain's entry into the **Common Market** unless better terms were obtained.

Trinidad–Tobago became independent states.

Tanganyika became a republic with **Mr. Nyerere** as first President.

1963   At the end of January **Mr. Macmillan** announced the breakdown of the talks for Britain's entry into the **Common Market** because of the opposition of the French Government.

Mr. Harold Wilson elected to leadership of the **Labour Party.**

Nyasaland became self-governing on February 1.

Government announced proposals for unifying the Ministry of Defence with abolition of Admiralty, War Office and Air Ministry.

Kenya formally proclaimed self-governing on May 31.

Mr. Profumo, Secretary of State for War, resigned because of his association with Miss Christine **Keeler.**

Zanzibar became self-governing on June 24.

Royal Assent given to **Peerage Bill** which allows peers to disclaim their title. The first to do this was Lord Stansgate (Mr. Wedgwood Benn).

Nuclear Test Ban Treaty signed by major powers.

Federation of **Malaysia** consisting of Malaya, Singapore, North Borneo and Sarawak established.

President John Kennedy assassinated by shooting at Dallas, Texas.

Mr. Macmillan resigned as Prime Minister because of ill health. **Lord Home** selected to become Prime Minister and renounced his peerage to become Sir Alec Douglas Home.

1964 **BBC 2,** the third television channel, began transmission.

March 10. Birth of Prince Edward Anthony Richard Louis.

The **Bahamas** became self-governing.

Northern Rhodesia became independent as the Republic of **Zambia.**

Malta became independent.

Harold Macmillan was offered (and declined) an earldom.

October 15. A General Election was won by the Labour Party. Harold Wilson became Prime Minister.

President **Makarios** of **Cyprus** announced his desire to terminate the treaties of 1960. Fighting broke out between the Greek and Turkish communities and the United Nations were asked to intervene.

1965 **Sir Winston Churchill** died on January 24, and was accorded a State funeral.

The Prices and Incomes Board was set up.

Sir Alec Douglas-Home resigned and **Edward Heath** was elected Leader of the Conservative Party.

Britain recognised **Singapore** as an independent State.

Further outbreaks of terrorism occurred in **Aden.** The constitution was suspended by Order in Council and the U.K. High Commissioner assumed control.

The Royal Assent was given to the **Murder (Abolition of Death Penalty) Bill.**

Unilateral Declaration of Independence was proclaimed by **Rhodesia.**

Ian Smith became Prime Minister. Harold Wilson announced economic sanctions against the Smith regime.

1966 **Malawi** became a republic. British Guiana became independent as **Guyana.** Bechuanaland became independent as **Botswana.** **Barbados** became independent.

HMS *Resolution*, the first British Polaris submarine was launched at Barrow-in-Furness.

England won the **Association Football World Cup** at Wembley Stadium.

The **Mountbatten Report** on prison security concluded that " there is no really secure prison in existence in this country ".

A.D.

Harold Wilson dissociated the British Government from the US policy of bombing the North Vietnamese cities of Hanoi and Haiphong.

Ian Smith and **Harold Wilson** held talks on board HMS *Tiger* in Gibraltar, but no agreement on the Rhodesian question was reached.

After continuous heavy rain, a coal tip engulfed part of the Welsh village of **Aberfan**. Most of the 144 dead were children and teachers in the village school, which was buried under tons of slurry.

1967 **Jeremy Thorpe** was elected Leader of the Liberal Party.

The Prime Minister announced that Britain would apply to join the **European Economic Community** (the **Common Market**). Five of the six member nations were in favour of British membership, but France vetoed the application.

Twenty Chinese officials attacked police outside the Chinese Legation in London. Foreign Secretary, **George Brown,** asked Peking to discuss a return to more normal relations.

South Arabia became independent.

In a referendum, **Gibraltarians** voted 12,138 to 44 to stay British rather than become part of Spain.

The £ was devalued by 14.3%.

1968 **Spain** closed her land frontier with **Gibraltar.**

The legal **age of majority** was reduced from 21 to 18 years.

The **Race Relations Bill** became law.

The Government announced plans for comprehensive education and the abolition of the 11-plus examination.
Mauritius and **Swaziland** became independent.
Hundreds were injured when fighting broke out between police and demonstrators outside the American Embassy in Grosvenor Square.

1969 The **Investiture** of the Prince of Wales took place at Caernarvon.

Neil Armstrong became the first man to set foot on the moon.

The Anglo-French supersonic airliner, **Concorde,** had its maiden flight.

The **Divorce Reform Act** became law.

Libya asked **Britain** to close down her military bases in that country.

A record balance of payments, £387 million, was reported.

Violence broke out in **Northern Ireland** and British troops were sent in to restore order. Bombings and shootings, based on political and religious rivalry, were to continue for many years.

1970 A Bill was published compelling Education Authorities to introduce **comprehensive education.**

A **National Dock strike** paralyzed ports and had an adverse effect on the balance of payments.

A **General Election** was won by the Conservative Party. **Edward Heath** became Prime Minister.

Guyana became a republic. **Fiji** and **Tonga** became independent.

Rhodesia declared itself a republic.

'**Arms for South Africa**' became a political issue. The Government insisted that only arms necessary for the defence of sea routes would be supplied.

Britain re-applied to join the **Common Market,** and reopened negotiations with the Community.

The **Industrial Relations Bill** had its second reading in the House of Commons. There were widespread strikes in protest against the Bill.

1971   **February 15.** Decimal currency was introduced.

Rolls-Royce went into voluntary liquidation.

A **Census** showed that Britain's population was 55,346,551.

Ninety Russian diplomats were expelled from Britain for spying.

The home of **Robert Carr,** Secretary of State for Employment and Productivity was damaged by a bomb. The responsibility for this and other attacks was claimed by a group calling themselves the **Angry Brigade.**

The **Queen** asked for an increase in the **Civil List** – a pay rise.

1972   Sanctions against **Rhodesia** continued. Foreign Secretary, **Sir Alec Douglas-Home,** renegotiated a settlement with Ian Smith. The **Pearce Commission** reported that the terms of settlement agreed were unacceptable to the majority of Rhodesian Africans.

Unemployment figures rose to 1,000,000 for the first time since 1947.

The Government published a White Paper on **Metrication.**

William Whitelaw was appointed Secretary of State for Northern Ireland, and met leaders of all political parties in attempts to find a solution to the Northern Ireland problem.

President Amin of **Uganda** expelled all Ugandan Asians. Many thousands entered Britain penniless.

Ceylon became the Republic of **Sri Lanka.**

1973   **Britain** became a member of the **European Economic Community** on **January 1.**

A wave of **bomb attacks** hit London and Birmingham, injuring hundreds of people. Various guerilla groups, including the Provisional IRA and anti-Israeli groups, claimed responsibility for the attacks.

Britain and **Iceland** quarrelled over **fishing rights** within the 50-mile limit. Live shots were fired by Icelandic gunboats, and British naval vessels were sent to protect the fishing fleet. After long and difficult negotiations, agreement was finally reached and the dispute settled.

Mortgage rates and food prices rose to unprecedented levels.

War broke out in the **Middle East.** Arab oil-producing countries cut oil supplies to America and European countries. A miners' overtime ban cut supplies of coal, and a state of emergency was declared.

The **Channel Tunnel Bill** was published.

The Army death roll in **Northern Ireland** rose to 200. Agreement was reached on the formation of a **Northern Ireland Assembly,** but the Assembly broke up in disorder when fighting broke out between political factions.

In America, **President Nixon** became deeply involved in the **Watergate affair.** Vice-President Agnew resigned when accused of income-tax evasion.

Princess Anne married Captain Mark Phillips in Westminster Abbey.

TABLE SHOWING EDWARD III's CLAIM TO THE FRENCH CROWN

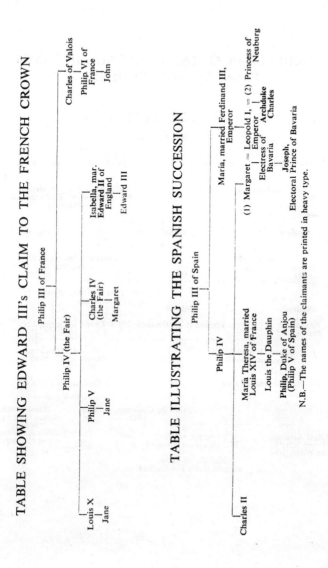

Philip III of France

Philip IV (the Fair) — Charles of Valois

Louis X — Philip V — Charles IV (the Fair) — Isabella, mar. Edward II of England — Philip VI of France

Jane — Jane — Margaret — Edward III — John

TABLE ILLUSTRATING THE SPANISH SUCCESSION

Philip III of Spain

Philip IV — Maria, married Ferdinand III, Emperor

Maria Theresa, married Louis XIV of France

(1) Margaret = Leopold I, = (2) Princess of Emperor Neuburg

Charles II

Louis the Dauphin

Electress of Bavaria — Archduke Charles

Philip, Duke of Anjou (Philip V of Spain)

Joseph, Electoral Prince of Bavaria

N.B.—The names of the claimants are printed in heavy type.

GENEALOGICAL TABLE OF ENGLISH KINGS
FROM EGBERT TO HENRY I

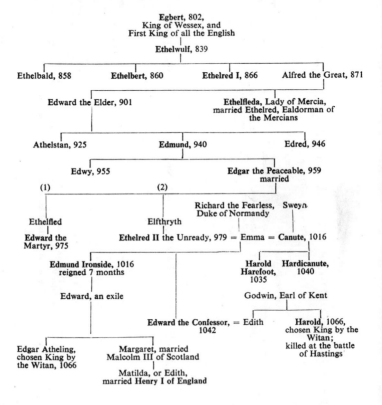

GENEALOGICAL TABLE OF THE NORMAN AND PLANTAGENET LINES

William I, 1066 = Matilda of Flanders

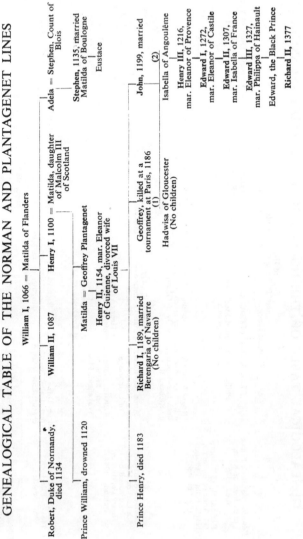

Robert, Duke of Normandy, died 1134

William II, 1087

Henry I, 1100 = Matilda, daughter of Malcolm III of Scotland

Adela = Stephen, Count of Blois

Prince William, drowned 1120

Matilda = Geoffrey Plantagenet

Henry II, 1154, mar. Eleanor of Guienne, divorced wife of Louis VII

Stephen, 1135, married Matilda of Boulogne

Eustace

Prince Henry, died 1183

Richard I, 1189, married Berengaria of Navarre (No children)

Geoffrey, killed at a tournament at Paris, 1186

Hadwisa of Gloucester (No children) (1)

John, 1199, married (2)

Isabella of Angoulême

Henry III, 1216, mar. Eleanor of Provence

Edward I, 1272, mar. Eleanor of Castile

Edward II, 1307, mar. Isabella of France

Edward III, 1327, mar. Philippa of Hainault

Edward, the Black Prince

Richard II, 1377

GENEALOGICAL TABLE OF THE HOUSES OF YORK AND LANCASTER

Edward III, 1327,
mar. Philippa of Hainault

(Yorkist Line) **(Lancastrian Line)**

Edward, the Black Prince, mar. Joan of Kent, died 1376

Lionel, Duke of Clarence

John of Gaunt, Duke of Lancaster, mar.

Edmund, Duke of York

Richard II, 1377, mar. (1) Anne of Bohemia, (2) Isabella of France (No children)

Philippa = Edmund Mortimer 3rd Earl of March

(1) Blanche of Lancaster

(2) Catherine Swynford

Richard, Earl of Cambridge, mar. Anne Mortimer, beheaded 1415 by Henry V for treason

Roger Mortimer, 4th Earl of March, decl. heir-apparent by Richard II, 1386

Sir Edmund Mortimer taken prisoner by Owen Glendower

Henry IV, 1399, mar. Mary de Bohun

John Beaufort, Earl of Somerset

John Beaufort, Duke of Somerset

Edmund Mortimer, 5th Earl of March, imprisoned by Henry IV, died in Ireland, 1424

Anne Mortimer, mar. Richard Earl of Cambridge

Henry V, 1413, mar. Catherine of France

John, Duke of Bedford, Regent of France

Humphrey, Duke of Gloucester

Margaret Beaufort, mar. Edmund Tudor, son of Owen Tudor

Richard, Duke of York, killed at Wakefield, 1460

Henry VI, 1422, mar. Margaret of Anjou

Henry VII, 1485, mar. Elizabeth of York, daughter of Edward IV

Prince Edward, slain at Tewkesbury, 1471

Edward IV, 1461 = Elizabeth Woodville

George, Duke of Clarence, mar. Isabel Neville: executed for treason

Richard III, 1483, mar. Anne Neville, daughter of the Earl of Warwick

Elizabeth = John De la Pole

Margaret = Charles the Bold, Duke of Burgundy

Edward V, 1483, murdered

Richard, Duke of York, murdered

Elizabeth = Henry VII, 1485

John De la Pole, Earl of Lincoln, declared heir-apparent by Richard III; killed at the Battle of Stoke

Henry VIII, 1509

GENEALOGICAL TABLE OF THE TUDOR LINE

Henry VII, 1485,
mar. Elizabeth of York, daughter of Edward IV

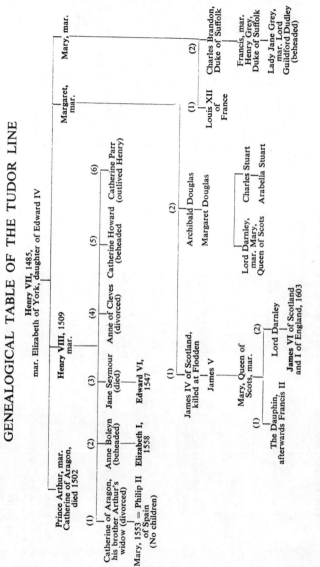

GENEALOGICAL TABLE OF THE STUART AND BRUNSWICK LINES

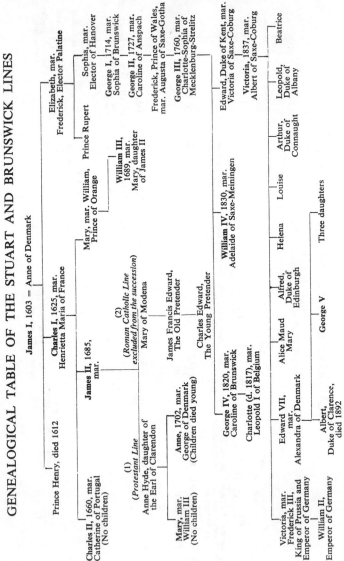

GENEALOGICAL TABLE OF THE DESCENDANTS OF QUEEN VICTORIA

Victoria (1837–1901),
mar. Albert of Saxe-Coburg, died 1861

Victoria, mar. Frederick III, King of Prussia, and German Emperor	Edward VII, mar. Alexandra, daughter of Christian IX of Denmark	Alice, mar. Louis, Grand D. of Hesse	Alfred, D. of Coburg and Edinburgh, mar. Marie, daughter of Alexander II of Russia	Helena, mar. Prince Christian of Schleswig-Holstein	Louise, mar. Marquis of Lorne	Arthur, D. of Connaught, mar. Louise Margaret, daughter of Prince Frederick Charles of Prussia	Leopold, D. of Albany, mar. Helen of Waldeck	Beatrice, mar. Prince Henry of Battenberg

William II, King of Prussia, and German Emperor

Six sons — **One daughter**

Victoria, mar. Prince Louis of Battenberg

Alix, mar. the Czar of Russia — **Four daughters and one son**

Christian — **Albert** — **Victoria** — **Louise**

Margaret — **Arthur** — **Victoria Patricia**

One son and one daughter

Three sons and one daughter

Albert Victor, D. of Clarence

George V, mar. Princess Victoria Mary of Teck

Louise, mar. the D. of Fife — **Three daughters**

Victoria

Maud, mar. King Haakon of Norway

Edward VIII

George VI, mar. Elizabeth Bowes-Lyon

Mary, mar. Viscount Lascelles

Henry

George, d. 1942

John, d. 1919

Alice, mar. Prince Andrew of Greece

Elizabeth II, mar. — **Margaret Rose,** mar. Anthony Armstrong-Jones

Philip Mountbatten

Charles — **Anne** — **Andrew** — **Edward**

TABLE OF THE SOVEREIGNS SINCE THE CONQUEST

House	Name	Accession	Years	Married	Children
Norman	William I	1066	21	Matilda of Flanders	Robert, William II, Henry I, Adela
	William II	1087	13		
	Henry I	1100	35	1. Matilda of Scotland 2. Adela of Louvain	William, Matilda
	Stephen	1135	19	Matilda of Boulogne	Eustace
Plantagenet	Henry II	1154	35	Eleanor of Guienne	Henry, Richard I, Geoffrey, John
	Richard I	1189	10	Berengaria of Navarre	
	John	1199	17	1. Hadwisa of Gloucester 2. Isabella of Angoulême	Henry III, Eleanor, mar. Simon de Montfort
	Henry III	1216	56	Eleanor of Provence	Edward I, Margaret, mar. Alexander III of Scotland
	Edward I	1272	35	1. Eleanor of Castile 2. Margaret of France	Edward II
	Edward II	1307	20	Isabella of France	Edward III
	Edward III	1327	50	Philippa of Hainault	Black Prince, Lionel, John of Gaunt, Edmund, Duke of York
	Richard II	1377	22	1. Anne of Bohemia 2. Isabella of France	
Lancaster	Henry IV	1399	14	1. Mary de Bohun 2. Joan of Navarre	Henry V, John, Duke of Bedford, Humphrey, Duke of Gloucester
	Henry V	1413	9	Catherine of France	Henry VI
	Henry VI	1422	39	Margaret of Anjou	Edward
York	Edward IV	1461	22	Elizabeth Woodville	Edward V, Richard, Duke of York. Elizabeth
	Edward V	1483	2 mths.		
	Richard III	1483	2	Anne Neville	
Tudor	Henry VII	1485	24	Elizabeth of York	Arthur, Henry VIII, Margaret, Mary
	Henry VIII	1509	38	1. Catherine of Aragon 2. Anne Boleyn 3. Jane Seymour 4. Anne of Cleves 5. Catherine Howard 6. Catherine Parr	Mary Elizabeth Edward VI
	Edward VI	1547	6		
	Mary	1553	5	Philip II of Spain	
	Elizabeth I	1558	45		
Stuart	James I	1603	22	Anne of Denmark	Henry, Charles I, Elizabeth
	Charles I	1625	24	Henrietta Maria of France	Charles II, James II, Mary
	Commonwealth	1649	4		
	Protectorate	1653	7		
	Charles II	1660	25	Catherine of Portugal	
	James II	1685	4	1. Anne Hyde 2. Mary of Modena	Mary, Anne James Francis Edward
	William and Mary	1689	13		
	Anne	1702	12	Prince George of Denmark	

House	Name	Accession	Years	Married	Children
Hanover	George I	1714	13	Sophia of Brunswick	George II
	George II	1727	33	Caroline of Anspach	Frederick, Prince of Wales, William, Duke of Cumberland
	George III	1760	60	Charlotte-Sophia of Mecklenburg-Strelitz	George IV, William IV, Edward, Duke of Kent
	George IV	1820	10	Caroline of Brunswick	
	William IV	1830	7	Adelaide of Saxe-Meiningen	
	Victoria	1837	64	Albert of Saxe-Coburg	Edward VII, Alfred, Arthur, Leopold, Victoria, Alice, Helena, Louise, Beatrice
	Edward VII	1901	9	Alexandra of Denmark	Albert, George V, Louise, Victoria, Maud
	George V	1910	26	Victoria Mary of Teck	Edward VIII, George VI, Mary, Henry, George, John
Windsor (from 1917)	Edward VIII (abdicated same year)	1936			
	George VI	1936	16	Elizabeth Bowes-Lyon	Elizabeth II, Margaret Rose
	Elizabeth II	1952		Philip Mountbatten (formerly Prince Philip of Greece and Denmark) created Duke of Edinburgh	Charles, Anne, Andrew, Edward

IMPORTANT EVENTS, WITH DATES

NORMAN PERIOD

Battle of Hastings (*Sussex*)	...	...	...	...	1066	William I
Bridal of Norwich (*Norfolk*)	...	...	...	...	1074	,,
Doomsday Book completed	...	...	...	...	1086	,,
First Crusade	...	...	...	...	1096	William II
Battle of Tenchebrai (*Normandy*)		...	...	...	1106	Henry I
Investiture dispute settled	...	...	...	...	1107	,,
Battle of **Northallerton** (*Yorkshire*)		...	...	...	1138	Stephen
,, Lincoln (*Lincolnshire*) ...		...	...	...	1141	,,

PLANTAGENET PERIOD

Constitutions of Clarendon (*Wilts*)		...	...	...	1164	Henry II
Murder of Becket	...	...	...	...	1170	,,
Itinerant Justices appointed, Assize of Northampton					1176	,,
Third Crusade ...	...	...	...	...	1190	Richard I
Loss of Normandy	...	...	...	...	1204	John
Magna Charta ...	...	...	...	...	1215	,,
Mad Parliament and the Provisions of Oxford				...	1258	Henry III
Battle of Lewes (*Sussex*) ...	...	...	...	...	1264	,,
First House of Commons ...	...	...	...	...	1265	,,
Battle of Evesham (*Worcestershire*)		...	...	...	—	,,
Dictum of Kenilworth (*Warwickshire*) ...		...	...	1266	,,
Statute of Mortmain	...	...	...	...	1279	Edward I
Conquest of Wales	...	...	...	...	1277–1284	,,
Struggle with Scotland	...	...	...	...	1291–1307	,,
First Complete Parliament	...	...	...	...	1295	,,
Battle of Dunbar (*Haddington*) ...		...	...	...	1296	,,
,, Cambuskenneth (*Stirlingshire*)		...	...	...	1297	,,
Confirmatio Cartarum	...	...	...	...	—	,,
Battle of Falkirk (*Stirlingshire*) ...		...	...	...	1298	,,
Organization of Law Courts	...	...	...	...	1300	,,
Lords Ordainers appointed	...	...	...	...	1310	Edward II
Battle of Bannockburn (*Stirlingshire*)		...	...	...	1314	,,
Battle of Halidon Hill (*Northumberland*)			...	...	1333	Edward III
Hundred Years' War	...	...	...	...	1337–1453	,,
Battle of Sluys (*Holland*) ...	...	...	...	...	1340	,,
,, **Crecy** (*France*) ...	...	...	...	...	1346	,,
,, Neville's Cross (*Durham*)		...	...	...	—	,,
Statute of Provisors	...	...	...	...	1351	,,
First Statute of Treason ...	...	...	...	...	1352	,,
Battle of Poitiers (*France*)	...	...	...	...	1356	,,
Peace of Bretigny (*France*)	...	...	...	...	1360	,,
The Good Parliament	...	...	...	...	1376	,,
Wat Tyler's Rebellion	...	...	...	...	1381	Richard II
Merciless Parliament	...	...	...	...	1388	,,
Statute of Præmunire	...	...	...	...	1393	,,

HOUSE OF LANCASTER

Battle of Homildon Hill (*Northumberland*)	...	...	1402	Henry IV
„ Shrewsbury (*Shropshire*)	...	...	1403	„
„ **Agincourt** (*France*)	...	...	1415	Henry V
Treaty of Troyes (*France*)	...	...	1420	„
Siege of Orleans raised (*France*)...	...	...	1429	Henry VI
Congress of Arras (*France*)	...	...	1435	„
Cade's Rebellion ...	...	...	1450	„
Wars of the Roses ...	...	...	1455–1485	„
First Battle of St. Albans (*Hertford*)	...	...	1455	„
Battle of Bloreheath (*Stafford*) ...	...	...	1459	„
„ Northampton ...	...	...	1460	„
„ Wakefield (*Yorkshire*) ...	...	...	—	„
„ Mortimer's Cross (*Hereford*) ...	...	...	1461	„
Second Battle of St. Albans	...	...	—	„

HOUSE OF YORK

Battle of **Towton** (*Yorkshire*)	...	...	1461	Edward IV
„ **Barnet** (*Hereford*)	...	...	1471	„
„ **Tewkesbury** (*Gloucestershire*)...	...	...	—	„
Treaty of Pecquigny (*France*)	...	...	1475	„
Battle of **Bosworth** (*Leicestershire*)	...	...	1485	Richard III

THE TUDOR PERIOD

Battle of Stoke (*Nottinghamshire*)	...	...	1487	Henry VII
Star Chamber established	...	...	—	„
Columbus discovered the Bahamas (*West Indies*)	...	1492	„
The Great Intercourse ...	...	...	1496	„
Sebastian Cabot discovered Labrador (*N. America*) ...	1497	„
Battle of Flodden Field (*Northumberland*)	...	1513	Henry VIII
Field of the Cloth of Gold (*France*)	...	...	1520	„
Papal Authority abolished in England	...	...	1534	„
Henry took the title of " Supreme Head of the Church of England "	...	...	1535	„
Pilgrimage of Grace	...	...	1536	„
Battle of Pinkie (*Edinburgh*)	...	...	1547	Edward VI
First Act of Uniformity ...	...	...	1549	„
Wyatt's Rebellion	...	...	1554	Mary
Cranmer burnt ...	...	...	1556	„
Loss of Calais (*France*) ...	...	...	1558	„
Second Act of Supremacy	...	...	1559	Elizabeth I
Second Act of Uniformity	...	...	—	„
Massacre of St. Bartholomew	...	...	1572	„
Complete establishment of the High Commission Court	1583	„
Execution of Mary, Queen of Scots	...	...	1587	„
Defeat of the Spanish Armada ...	...	...	1588	„
Establishment of the East India Company	...	1600	„

THE STUART PERIOD

Union of the English and Scottish Crowns	1603	James I
Hampton Court Conference	1604	,,
Gunpowder Plot	1605	,,
Thirty Years' War begins	1618	,,
Landing of the Pilgrim Fathers in America	1620	,,
Impeachment of Lord Bacon	1621	,,
Petition of Right	1628	Charles I
Long Parliament	1640	,,
Triennial Act	1641	,,
Grand Remonstrance	—	,,
First Civil War or Great Rebellion begins	1642	,,
Battle of Edgehill (*Warwickshire*)	—	,,
,, Chalgrove Field (*Oxfordshire*)	1643	,,
First Battle of Newbury (*Berkshire*)	—	,,
Battle of Marston Moor (*Yorkshire*)	1644	,,
Second Battle of Newbury	—	,,
Self-denying Ordinance	1645	,,
Battle of Naseby (*Northamptonshire*)	—	,,
Second Civil War	1648	,,
Pride's Purge	—	,,
Execution of Charles I	1649	,,
Battle of Dunbar	1650	The Commonwealth
,, Worcester	1651	,,
First Dutch War	1652–1653	,,
Expulsion of the Rump	1653	,,
Little or Barebone's Parliament	—	Protectorate
Instrument of Government	—	,,
Humble Petition and Advice	1657	,,
Declaration of Breda (*Holland*)	1660	,,
The Restoration	—	,,
Pension Parliament	1661	Charles II
Corporation Act	1661	,,
Third Act of Uniformity	1662	,,
Conventicle Act	1664	,,
Great Plague of London	1665	,,
Five-Mile Act	—	,,
Second Dutch War	1665–1667	,,
The Great Fire of London	1666	,,
Cabal Ministry formed	1667	,,
Triple Alliance	1668	,,
First Declaration of Indulgence	1672	,,
Third Dutch War	1672–1674	,,
Test Act	1673	,,
Titus Oates' Plot	1678	,,
Habeas Corpus Act	1679	,,
Rye House Plot	1683	,,
Rebellions of Argyle and Monmouth	1685	James II
Bloody Assize	—	,,
Second Declaration of Indulgence	1688	,,
Trial of the Seven Bishops	—	,,
The Revolution	1689	,,

First Mutiny Bill	—	William III
Toleration Act	—	and Mary
Battle of Killiecrankie (*Perthshire*)	—	,,
Siege of Londonderry (*Ireland*)	—	,,
Bill of Rights	—	,,
Battle of the Boyne (*Ireland*)	1690	,,
,, La Hogue (*France*)	1692	,,
National Debt originated	1693	,,
Bank of England established	1694	,,
Triennial Act	—	,,
Second Treason Bill	1696	,,
Peace of Ryswick (*Holland*)	1697	,,
First Partition Treaty	1698	,,
Darien Scheme	1699	,,
Second Partition Treaty	1700	,,
Act of Settlement or Succession Act	1701	,,
Grand Alliance	—	,,
War of the Spanish Succession	1702–1713	Anne
The Methuen or Port Wine Treaty	1703	,,
Queen Anne's Bounty instituted	1704	,,
Gibraltar taken	—	,,
Battle of Blenheim (*West Bavaria*)	—	,,
Battle of Ramillies (*Belgium*)	1706	,,
Act for the Union of England and Scotland	1707	,,
Battle of Oudenarde (*Belgium*)	1708	,,
,, Malplaquet (*France*)	1709	,,
Treaty of Utrecht (*Holland*)	1713	,,

HANOVERIAN PERIOD

The Rebellion of Fifteen	1715	George I
Septennial Act	1716	,,
Quadruple Alliance	1718	,,
South Sea Scheme	1720	,,

PRIME MINISTERS

Sir Robert Walpole (*Whig*), 1727–1742

Bill of Indemnity for non-observance of Test and Corporation Acts	1727	George II
Walpole fails to pass his Excise Bill	1733	,,
Porteous Riots in Edinburgh	1736	,,
War with Spain (*Jenkins' Ear War*)	1739	,,

Lord Wilmington (*Whig*), 1742–1743

The Place Bill passed, limiting the number of offices to be held by members of Parliament	1742	,,
War of the **Austrian Succession** begins	1743	,,
Battle of Dettingen (*Bavaria*)	—	,,

Henry Pelham (*Whig*), 1743–1754

The "Broad Bottom Ministry" formed under the Pelhams (Henry and Thomas)	1744	,,
Battle of Fontenoy (*Belgium*)	1745	,,
The **Rebellion of Forty-Five**	—	,,

Battle of Preston Pans (*Haddington*)	—	George II
,, Falkirk (*Stirlingshire*)	1746	,,
,, Culloden (*Nairn*)	—	,,
Peace of Aix-la-Chapelle (*Rhenish Prussia*)	1748	,,
Duke of Newcastle, Thomas Pelham (*Whig*), 1754–1756		
Byng fails to relieve Minorca	1756	,,
Seven Years' War begins	—	,,
Duke of Devonshire (*Whig*), 1756–1757		
Pitt becomes Secretary of State	—	,,
Execution of Byng	1757	,,
Duke of Newcastle, 1757–1762		
Battles of Hastenbeck and Klosterseven	—	,,
Battle of **Plassy** (*India*)	—	,,
,, Minden (*Germany*)	1759	,,
Capture of Quebec (*Canada*)	—	,,
Victories off Lagos (*Portugal*) and in Quiberon Bay		
(*France*)	—	,,
Battle of Wandewash (*India*)	1760	,,
Family Compact between France and Spain formed ...	1761	George III
Lord Bute (*Tory*), 1762–1763		
First Treaty of Paris, or Fontainebleau	1763	,,
George Grenville (*Whig*), 1763–1765		
Prosecution of Wilkes	—	,,
Quarrel with the American Colonists begins	1764	,,
The American Stamp Act passed	1765	,,
Lord Rockingham (*Whig*), 1765–1766		
Repeal of the American Stamp Act	1766	,,
Duke of Grafton (*Whig*), 1766–1770		
The American Revenue Act passed	1767	,,
Riots in favour of Wilkes	1768	,,
Lord North (*Tory*), 1770–1782		
The American import duties abolished, except that on		
tea	1770	,,
The Royal Marriage Act passed	1772	,,
The Boston Tea-party	1773	,,
American Declaration of Rights	1774	,,
American War of Independence begins	1775	,,
Battles of Lexington and Bunker's Hill (*United States*)	—	,,
American Declaration of Independence	1776	,,
Battle of Brandywine (*United States*)	1777	,,
Convention of Saratoga (*United States*)	—	,,
Savile's Roman Catholic Relief Bill passed	1778	,,
Siege of Gibraltar (*Spain*)	1779–1782	,,
The Armed Neutrality	1780	,,
Rodney's victory off Cape St. Vincent	—	,,
The Gordon Riots in London	—	,,
Capitulation of Cornwallis at Yorktown	1781	,,
Grattan's Bill, called the Declaration of Right, passed	1782	,,
Lord Rockingham (*Whig*), 1782		
Rodney's victory off St. Lucia (*West Indies*)	—	,,
Lord Shelburne (*Whig*), 1782		
Treaty of Versailles (*France*)	1783	,,

Duke of Portland (Whig), 1783

Fox's India Bill passes the Commons but is thrown out
by the Lords ... ... — George III

William Pitt (Whig), 1783–1801

Pitt's India Bill passed	1784	,,
Impeachment of Warren Hastings	1786	,,
Commencement of the French Revolution	1789	,,
War with the French Republic	1793–1797	,,
Lord Howe's victory off Brest	1794	,,
Sir John Jervis' victory off Cape St. Vincent	1797	,,
Mutinies at Spithead and the Nore	—	,,
Admiral Duncan's victory off Camperdown (*North Holland*)	—	,,
Irish Rebellion and Battle of Vinegar Hill (*Wexford*)	1798	,,
First War with Napoleon begins	—	,,
Nelson's victory of the Battle of the Nile (*Egypt*) ...	—	,,
Capture of Seringapatam (*India*)	1799	,,
Pitt's Bill for the **Union of Great Britain and Ireland** passed	1800	,,
The Armed Neutrality of 1780 revived	1800	,,

Addington (Tory), 1801–1804

Abercrombie's victory at Alexandria (*Egypt*)	1801	,,
Nelson's victory off Copenhagen	—	,,
Peace of Amiens	1802	,,
Wellesley's victory at Assaye	1803	,,

William Pitt, 1804–1806

Second War with Napoleon begins	1805	,,
Battle of Trafalgar (Spain) and Death of Nelson ...	—	,,

Lord Grenville (Tory), 1806–1807

Ministry of All the Talents formed under Grenville and Fox	1806	,,
Napoleon issues his Berlin Decrees	—	,,
Act passed for the Abolition of the Slave Trade ...	1807	,,

Duke of Portland (Whig), 1807–1809

The Peninsular War begins	1808	,,
Battles of Rolica and Vimiero (*Portugal*)	—	,,
Convention of Cintra (*Portugal*)	—	,,
Battle of Corunna (*Spain*) and death of Sir John Moore	1809	,,
Battle of Talavera (*Spain*)	—	,,
Failure of the Walcheren Expedition	—	,,

Perceval (Tory), 1809–1812

Battle of Bussaco (*Portugal*)	1810	,,
Wellington storms Badajoz (*Spain*)	1812	,,
Perceval assassinated	—	,,

Lord Liverpool (Tory), 1812–1827

Battle of Salamanca (*Spain*)	—	,,
,, Vittoria (*Spain*)	1813	,,
Battles of Orthez (*France*) and Toulouse (*France*) ...	1814	,,
First Peace of Paris	—	,,
Abdication of Napoleon	—	,,
Congress of Vienna (*Austria*)	—	,,
Battle of Waterloo (Belgium)	1815	,,

The Holy Alliance	—	George III
Second Peace of Paris	—	,,
Bombardment of Algiers	1816	,,
Bill passed to suspend the Habeas Corpus Act ...	1817	,,
The Peterloo Massacre	1819	,,
The Six Acts	—	George IV
Cato Street Conspiracy	1820	,,
Reciprocity of Duties Bill	1823	,,
Great Money Panic in England	1825	,,

Canning (Tory), 1827

Treaty of London between England, France, and Russia to bring about peace between Turkey and Greece	1827	,,

Lord Goderich (Whig), 1827

Battle of Navarino (*Greece*)	1827	,,

Duke of Wellington (Tory), 1828–1830

Repeal of the Test and Corporation Acts	1828	,,
Roman Catholic Relief Bill passed	1829	,,
Independence of Greece acknowledged	—	,,

Lord Grey (Liberal), 1830–1834

Second French Revolution	1830	William IV
The First Reform Bill	1832	,,
Act for the Emancipation of Slaves in all the British Dominions	1833	,,
New Poor Law Act	1834	,,

Lord Melbourne (Whig), 1834
Sir Robert Peel (Conservative), 1834
Lord Melbourne, 1835–1841

Municipal Reform Act	1835	,,
Marriage Act	1836	,,
Tithe Commutation Bill	—	,,
Insurrection in the Canadas	1837	Victoria
New Postage Scheme adopted	1839	,,
First War with China	—	,,

Sir Robert Peel, 1841–1846

First Afghan War	1839–1842	,,
Income Tax introduced	1842	,,
Establishment of the Free Church in Scotland ...	1843	,,
War with and conquest of Sindh	—	,,
First Sikh War begins	1845	,,
Repeal of the Corn Laws	1846	,,

Lord John Russell (Liberal), 1846–1852
(Lord Palmerston Foreign Secretary)

The Third French Revolution	1848	,,
Great Chartist Demonstration in London	—	,,
Rebellion of the " Young Ireland Party " in Ireland ...	—	,,
Second Sikh War and Annexation of the Punjab ...	1849	,,
The **Great Exhibition**	1851	,,
Coup d'état in Paris	—	,,

Lord Derby (Conservative), 1852

Death of the Duke of Wellington	1852	,,

Lord Aberdeen (Liberal), 1852–1855

Crimean War begins	1853	,,
Battles of Alma, Balaclava, and Inkerman (*Crimea*) ...	1854	,,

Lord Palmerston (Whig), 1855–1858
 Fall of Sebastopol (*Crimea*) ... ... 1855 Victoria
 Third Treaty of Paris ... ... 1856 ,,
 Second War with China ... ... — ,,
 The **Indian Mutiny** ... ... 1857–1858 ,,
 Conspiracy to Murder Bill defeated ... ... 1858 ,,
Lord Derby, 1858–1859
 Bill admitting Jews to Parliament ... ... — ,,
 The Volunteer Movement begins ... ... 1859 ,,
 Disraeli's Reform Bill defeated ... ... — ,,
Lord Palmerston, 1859–1865
 Italian War of Liberation ... ... 1859–1861 ,,
 Cobden's Treaty with France ... ... 1860 ,,
 American Civil War ... ... 1861–1865 ,,
 Death of the Prince Consort ... ... 1861 ,,
 Cotton famine in Lancashire ... ... 1862 ,,
 The Ionian Islands separate from England and unite
  with Greece ... ... 1863 ,,
 Death of Lord Palmerston ... ... 1865 ,,
Lord John Russell, 1865–1866
 Gladstone's Reform Bill defeated ... ... 1866 ,,
Lord Derby, 1866–1868
 The **Second Great Reform Bill** ... ... 1867 ,,
 The Fenian Conspiracy ... ... — ,,
Disraeli (Conservative), 1868
 Abyssinian Expedition ... ... 1868 ,,
Gladstone (Liberal) 1868–1874
 Disestablishment and Disendowment of the Irish Church 1869 ,,
 First Irish Land Act ... ... 1870 ,,
 Elementary Education Act ... ... — ,,
 Franco-Prussian War ... ... 1870–1871 ,,
 Abolition of Religious Tests in the Universities ... 1871 ,,
 Abolition of Army Purchase ... ... — ,,
 The Ballot Act ... ... 1872 ,,
 The Alabama Claims settled ... ... — ,,
 Second Ashanti War ... ... 1873 ,,
 Supreme Court of Judicature Act ... ... — ,,
Disraeli, 1874–1880
 Public Worship Regulation Act ... ... 1874 ,,
 Fiji Islands annexed ... ... 1875 ,,
 Unseaworthy Ships Bill ... ... — ,,
 The English Government purchases shares in the Suez
  Canal ... ... — ,,
 The Prince of Wales visits India ... ... — ,,
 The Queen assumes the title of **Empress of India** ... 1876 ,,
 Russo-Turkish War ... ... 1877–1878 ,,
 Congress and **Treaty of Berlin** ... ... 1878 ,,
 Second War with Afghanistan ... ... 1878–1879 ,,
 Zulu War ... ... 1879 ,,
Gladstone, 1880–1885
 Organization of the Land League in Ireland ... ... 1880 ,,
 Gladstone's Second Irish Land Act ... ... 1881 ,,
 Assassination of Lord Frederick Cavendish and Mr.
  Burke ... ... 1882 ,,

Closure Bill	—	Victoria
Arabi Pasha's Insurrection in Egypt and Bombardment		
of Alexandria	—	,,
Revolt of the Mahdi in the Sudan	1883	,,
Third Great Reform Bill	1884	,,
Fall of Khartoum and Murder of Gordon	1885	,,

Lord Salisbury (*Conservative*), 1885
Gladstone, 1886

Gladstone's Home Rule Bill for Ireland defeated ...	1886	,,

Lord Salisbury, 1886–1892

" Plan of Campaign " in Ireland	—	,,
New Rules of House of Commons Procedure ...	1887	,,
Celebration of the Queen's Jubilee	—	,,
Third Irish Land Bill	—	,,
Nationalist Meeting at Mitchelstown	—	,,
Goschen's National Debt Scheme	1888	,,
Special Commission on Parnellism and Crime ...	1889	,,
County Councils established	—	,,

Gladstone, 1892–1894

Gladstone's Second Home Rule Bill defeated ...	1893	,,
Parish Councils Bill	1894	,,

Lord Rosebery (*Liberal*), 1894–1895

Bill regulating Death Duties	—	,,
Factory and Workshops Bill	1895	,,

Lord Salisbury, 1895

The Jameson Raid	1896	,,
Expedition to Coomassie	—	,,
The Venezuelan Dispute	—	,,
The Cretan Question	1897	,,
Queen's Diamond Jubilee, June 22	—	,,
Spanish–American War	1898	,,
Battle of **Omdurman**	—	,,
Major Marchand evacuates **Fashoda**	—	,,
The **Imperial Penny Postage** comes into operation ...	—	,,
The Niger Territories Bill passed	1899	,,
Outbreak of Boer War; British defeated at Stormberg,		
Magersfontein, and Colenso	—	,,
Surrender of Cronje, relief of Ladysmith and Mafe-		
king	1900	,,
End of full-scale fighting...	—	,,
Boxer rebellion in China...	—	,,
Inauguration of **Australian Commonwealth**	1901	,,
Taff Vale decision...	—	,,
Anglo–Japanese Alliance...	1902	Edward VII

Balfour (*Conservative*)

Education Bill	—	,,
Peace Conference with Boers	—	,,
Irish Land Purchase Bill	1903	,,
" Entente Cordiale "	1904	,,
Outbreak of Russo–Japanese War (1904–1905) ...	—	,,
Younghusband Mission to Tibet	—	,,

Sir Henry Campbell-Bannerman (*Liberal*)

First Parliamentary Labour Party	1905	,,
Aliens Bill	—	,,

Trades Disputes Act	...	...	...	...	—	Edward VII
Workmen's Compensation Act	...	...	...	...	—	,,
Haldane's reorganization of the army	...	...	...	1907	,,
Court of Criminal Appeal established	...	...	...	—	,,
Office of Public Trustee established	...	...	...	1908	,,

Asquith (*Liberal*)

Old Age Pensions Act	...	...	...	...	1909	,,
Labour Exchanges established	...	...	...	—	,,
Osborne judgment	...	...	...	...	—	,,
Federation in South Africa	...	...	...	1910	George V
Parliament Act	...	...	...	...	1911	,,
Insurance Act	...	...	...	...	—	,,
Payment of M.P.s	...	...	...	...	—	,,
Coal mines minimum wages	...	...	...	1912	,,
Panama Canal opened	...	...	...	...	1913	,,
Trade Union Act	...	...	...	...	—	,,
Outbreak of First World War, 1914–1918	...	...	1914	,,
Battle of the Marne	...	...	...	...	—	,,
Gallipoli Landing	...	...	...	...	1915	,,
Battle of Jutland (North Sea)	...	...	...	1916	,,
First Battle of the Somme	...	...	...	—	,,
United States declares war on Germany	...	...	1917	,,
Russian Revolution	...	...	...	...	—	,,
Allied victory in Palestine	...	...	...	—	,,
Last German offensive defeated	...	...	...	1918	,,
Armistice, November 11	...	...	...	...	1918	,,
Education Act	...	...	...	...	—	,,
Parliamentary Reform Act	...	...	...	—	,,

Lloyd George (*Coalition*), 1918

Versailles Peace Treaties	...	...	...	1919	,,
League of Nations established	...	...	...	—	,,
Partition of Ireland	...	...	...	...	1920	,,
Establishment of **Irish Free State**	...	...	1921	,,
Government of India Act	...	...	...	—	,,

Bonar Law (*Conservative*), 1922

Mussolini seizes power in Italy	...	...	...	1922	,,

Stanley Baldwin (*Conservative*), 1923

Treaty of Lausanne	...	...	...	...	1923	,,

Ramsay MacDonald (*Labour*), 1924
Stanley Baldwin (*Conservative*), 1924

Return to Gold Standard	...	...	...	1925	,,
Widows Pensions Act	...	...	...	...	—	,,
Treaty of Locarno	...	...	...	...	—	,,
General Strike	...	...	...	...	1926	,,
Trade Union Act	...	...	...	...	1927	,,
Equal Franchise Act	...	...	...	...	1928	,,
Kellogg Pact	...	...	...	...	—	,,
Local Government Act	...	...	...	1929	,,

Ramsay MacDonald (*Labour*), 1929

Simon Report on India	...	...	...	1930	,,
Beginning of Great Depression	...	...	...	1931	,,

Ramsay MacDonald (" *National*," *chiefly Conservative*), 1931

Japan invaded Manchuria	...	...	...	...	—	,,

G

Statute of Westminster	—	George V
Import Duties Act	1932	,,
Means Test	—	,,
Ottawa Conference	—	,,
Lausanne Conference	—	,,
Adolf Hitler seizes power in Germany	1933	,,
Unemployment Assistance Board	1934	,,
Italian invasion of Abyssinia	1935	,,

Stanley Baldwin (" National," chiefly Conservative), 1935

Hoare–Laval Pact	1935	,,
King George V's Silver Jubilee	—	,,
Government of India Act	—	,,
Death of King George V	1936	,,
Accession and Abdication of King Edward VIII ...	—	George VI
German occupation of Rhineland	1936	,,
Spanish Civil War	—	,,
Factory Act	1937	,,

Neville Chamberlain (" National," chiefly Conservative), 1937

German annexation of Austria	1938	,,
Munich Agreement	—	,,
German occupation of Czechoslovakia	1939	,,
Italian occupation of Albania	—	,,
Royal Visit to Canada and United States	—	,,
Russo–German Pact	—	,,
Outbreak of Second World War, 1939–1945	—	,,
German conquest of Denmark, Norway, Holland, and Belgium	1940	,,

Winston Churchill (Coalition), 1940

German conquest of France	1940	,,
Axis conquest of Greece and Crete	—	,,
" Battle of Britain " (air)	—	,,
America Lend-Lease Bill	1941	,,
German conquest of Jugoslavia	—	,,
German invasion of Russia	—	,,
Japanese attack Pearl Harbour; United States joins the Allies	—	,,
Beveridge Report	1942	,,
Allied naval victories of Coral Sea and Midway (Pacific)	—	,,
Liberation of Abyssinia; capture of Italian Somaliland	—	,,
Allied victory of **El Alamein,** and landing in North-West Africa	—	,,
Russian victory at **Stalingrad**	—	,,
Final Allied victory in Tunisia	1943	,,
Allied invasion of Italy against German troops, Italy having concluded Armistice; fall of Mussolini ...	—	,,
Allied offensive begins in Pacific	—	,,
Allied offensive in Burma	1944	,,
Russian advance into Poland	—	,,
Rome captured	—	,,
Allied landing in **Normandy** (June 6)	—	,,
Liberation of France	—	,,

Education Act	—	George VI
Germany invaded from East and West; unconditional surrender May 7	1945	,,
First atomic bomb August 6	—	,,
Japan surrenders September 12	—	,,

Clement Attlee (Labour), 1945

Bank of England nationalized	1945	,,
United Nations Organization established	—	,,
National Insurance Act	1946	,,
National Health Service established	—	,,
Nationalization of coal mines, road and rail transport, and Cable Wireless Ltd.	—	,,
First meeting of United Nations Assembly	—	,,
Nationalization of electricity industry	1947	,,
Overseas Resources Bill	—	,,
Cominform established (eastern Europe) ...	—	,,
Marshall Aid set up	—	,,
Dunkirk Treaty	—	,,
Establishment of independent states of **India** and **Pakistan**	—	,,
Ceylon gains Dominion status	—	,,
Independence of **Burma**	—	,,
Representation of the People Bill	1948	,,
Monopolies Bill	—	,,
Legal Aid Scheme	—	,,
Nationalization of gas industry	—	,,
Childrens Bill	—	,,
Colonial Development and Welfare Act	—	,,
Treaty of Brussels...	—	,,
Organization for European Economic Co-operation (O.E.E.C.) established	—	,,
Russian blockade of Berlin	—	,,
First meeting of Central Legislative Assembly of East Africa	—	,,
Terrorism in Malaya	—	,,
State of Israel established	—	,,
Parliament Act	1949	,,
North Atlantic Treaty	—	,,
Council of Europe established	—	,,
Communist Government set up in China	—	,,

Clement Attlee (Labour), 1950

Iron and Steel industry nationalized	1950	,,
Invasion of South Korea by Communist North Korea ...	—	,,
European Payments Union established...	—	,,
Colombo Plan	—	,,
Festival of Britain	1951	,,
European Coal and Steel Community established ...	—	,,
Japanese Peace Treaty	—	,,

Winston Churchill (Conservative), 1951

Death of King George VI, February 6...	1952	,,
Accession of **Queen Elizabeth II**	—	Elizabeth II
De-nationalization of iron and steel, and road transport planned	—	,,
Mau Mau terrorism in Kenya	—	,,

G 2

Conquest of Mount Everest	1953	Elizabeth II
Death of J. V. Stalin	—	,,
Armistice in **Korea**	—	,,
End of food rationing	1954	,,
Establishment of Independent Television Authority ...	—	,,
Agreement for entry of a re-armed West Germany into Western alliance	—	,,
Cease-fire in **Indo-China**	—	,,
South-East Asia Defence Treaty signed	—	,,

Sir Anthony Eden (Conservative), 1955

Plans for road and rail modernization	1955	,,
Violence in Cyprus	—	,,
Calder Hall nuclear power station opened ...	1956	,,
Anglo–French attack on **Egypt**	—	,,

Harold Macmillan (Conservative), 1957

Britain's first **hydrogen bomb** exploded	1957	,,
New Homicide Act	—	,,
Commonwealth Antarctic Expedition	—	,,
Life peerages inaugurated	1958	,,
Clean Air Act	—	,,
West Indies Federation established	—	,,
Common Market set up	—	,,

Harold Macmillan (Conservative), 1959

First motorway opened	1959	,,
Singapore becomes a state	—	,,
Nigeria achieves independence	1960	,,
Cyprus becomes independent republic	—	,,
Somaliland achieves independence	—	,,
European Free Trade Association established ...	—	,,
Last National Service men called up	—	,,
Sierra Leone becomes an independent state ...	1961	,,
Tanganyika becomes an independent state ...	—	,,
Uganda becomes fully independent	1962	,,
Trinidad and Tobago become independent states ...	—	,,
Tanganyika becomes a republic	—	,,
Harold Wilson elected Leader of Labour Party ...	1963	,,
Nyasaland becomes an independent state ...	—	,,
Kenya becomes an independent state	—	,,
Zanzibar becomes an independent state ...	—	,,
Federation of Malaysia established	—	,,
President John Kennedy assassinated in Texas ...	—	,,
Harold Macmillan resigns premiership ...	—	,,

Sir Alec Douglas Home (Conservative), 1963

Bahamas becomes self-governing	1964	,,
Northern Rhodesia becomes independent	—	,,
Malta becomes independent	—	,,

Harold Wilson (Labour), 1964

Sir Winston Churchill died	1965	,,
Prices and Incomes Board set up	—	,,
Terrorism in Aden	—	,,
Rhodesia proclaims UDA	—	,,
Malawi becomes a republic	1966	,,
British Guiana becomes independent	—	,,
Bechuanaland becomes independent	—	,,

197

Barbados becomes independent ...	...	...	...	...	—	Elizabeth II
Mountbatten report on prison security	...	...	...	...	—	,,
Britain applies to join Common Market		...	...	1967		,,
South Arabia becomes independent	...	...	...	—		,,
£ devalued by 14.3%	...	...	...	—		,,
Legal age of majority reduced to 18	...	...	...	1968		,,
Race Relations Act	...	...	...	—		,,
Plans for comprehensive education	...	...	...	—		,,
Mauritius becomes independent	...	...	...	—		,,
Swaziland becomes independent	...	...	...	—		,,
Investiture of Prince of Wales ...	...	...	...	1969		,,
First man on the moon	...	...	...	—		,,
Divorce Reform Act	...	...	...	—		,,
Violence in Northern Ireland ...	...	...	...	—		,,

Edward Heath (Conservative) 1970

Britain reapplied to join Common Market		...	...	1970		,,
Industrial Relations Act	...	...	...	—		,,
Decimal currency introduced ...	...	...	...	1971		,,
Population census... ...	...	...	...	—		,,
Angry Brigade bomb attacks ...	...	...	...	—		,,
Pearce Commission in Rhodesia	...	...	...	1972		,,
1,000,000 unemployed	...	...	...	—		,,
White Paper on Metrication ...	...	...	...	—		,,
Ugandan Asians expelled ...	...	...	...	—		,,
Ceylon becomes republic of **Sri Lanka** ...		...	...	—		,,
Britain becomes member of EEC ...	...	...	1973		,,
Widespread bomb attacks in Britain ...		...	...	—		,,
' Cod War ' with Iceland...		...	...	—		,,
War in Middle-East		...	...	—		,,
Channel Tunnel Bill		...	...	—		,,
Army death roll in Northern Ireland, 200		...	...	—		,,
Agreement on Northern Ireland Assembly		...	...	—		,,
Watergate Affair		...	...	—		,,
State of emergency declared after oil embargo and miners' overtime ban caused power crisis ...			...	...	—	,,

ACTS LIMITING THE ROYAL POWER

Charter of Liberties ...	... ...	1100	Henry I
Magna Charta ...	... ...	1215	John
Provisions of Oxford	... ...	1258	Henry III
Confirmatio Cartarum	... ...	1297	Edward I
Lords Ordainers appointed	... ...	1310	Edward II
Petition of Right ...	... ...	1628	Charles I
Habeas Corpus ...	... ...	1679	Charles II
Bill of Rights ...	... ...	1689	William III
First Mutiny Bill ...	... ...	—	and Mary
Act of Settlement ...	... ...	1701	,,

ACTS LIMITING THE PAPAL POWER

Constitutions of Clarendon	... ...	1164	Henry II
Statute of Mortmain ...	... ...	1279	Edward I
,, Provisors ...	... ...	1351	Edward III
,, Præmunire ...	... ...	1393	Richard II
Act forbidding all appeals to Rome	... ...	1533	Henry VIII
Act forbidding the Payment of Annates ...	... ...	1534	,,
Act abolishing the Authority of the Pope	... ...	—	,,
First Act of Supremacy ...	... ...	1535	,,
Second ,, ,,	... ...	1559	Elizabeth I

ACTS OF RELIGIOUS INTOLERANCE

De Heretico Comburendo ...	... ...	1401	Henry IV
Six Articles	... ...	1539	Henry VIII
First Act of Uniformity	... ...	1549	Edward VI
Second ,, ,,	... ...	1559	Elizabeth I
Corporation Act ...	... ...	1661	Charles II
Third Act of Uniformity	... ...	1662	,,
Conventicle Act ...	... ...	1664	,,
Five-Mile Act ...	... ...	1665	,,
Test Act	... ...	1673	,,
Occasional Conformity Act	... ...	1711	Anne
Schism Act	... ...	1714	,,

SHORT BIOGRAPHICAL SKETCHES

THE ROMAN PERIOD

Julius Cæsar, the greatest of all the Roman generals, undertook two invasions of Britain, probably with the intention: (1) of punishing the Britons for having sent assistance to their kinsmen the Belgæ, with whom he was at war; (2) of annexing to the Roman Empire a country reputed to be wealthy. His first invasion (55 B.C.) was merely for the purpose of reconnoitring; in his second invasion (54 B.C.) he pushed far into the interior, and having defeated the natives under their brave leader **Cassivellaunus,** and destroyed their stronghold **Verulamium** (St. Albans), he imposed a tribute, received hostages, and returned to Gaul. *For about ninety years after these events the Romans left the Britons unmolested.*

Aulus Plautius, a general of the Emperor Claudius, in A.D. 43 was sent to conquer Britain. He took **Vectis** (Isle of Wight), stormed the stockaded village of **Camulodunum** (Colchester), which afterwards became a Roman town, *and subdued all the districts lying between the Wash and Southampton Water.*

Caractacus was one of the sons of Cunobelinus, who, after the capture of his capital Camulodunum, became King of the warlike Silures. He was subsequently defeated, taken prisoner by Aulus Plautius, and sent a prisoner to Rome.

Suetonius Paullinus, a Roman general, who in A.D. 61 became governor of Britain. To complete the subjugation of the West he took the **Isle of Mona** (Anglesey), and put to death all the Druids, who lived there, and who encouraged the Britons to resist the Roman Government. He also crushed the rebellion raised by **Boadicea,** but was recalled in disgrace by the Emperor Nero.

Boadicea was Queen of the Iceni. Roused by the indignities she had received at the hands of the Romans, she rose in rebellion against her cruel oppressors, but was defeated by Suetonius Paullinus, and took her own life.

Julius Agricola was the father-in-law of the Roman historian Tacitus, and the *best and ablest of all the Roman governors of Britain.* His rule lasted from 78 to 85, and during that time he completed the conquest of the country. He induced the noblemen among the Britons to adopt the Roman manners and customs. He constructed excellent roads, built many strong towns, administered strict justice, " put an end to the power of the grasping Roman tax-gatherers," and did much to reconcile the Britons to the Roman rule. The Emperor Domitian, however, being jealous of his fame, recalled him.

Hadrian was a Roman Emperor, who in 119 visited Britain. " *He was more disposed to defend the empire than to extend it,*" and to hinder the Caledonians from plundering Britain, he erected a solid stone wall known as *Hadrian's Wall,* eighty miles in length, from Newcastle to Carlisle, and furnished it with forts at convenient intervals, well garrisoned with troops drawn from the Moors, Spaniards, Thracians, and other tribes who had been subdued by the Romans. The remains of this wall are still to be seen.

Carausius was one of the " *Counts of the Saxon Shore*," an officer whose duty it was to guard the eastern coast of England from the Wash to Beachy Head. Carausius kept off the Saxons, drove back the Picts and Scots, proclaimed Britain an independent state in 288, and reigned over it as " *Emperor*." After a reign of seven years he was murdered, and Britain was again annexed to the Roman Empire.

St. Alban was one of the missionaries who preached Christianity in Britain during the Roman occupation. He is said to have suffered martyrdom in 305 at Verulamium (St. Albans), where a noble abbey now stands bearing his name.

THE SAXON PERIOD

Cerdic was the leader of a band of Saxon adventurers who in 495 landed on the shores of Southampton Water and after a hard fight with the Britons captured Winchester and took the title of *King of Wessex*. *He was the ancestor of Egbert, the first King of the English.*

St. Augustine was a zealous Roman monk who was sent by Pope Gregory to convert the English. Twenty years before, when Gregory was an abbot, he had been attracted by the fair faces and golden hair of some beautiful boys exposed for sale in the slave-market at Rome. " *Who are these children*? " he asked of the slave-dealer. " *Angles*," he replied. " *They should be angels*," said Gregory, " *they are so fair*." When Gregory became Pope he remembered those beautiful children, and sent his friend Augustine to convert the English. Augustine and his band of forty missionaries landed at **Ebbsfleet**, in the Isle of Thanet. He chose Kent as the scene of his labours because: (1) **Ethelbert**, the King of Kent, was at that time the most powerful chief in Britain; (2) he had married **Bertha**, a Christian princess, and the daughter of Charibert, King of Paris. In the end Ethelbert was converted to Christianity, and he and many of his Kentish subjects received baptism. Augustine became the **first Archbishop of Canterbury,** and from his zeal in trying to convert the English he was called " *the Apostle of the English*."

Bede, or Baeda, usually called the " *Venerable Bede*," was a monk of Jarrow-on-Tyne, and the *first great English scholar and historian*. His greatest work is the **Ecclesiastical History of the English Nation.** He wrote many books for the use of students, and translated the Gospel of St. John into English. Bede was of a patient and loving disposition, zealous in the cause of learning, and one who did much towards civilizing the English people and uniting them into one nation. He died in 753.

Cædmon was a poor monk of the monastery of **Whitby,** who sang the Bible History in English poems. *He has been called the founder of English poetry.* He died about 680.

Alcuin was a native of Northumbria, and so renowned for his learning that the Emperor, Charles the Great (Charlemagne), sent for him to go to France and teach his subjects.

Egbert was a powerful King of Wessex, and the lineal descendant of Cerdic. In his youth he had been compelled to take refuge at the Court of Charles the Great, but in 802 he returned to England, and at the request of his countrymen he took the crown. During the thirty-seven years of his reign (802–839) his whole aim was to bring the neighbouring kings under his sway, as Edwin and Offa had done. He defeated the Northumbrians, under the King Beornwulf, in a battle at **Ellandun.** This was followed by the submission of all the under-kings of Kent, Sussex, Essex, and East Anglia. Northumbria also, weakened by the repeated invasions of the Northmen, offered him obedience and allegiance. His last great victory was that gained over the combined forces of the Northmen and the West Welsh at **Hengist's Down,** after which the Welsh Prince of Cornwall did him homage. Egbert thus became **Overlord of Britain.** *He is generally considered to be the first King of the English.*

Alfred the Great was the son of Ethelwulf and Osberga and was born at Wantage, in 849. When he was quite a child he was sent by his father to Rome, where he attracted the attention of Pope Leo IV, who foretold that he would one day be a king.

(1) On his return home he joined his brother Ethelred in his campaigns against the Danes, who had overrun almost the whole of England and now threatened Wessex. In a single year (871) the two warrior-brothers fought no less than *six battles* with the invaders, in one of which, at **Ashdown,** they won a great victory, but were unable to drive the Danes out of their stronghold at Reading. Shortly after Ethelred received his death-wound at Merton (Surrey), and the army of Wessex was broken up.

(2) To Alfred, who succeeded his brother as king, was bequeathed the task of saving his country from ruin. The " Great Army " of Danes now forced its way up the Thames and defeated the men of Wessex at **Wilton.** Alfred then paid an immense amount of treasure as the price of peace, and the marauders turned northwards to seize and occupy Mercia.

(3) In 878 part of the " Great Army " under Guthrum returned to renew their attacks upon their old enemies the men of Wessex. Two years of desperate fighting followed, till at last Alfred was so completely crushed that he fled for safety to the little island of **Athelney.** The stories of his adventures in the swine-herd's hut and in the Danish camp are well known. A few weeks later he issued forth from his hiding-place, and being joined by levies from Somerset, Wilts, and Hants, utterly defeated **Guthrum** at **Ethandun,** and stormed the strong Danish Camp at **Chippenham.** Guthrum was compelled to make a treaty with Alfred at **Wedmore.** Alfred spent the remainder of his life in making wise and good laws, organizing the military resources of the country, and in encouraging learning. His bravery in battle, his self-denial, and patient endurance in adversity, his deep religious feeling and high sense of duty endeared him to his people, while his many-sided activity and his ability as an organizer, legislator, and scholar have gained for him an undying fame, and the reputation of being *one of the greatest and noblest kings that ever sat on the English throne.* He died in 901.

Dunstan was the *first ecclesiastical statesman to leave his mark on the history of the English nation.* He was a monk of Glastonbury, and a man of great learning and ability. Under Edmund I he became **Abbot of Glastonbury,** and his great aim was to reform the Church. He tried to enforce celibacy on the secular clergy, and the rule of St.

Benedict, "*poverty, chastity, and obedience,*" on the monks. He opposed the marriage of Edwy and his near kinswoman Elgiva, because it was within the forbidden degrees of marriage. This ultimately led to his banishment by the king, but Edgar recalled him and made him **Archbishop of Canterbury** and his chief adviser. *His wise government contributed much towards making the Anglo-Saxon and Danish races one nation.* He died in 988.

Sweyn was a king of the Danes, who in 994 appeared with a host of invaders on the east coast of England, but was bought off by the Saxon Witan, by the payment of £16,000. Meanwhile Ethelred, the Saxon King, ordered all the Danes in England to be massacred. This unwise plan was actually carried out on **St. Brice's Day.**

In 1003 Sweyn returned to England with the determination to avenge the death of his countrymen, and to conquer England. For four years he ravaged the whole country with fire and sword, and when Ethelred fled to Normandy **he was chosen King by the Witan.** He died in 1014, leaving his dominion to his son Canute.

Canute was the son of Sweyn, the Danish King. On the death of his father, the Danish warriors chose him King of England; but the Witan sent for Ethelred the Unready, who had fled to Normandy, to return to England. Two years after, however, Ethelred died, and his son, **Edmund Ironside,** was chosen king by the people of London, while those of the other parts of England elected Canute. Edmund died soon after and the **Witan then chose Canute as King of all England.**

Canute's early life had contained many acts of violence, but on coming to the English throne, he ruled with moderation. His **policy** was *to rule as an English King,* and his impartial government soon made the English respect and trust him. Besides being King of **England,** he ruled over **Norway** and **Denmark.** His reign was one of peace and prosperity; towns, hitherto mere fortresses, became the centres of English life, commerce was opened with the Continent, fens were drained, and many churches, towers, and bridges were built. So peaceful was the country that in 1027 he made a **pilgrimage to Rome,** where he was honourably received by the Pope and Emperor. At his death in 1035 his extensive dominions were divided between his three sons.

Godwin, Earl of Wessex, was a very prominent figure during the reigns of Canute and Edward the Confessor. Canute placed the greatest confidence in him, and made him ruler of the kingdom during his absence on a pilgrimage to Rome. Under Edward the Confessor, who had married his daughter, Godwin became practically the **Governor of England.** His refusal to punish the men of Dover for an attack on Eustace of Boulogne, Edward's brother-in-law, and his *extreme dislike for the Norman favourites of the King* led to an open rupture between the King and his minister. *The Earl and all his family were banished and the Queen sent to a nunnery.* The next year, however, he returned with a large army, and Edward, unable to resist the popular feeling, reinstated him in his earldom and former position of power. In 1053 the Earl died suddenly at a great feast at Winchester, and his son Harold succeeded to his earldom and power. "He was a man sagacious in counsel, strenuous in war, diligent in business, weighty in speech, of winning manner and of admirable temper."

THE NORMAN PERIOD
WILLIAM I

Stigand, appointed Archbishop of Canterbury by Edward the Confessor in 1052, was a leading **member of the Witan** at the time of the Conquest. After the Battle of Hastings he **proclaimed Edgar Atheling** as king, but was compelled to submit to William, who, however, refused to be crowned by him, because he had been appointed to his see by the Anti-pope Benedict X. He was **deposed** in 1070, and kept a prisoner at Winchester.

Lanfranc, a native of Pavia and Abbot of Bec, was appointed **Archbishop of Canterbury** by William I on the deposition of Stigand. He supported the power of the monarchy and its control of the Church, which he reorganized and reformed.

Waltheof, son of Siward, was a famous Saxon noble and Earl of Northumberland. He submitted to William I, but was concerned in the **great Saxon revolt** of 1069, and took the City of York from the Normans. William afterwards became reconciled to him, and gave his niece **Judith** in marriage. Becoming implicated in the **Bridal of Norwich,** he confessed his guilt to Lanfranc, and was shortly afterwards executed; the last powerful English noble was thus removed.

Hereward the Wake, a Saxon patriot who had been deprived of his possessions by a Norman intruder. With a small Saxon following he formed the **Camp of Refuge** in the Fen Country. After the taking of this stronghold in 1071 he was pardoned and **restored to his estates.**

Edgar Atheling was grandson of Edmund Ironside, and rightful heir to the English throne on the death of Edward the Confessor. After the Battle of Hastings he was **proclaimed King,** but soon submitted to William. He was concerned in the great rebellion of 1069, but, on again yielding to William, retired to Normandy. Subsequently he **joined Robert,** Duke of Normandy, and at the battle of **Tenchebrai** was taken prisoner by Henry I, but afterwards liberated, and died in peace in England.

WILLIAM II

Anselm, an eminent Piedmontese monk, succeeded Lanfranc as **Abbot of Bec.** After Lanfranc's death William II kept the see of Canterbury vacant for four years, but, on becoming ill in 1093, and for the time penitent, he appointed **Anselm,** as **Archbishop.** Anselm, however, accepted the office somewhat reluctantly, remarking, " *that he, a poor feeble sheep, was to be yoked to a wild bull.*" In 1097 Anselm was exiled after a quarrel with the King over the Archbishop's feudal obligations. He returned on the accession of Henry I, with whom he quarrelled about the **right of appointing Bishops.** In 1107 the dispute was settled by a compromise at **Bec,** by which the King gave up the right of investing the Bishops with ring and crozier, but retained the claim of homage from them for their temporal possessions.

Ralph Flambard succeeded Lanfranc as chief adviser of **William II.** A more accurate completion of the Doomsday Book is attributed to him. He held the office of **Justiciar,** and was the chief instrument of the King's extortions. Henry I imprisoned him, but he escaped and took refuge in Normandy, and died Bishop of Lisieux in 1089.

Peter the Hermit was a French monk who, having suffered many trials and hardships on a pilgrimage to the Holy Land, **preached the Crusades** in the principal countries of Europe. **Pope Urban II** gave his sanction to the Crusade movement, and Peter led an irregular host of Crusaders, to the number, it is said, of 100,000, to the Holy Land, but accomplished nothing.

STEPHEN

Thurstan, Archbishop of York, won the **Battle of the Standard,** near Northallerton, 1138, defeating the Scots, who had invaded England, under David I, in support of Matilda.

Robert of Gloucester was an illegitimate son of Henry I. He supported the cause of his half-sister Matilda against Stephen. In 1139 he **invaded England,** took Stephen prisoner at **Lincoln,** but shortly after was himself captured. An exchange of prisoners was followed by a renewal of the war, which continued until Robert's death in 1147.

THE PLANTAGENET PERIOD

HENRY II

Thomas à Becket, the son of a London citizen, was the first **Englishman** who rose to any eminence under the Norman rule. He was introduced to Henry's notice by Theobald, and became **Chancellor;** and to such a degree had he won the personal favour and friendship of the King that Theobald said, " *The King and Becket have but one heart and mind.*" Henry loaded his favourite with riches and honour, so that he outshone his royal master in his magnificence. Being anxious to carry out reforms respecting the **trial of the Clergy,** and thinking that Becket would assist him, Henry made him **Archbishop of Canterbury.** Becket received the appointment with some hesitation. " *You will soon hate me,*" said he to Henry, " *as much as you love me now.*" Taking **Anselm as his model,** he stood up boldly as the champion of the Church, and opposed Henry. He reluctantly gave his consent to the **Constitutions of Clarendon,** shortly after rejected them, and appealed to the Pope to absolve him from his oath. At the **Council of Northampton** he openly defied the King's authority, and, fearing for his life, fled to France, and there continued the bitter contest for six years. At last the Pope threatened to excommunicate Henry, and so a hollow **reconciliation** was effected between the King and the Primate, and Becket returned to England. He, however, renewed the struggle by excommunicating Roger, Archbishop of York, for having crowned Prince Henry in his absence, and two other Bishops for having taken the King's side against him. On hearing of this, Henry, in a burst of passion, exclaimed, " *Will no one rid me of this turbulent priest?* " Four knights took him at his word, hurried across to England, and, after an angry interview with the Archbishop, **murdered** him on the altar steps of his own cathedral. Subsequently Becket was canonized, and his shrine became the resort of thousands of pilgrims.

Strongbow, Earl of Pembroke (Richard de Clare), was a bankrupt nobleman who, with a small body of Welshmen, landed in Ireland **to reinstate Dermot,** the expelled King of Leinster. Having recovered Dermot's possessions, he married his daughter Eva, and succeeded to the **crown of Leinster.** In 1171 Henry, being jealous of the success of Strongbow, visited Ireland in person, and received the **submission of Strongbow** and the Irish chiefs. **Prince John** was afterwards nominated Lord of Ireland, but the English were only masters of the counties round Dublin, and it was not till the time of the Tudors that the real conquest of Ireland took place.

Ralph de Glanville, Justiciar, and the greatest of Henry II's generals, surprised and **captured William the Lion of Scotland,** near **Alnwick Castle,** under cover of a mist.

Nicolas Breakspear (Adrian IV) was the only Englishman who ever ascended the **Papal throne.** Under his rule England was drawn into a much closer connection with the Papal See, and in 1154 Adrian granted a Bull to Henry II, authorizing him to conquer Ireland.

RICHARD I

William Longchamp, Bishop of Ely, a man of low extraction, and a favourite of Richard I, was made **Regent of England** during Richard's absence. He also became Chancellor, Justiciar, and Papal Legate, thus holding the chief civil and ecclesiastical authority in England. With the aid of Geoffrey, Archbishop of York, Prince John raised the Barons against **Longchamp,** and he was **expelled from office** and retired to Normandy.

William Fitz-Osbert (Longbeard) **headed a rebellion** of the poorer citizens of London, who rose against unjust taxation of craftsmen. Fitz-Osbert was captured and hanged, and the rebellion easily suppressed.

NOTE.—This was the first rising of the "Commons" in England.

JOHN

Stephen Langton was an eminent Englishman who became **Chancellor of the University of Paris,** and on the death of Hubert of Canterbury was elected **Archbishop** by Pope Innocent III, his old friend and fellow-student. John refused to confirm the election, and the kingdom was placed under an **Interdict,** which continued four years, when John submitted to the Pope's decision, and received Langton as Archbishop. Langton afterwards **took a leading part** in the struggle with John to obtain the **Great Charter.** In 1213 he laid before the Barons, who were assembled at St. Paul's, the Coronation Charter of Henry I, which was considered as the basis of their demands from the King. Subsequently the **Pope suspended Langton** for taking part against John.

HENRY III

William Marshall, Earl of Pembroke, was chosen **Regent** during the minority of Henry III, and ruled well for two years. He **overthrew Louis** in a battle fought in the streets of Lincoln, commonly called the **Fair of Lincoln.** The defeat of a great French fleet of eighty ships, which was bringing assistance to Louis, compelled him to make terms with Pembroke, and he left the country. Pembroke died in 1219.

Hubert de Burgh, one of the twenty-four Guardians of the Great Charter, appointed in the reign of John, succeeded Pembroke as Regent. He **defeated the French fleet** sent to help Louis. When Henry was twenty years of age he declared himself old enough to govern, and caused Hubert to resign the office of Regent, but retained him as his **Justiciar.** In the discharge of his duties he was **constantly opposed** by **Peter des Roches,** Bishop of Winchester. In 1232 he was accused of peculation, and deprived of all his offices. " He was the last of the great Justiciars, who had acted as the King's chief ministers since the time of William II."

Peter des Roches, Bishop of Winchester, was a Poitevin, and the rival of Hubert de Burgh. On the downfall of Hubert he became the **King's chief minister,** and obtained for his countrymen many influential offices in England. This caused the Barons to form an opposition under **Edmund Rich,** Archbishop of Canterbury, and Des Roches and his friends were dismissed.

Simon de Montfort, Earl of Leicester, was a Frenchman, and brother-in-law to Henry III. As Governor of Gascony his rule was harsh. He became **leader of the opposition Barons** in 1258, and was at the **head of the Mad Parliament.** In 1264 the Barons' War broke out, and at the **Battle of Lewes** De Montfort defeated the King and took him prisoner. The following year De Montfort called together his **famous Parliament,** representatives being summoned from the towns as well as the counties.

A **quarrel having arisen** between the **Earl of Gloucester** and **De Montfort,** many of the nobles deserted the latter, and at **Evesham** " *Sir Simon the Righteous,*" as the people called De Montfort, was slain, fighting over the dead body of his son. All contemporary writers speak of him with admiration.

NOTE.—Montfort's rebellion led to three good results: (1) There were no more inroads of foreigners. (2) The Pope no longer interfered with England as overlord. (3) The idea of " popular representation " was for the first time brought before the nation.

Roger Bacon (1214–1294), a Franciscan monk, was a man of wide learning with a passion for science and mathematics. He valued practical experiment, unlike most contemporary philosophers, and was much influenced by Arab scholars. He was imprisoned for fourteen years and his books condemned, on suspicion of magic and heresy, and because of his attacks on clerical ignorance.

Robert Grosseteste was Bishop of Lincoln, and eminent for his learning. He strenuously opposed the Papal extortions in the reign of Henry III, and laboured hard to reform the demoralized clergy. He was the **friend and supporter** of Simon de Montfort.

EDWARD I

Llewellyn, the last native prince of Wales, took part with the Barons in their struggle with Henry III. In 1277 Edward I invaded Wales, and compelled Llewellyn to submit. Soon afterwards a fresh insurrection broke out, which ended in the defeat and death of Llewellyn. By the Statute of Wales, enacted at Rhuddlan, Wales was annexed to England.

John Balliol, a rival of Robert Bruce the elder for the throne of Scotland, was chosen by Edward I as King. Subsequently, however, he rebelled against Edward, but was defeated at **Dunbar** and sent a prisoner to England.

Sir William Wallace was a brave outlawed knight who raised the standard of rebellion against Edward's rule in Scotland. He defeated the English at **Cambuskenneth**, and ravaged the north of England. He then proclaimed himself " *Guardian of the Kingdom* " in Balliol's name, but having been utterly routed by Edward at **Falkirk**, 1298, he resumed his outlawed life, and was ultimately betrayed by his own servant to the English and executed.

Robert Bruce the younger was the **grandson** of Robert Bruce the elder, the rival of Balliol. Suspecting **John Comyn** of treachery, he murdered him in the Grey Friars Church at Dumfries, and was **crowned King** at Scone. Edward I marched against him, but his death at Burgh-on-Sands saved Scotland's freedom. In 1314 Bruce gained a signal victory over Edward II at **Bannockburn,** and Scotland regained her independence.

EDWARD II

Roger Mortimer, 1st Earl of March, and paramour of Queen Isabella, fled to France after the rebellion of the Barons against the Despensers. In 1326 he returned with Isabella, and Edward II was deposed. For the next three years the **Government** was in the **hands of Mortimer** and the **Queen,** but in 1330 Edward III rose against them, and Mortimer was seized at **Nottingham Castle** and hanged at Tyburn.

Piers Gaveston, a gay and dissolute Gascon knight, was banished by Edward I, but recalled by his son, Edward II, made a favourite, and created **Earl of Cornwall.** His insolent conduct towards the Barons caused them to rebel under **Thomas, Earl of Lancaster,** and demand his dismissal. Edward II banished him, but made him **Lord-Deputy of Ireland.** He was again recalled, but seized by the Earl of Warwick, and executed on Blacklow Hill.

Hugh Despenser and his son were the favourites of Edward II in the latter part of his reign. They were both banished in 1321, but recalled the following year, when the Barons, under Lancaster, rebelled, but were defeated by Edward at **Boroughbridge,** and Lancaster, whom Edward had never forgiven for Gaveston's death, was beheaded. On the deposition of Edward, both the Despensers were captured and executed by the Barons under Mortimer.

EDWARD III

John Wycliffe, the " *Morning Star of the Reformation,*" was an eminent reformer, born in Yorkshire, and educated at Oxford. He became **Master of Balliol College,** and wrote against the **abuses in the Church** and the corruption of the Clergy, especially the Friars, who called him a " *sower of strife.*" He also attacked the doctrine of Transubstantiation. A few years later he translated the **Bible into English,** and trained and sent out " *simple priests barefooted and in russet gowns,*" who taught that all men were equal in the sight of God and that the doctrines and practices of religion should be in accordance with the teaching of Holy Scripture. Wat Tyler's rebellion increased the alarm which his opinions had excited, and he was summoned by the Bishops to **appear at St. Paul's** and answer for his heretical teaching. The **protection of John of Gaunt** saved his life. He afterwards retired to his own parish at **Lutterworth,** where he died in 1384. The followers of Wycliffe, " **Lollards,**" as they were called, belonged to every class of society.

William of Wykeham, Bishop of Winchester, and Chancellor from 1367 to 1371, was the founder of St. Mary's College, Winchester, and of New College, Oxford.

Geoffrey Chaucer, the " *Father of English poetry,*" was born in London. His chief work is the *Canterbury Tales,* supposed to be told by pilgrims going to see the shrine of Thomas à Becket. Chaucer died in 1400.

RICHARD II

Wat Tyler, the leader of the peasant revolt in Kent in 1381, was killed at Smithfield by **Sir William Walworth,** the Lord Mayor.

THE HOUSE OF LANCASTER

HENRY IV

Owen Glendower was a Welsh chief who claimed to be a descendant of Llewellyn, Prince of Wales in the reign of Edward I. He had been a **faithful squire to Richard II,** and, on the deposition of his master, he retired to Wales, and **raised the standard of rebellion** against Henry IV. The Welsh from all parts of the country flocked to support him, and all attempts on the part of Henry to reduce him failed. He **joined the Percies** in their rebellion, and, on the defeat of Northumberland, he maintained his independence in the Welsh Mountains for many years, but at last died miserably in 1415.

Henry Percy, "*Hotspur,*" so called from his fiery temper, was the son of the Earl of Northumberland. He was defeated by the Scots at **Chevy Chase,** but gained a victory over them at **Homildon Hill,** and took Earl Douglas prisoner. He took part in the great rebellion of 1403 against Henry IV, and was killed at **Shrewsbury.**

HENRY V

Sir John Oldcastle, Lord Cobham, was the **leader of the Lollards** in the reign of Henry V. He was accused of heresy and treason, and condemned to death, but escaped into Wales. Four years later he was captured and executed as a traitor and heretic.

Edmund Mortimer, 5th Earl of March, and rightful heir to the throne on the deposition of Richard II, was **imprisoned by Henry IV.** A conspiracy was made in his favour in 1405 by **Archbishop Scrope** and others, but it failed. On the accession of Henry V, he was freed, but a second conspiracy was made in his favour by **Richard, Earl of Cambridge,** Lord Scrope, and Sir Thomas Grey, all of whom were executed. Mortimer died in 1424.

HENRY VI

John, Duke of Bedford, brother of Henry V, was Protector of England and Regent of France during the minority of his nephew, Henry VI. He strengthened the English alliance with Burgundy by **marrying Anne, sister of Philip the Good,** Duke of Burgundy, overthrew the French at **Verneuil,** but at the siege of Orleans was baffled by **Joan of Arc,** and compelled to raise the siege. Joan was captured at Compiegne and burnt at Rouen with Bedford's approval. Afterwards Bedford's rule was very unsuccessful, and although Henry VI was crowned in Paris in 1431, the **English gradually lost** all their acquired **possessions.** Bedford died at Rouen in 1435.

John Talbot, Earl of Salisbury, was a distinguished general in the French War in the reign of Henry VI. He gained the victory of **Crevant,** took part in the **siege of Orleans,** was taken prisoner at **Pataye,** but afterwards released, and defeated and slain at **Châtillon** in 1453.

William de la Pole, Duke of Suffolk, was the chief minister of Henry VI after Gloucester's death. He arranged an **unpopular marriage** between **Henry VI** and **Margaret** of Anjou, and his enemies accused him of having made a **disgraceful peace with France.** He was impeached, and Henry, to save his life, banished him for five years, but he was overtaken by his enemies while crossing the Channel and murdered.

Richard, Baron Mortimer and Duke of York, was the father of Edward IV. He became **Protector** in 1454 owing to the imbecility of Henry VI, and when displaced by Somerset took up arms. The rivalry between York and Somerset was one of the causes of the " *Wars of the Roses.*" He defeated the Lancastrians at **St. Albans,** but shortly after fled to the Continent. He returned in 1460, and won the battle of **Northampton,** after which he publicly claimed the throne, and was **acknowledged heir-apparent.** At **Wakefield** he suffered a severe defeat, was taken prisoner, and beheaded.

Jack Cade was the leader of the Kentish revolt against the rule of Somerset in 1450. He defeated the royal forces at **Sevenoaks,** and entered London. His followers, however, soon dispersed, and he was slain near Lewes by the Sheriff of Kent.

THE HOUSE OF YORK

EDWARD IV

Richard Neville, Earl of Warwick, the " *King-maker,*" was the most powerful adherent of the Yorkist faction in the Wars of the Roses. His retainers are said to have numbered 30,000. He fought in the battles of **Northampton, Second St. Albans,** and **Towton,** and was largely rewarded by Edward IV. He became Governor of Calais, Lord Deputy of Ireland, and Warden of the Welsh Marches. Being greatly displeased with the favour shown to the Woodvilles, he **joined the Lancastrian party.** In 1470 Warwick, with Clarence, Edward's brother, fled to France. They made common cause with Margaret of Anjou, and **invaded England** in her favour. Edward IV was compelled to fly the country, but returned soon after and encountered Warwick at **Barnet,** where the latter was slain.

William Caxton, the first English printer, introduced printing into England from Flanders in 1476. He set up a press in Westminster Abbey, and the first book printed in England was the *Dictes and Sayings of Philosophers, 1477.*

THE TUDOR PERIOD

HENRY VII

John Morton, Archbishop of Canterbury, was one of the chief advisers of Henry VII. He became **Chancellor** and **Cardinal,** and his device of extorting money from the people was known as " *Morton's Fork.*"

Sir Richard Empson and **Edmund Dudley** were two lawyers, who assisted Henry VII in his extortions. They were much hated by the people, and were both executed by Henry VIII in 1510.

Lambert Simnel was an imposter, who personated the Earl of Warwick, son of the Duke of Clarence. He was assisted by Margaret, Duchess of Burgundy, and was actually **crowned in Dublin Cathedral** as Edward VI. Landing in England, he was defeated by the royal forces at **Stoke,** and Henry, to show his contempt for his rival, made him a scullion in the royal kitchen.

Perkin Warbeck gave himself out to be the Duke of York, son of Edward IV, and was favourably received in **Ireland** and in **France.** The **Duchess of Burgundy** received him as her nephew. Leaving Flanders, he took refuge with **James IV of Scotland,** who gave him his own kinswoman, Lady Catherine Gordon, in marriage, and invaded England in his behalf, but the people rose against the invader, and the Scottish army withdrew. Having lost his asylum in Scotland in consequence of a truce between Henry and James, Warbeck landed at **Whitsand Bay,** near Penzance, seized St. Michael's Mount, and marched against Exeter. His assaults upon that city failed, and, on the desertion of his troops and the approach of the royal army, he fled by night to the **Abbey of Beaulieu,** in the New Forest. Here he surrendered and,.having confessed his imposture, he was placed in the Tower. While there, he formed the acquaintance of the **Earl of Warwick,** and both prisoners tried to escape, but failed. Warbeck was hanged at Tyburn and Warwick beheaded in the Tower.

HENRY VIII

Erasmus, a Dutch scholar and theologian, visited England, and from 1511 to 1513 was Divinity Professor at Cambridge. In his Greek New Testament he began modern Biblical scholarship.

Thomas Wolsey, the son of a **wealthy citizen of Ipswich,** was educated at Oxford, and became a Fellow of Magdalen College. He was chaplain to Henry VII, and incumbent of Lymington. His ability was appreciated by Henry VIII, who entrusted the **management of the French War** in 1511 almost entirely to his care. On the capture of Tournay he was made Bishop of that city, and when he returned to England became **Archbishop of York** and **Chancellor.** Afterwards he was made **Cardinal** and **Papal Legate,** and enjoyed a revenue equal to that of the Crown. His rule was most arbitrary; from 1515 to 1523 no Parliament was summoned, and he raised money for the King's use by means of benevolences and fines. His **neutral conduct** in the matter of the King's divorce cost him the favour of the King. He was indicted under the **Act of Præmunire,** compelled to resign the Great Seal, and retired to his own Diocese of York. Suddenly he was arrested on a charge of treason, founded on his correspondence with the Pope and the King of France, and died at **Leicester Abbey** while on his way to London (1530) to answer the charge. On his death-bed he uttered these memorable words, " *Had I served God as diligently as I have served my King, He would not have given me over in my grey hairs. But this is my just reward.*"

Wolsey was an able and enlightened man, and a " *ripe and good scholar* "; he founded **Christ Church** at Oxford, and a college at Ipswich, " *which fell with him.*" He also built two magnificent palaces, Hampton Court and York House (afterwards Whitehall). His policy was to uphold the **supremacy of the Church,** and his greatest ambition was to **become Pope.**

Thomas Cromwell was the **private secretary** of Wolsey, and when his master fell under the King's displeasure he ably defended him. Henry recognized and appreciated his honest ability, and immediately took him into his service. *Cromwell suggested that Henry should declare himself supreme Head of the Church,* a suggestion which Henry carried out in 1535. During his ten years' administration, " in some respects the most momentous period of English history," the **Church of England was separated from that of Rome.** As Vicar-General Cromwell carried out the **suppression of the monasteries,** but incurred Henry's displeasure in advising him to marry Anne of Cleves, and he was arrested in the Council Chamber on a charge of treason. A few days later he was condemned by a **Bill of Attainder, and executed.**

Thomas Cranmer, Fellow of Jesus College, Cambridge, first came into the notice and favour of Henry VIII by suggesting that *the question of the King's divorce should be referred to the Universities of Europe.* This was accordingly done, and it was found that most of them gave a verdict in the King's favour.

In 1533 Henry married Anne Boleyn, and Cranmer was made **Archbishop of Canterbury.** In the reign of Edward VI Cranmer vigorously **pushed forward the Reformation,** and played an important part in drawing up the First Prayer Book of Edward VI and the Articles of Religion.

On the accession of Mary he was **imprisoned,** and, being tempted by a promise of pardon, he signed no less than **six recantations** of his religious opinions. His enemies, however, were determined that he should die, and the day was fixed for his execution. At **St. Mary's Church, Oxford,** he was called upon to make a public confession of his faith, but, instead of the expected recantation, he said, " *As for the Pope, I utterly refuse him as Christ's enemy, and Antichrist, with all his false doctrine.*" He was at once hurried off to the stake and burnt, steadily holding his right hand in the flames, and crying out with a loud voice, " *This hand hath offended.*" No man contributed more towards the establishment and independence of the English Church than Cranmer.

Martin Luther, the great German Reformer, was born in Saxony in 1483. At the age of twenty-one he became an **Augustine Friar,** and, having devoted himself to the study of the Holy Scriptures, he became convinced of many of the errors which had crept into the Roman Catholic Church. He **opposed the sale of indulgences,** and maintained the authority of the Bible as the only rule of religious faith; and when Pope Leo X excommunicated him, he **burnt the Papal Bull** containing his excommunication before the gate of Wittenberg Castle. Being summoned to appear before the Emperor at the **Diet of Worms,** he ably defended himself, and was protected by the Elector of Saxony. He died in 1546.

John Calvin (1509–1564), a French scholar and theologian, evolved a religious system based on councils of elders and ministers, and putting great stress on the doctrine of predestination. The Presbyterian Churches of Scotland and elsewhere are Calvinistic, as were the Huguenots and the English Puritans.

Thomas Howard, 2nd Duke of Norfolk. When Earl of Surrey he defeated the Scots at the **Battle of Flodden,** 1513. His son, **Thomas Howard,** third Duke of Norfolk, was condemned to death together with his son, **Henry, Earl of Surrey,** by Henry VIII for treason, and was only saved by the death of the King, 1547.

Robert Aske, a young lawyer, was leader of the **Pilgrimage of Grace** in 1536. He was executed the following year.

William Tyndale, called the " *Apostle of England,*" published the **first printed English New Testament.** With the assistance of **Miles Coverdale** he also translated the Pentateuch. He was burnt as a heretic near Brussels.

John Fisher, Bishop of Rochester, was executed in 1535 for denying the King's supremacy.

Sir Thomas More, the wisest and noblest Englishman of his time, succeeded Wolsey as **Chancellor** in 1529. He was beheaded for denying the King's supremacy. Besides his *History of King Richard III,* he was the author of *Utopia,* describing an imaginary perfect society.

EDWARD VI

Edward Seymour, Duke of Somerset, was the brother of Jane Seymour. While Earl of Hertford, he was appointed **Protector** to his nephew, Edward VI, and, having invaded Scotland, won the battle of **Pinkie.** Under his administration the **Reformation made great progress,** but, becoming unpopular with the Council, he was supplanted by Warwick. Ultimately he was accused of treason and executed.

John Dudley, Earl of Warwick and Duke of Northumberland, was the son of the famous lawyer in the reign of Henry VIII. He suppressed the **insurrection of Kett,** and, on the fall of Somerset, became **Protector.** On the **failure of his plan** to place Lady Jane Grey on the throne to the exclusion of Mary, he was arrested, tried, and executed.

Lord Seymour, brother of Edward Seymour, married Catherine Parr, widow of Henry VIII. Having plotted to overthrow his brother, he was executed in 1549.

Lady Jane Grey was the grand-daughter of Mary, sister of Henry VIII. She married **Lord Guildford Dudley,** fourth son of the Duke of Northumberland, and, on the death of Edward VI, was proclaimed Queen, but **reigned only ten days.** She was imprisoned by Mary, and after Wyatt's rebellion, she and her husband were executed. She was only seventeen when she died.

MARY

Hugh Latimer, Bishop of Worcester, took part with Cranmer in the establishment of Protestantism in the reign of Edward VI. On the accession of Mary he was imprisoned, and in 1555 was chained back to back with **Ridley, Bishop of London,** to the same stake at Oxford, and so burnt. "*Play the game, Master Ridley,*" said Latimer; "*we shall this day light such a candle in England as by the grace of God shall never be put out.*"

Cardinal Pole was the son of the Marchioness of Salisbury who was beheaded for treason in Henry VIII's reign. He pronounced absolution over the assembled Parliament in 1553, and became **Archbishop of Canterbury** on the death of Cranmer. He took a leading part in the burning of " heretics," especially after the death of Gardiner in 1555.

Stephen Gardiner, Bishop of Winchester, and **Bonner, Bishop of London,** were strong supporters of the Roman Catholic religion in Mary's reign, and both cruelly persecuted the Protestants. Gardiner died in 1555, and Bonner, on the accession of Elizabeth, was imprisoned for life.

Sir Thomas Wyatt was the leader of the Kentish revolt against the marriage of Mary with Philip II of Spain. He was beheaded in 1554.

ELIZABETH I

Sir Nicholas Bacon, the father of Francis Bacon, was **Keeper of the Great Seal** in Elizabeth's reign for twenty years.

William Cecil, Lord Burleigh, was **Secretary of State** and privy councillor to Elizabeth for forty years. He was raised to the peerage in 1571 and died in 1598.

Sir Francis Walsingham became **Secretary of State** in 1573. He played an important part in the discovery of **Babington's plot.**

Thomas Howard, 4th Duke of Norfolk, was the head of the Roman Catholic party in England in Elizabeth's reign. He **aspired to a marriage with Mary Queen of Scots,** and for this he was sent to the Tower, but subsequently liberated. On becoming implicated in the **Ridolfi Plot** he was tried and executed.

Robert Dudley, Earl of Leicester, was the son of the Duke of Northumberland, who was executed in Mary's reign. He was a **favourite of Elizabeth,** who proposed that he should marry Mary Queen of Scots. He unsuccessfully commanded the expedition sent to aid the Dutch in 1585, but was appointed general of the army at **Tilbury** during the attempted Spanish invasion of 1588.

Robert Devereux, Earl of Essex, a favourite of Elizabeth, was the rival of the younger Cecil. He was appointed Viceroy of Ireland, with orders to suppress the rebellion of **Hugh O'Neill,** Earl of Tyrone, but failed, and thus lost the Queen's favour. On his return, he made an unsuccessful attempt to raise a rebellion in London, but was taken prisoner and executed.

Sir Philip Sidney, a soldier, courtier, author, and the "*jewel of Elizabeth's court,*" took part in the campaign of 1585 to assist the Dutch in the Netherlands, and was slain at **Zutphen.** He wrote *Arcadia,* a prose romance, and *Defence of Poesie.* He was regarded, both in England and on the Continent, as the type of a true and chivalrous gentleman.

Lord Howard of Effingham, a Roman Catholic nobleman, was the commander of the English fleet which defeated the **Spanish Armada.**

Sir Francis Drake was the first Englishman who **sailed round the world.** On his return Elizabeth welcomed him on his own ship and knighted him. He took part in the contest with the Spanish Armada.

Sir Martin Frobisher, one of the earliest explorers of the **North-West Passage.** He also served against the Armada.

Sir John Hawkins, a distinguished naval captain, who took part in the fight with the Armada. He did much to improve the navy, by building the ships on a plan which more nearly resembled modern vessels than those previously used.

Anthony Babington, a gentleman of Derbyshire, who, with a Jesuit named Ballard, and others, formed a plot to assassinate Elizabeth and place Mary Queen of Scots on the throne. The plot was discovered, and Babington and his accomplices were executed.

William Shakespeare (1564–1616), "*the greatest name in our Literature,*" and "*the prince of dramatists,*" was born at Stratford-on-Avon, and became an actor and playwright in London. He wrote thirty-seven plays, including the following: (1) **Historical Plays**—*Richard II, Henry V,* and *Richard III;* (2) **Comedies**—*Merchant of Venice, As you Like It, Midsummer Night's Dream, Much Ado about Nothing,* and *The Tempest;* (3) **Tragedies**—*Romeo and Juliet, Julius Cæsar, Macbeth, Hamlet, King Lear, Othello,* and *Cymbeline,* besides his *Sonnets.* About 1610 he retired to Stratford, where he died, and was buried in the church of that town.

Ben Jonson, a poet and dramatist, was the intimate friend of Shakespeare. His principal plays are: *Sejanus, The Alchemist, Volpone,* and *Every Man in his Humour.* He died in 1637, and was buried in Westminster Abbey, where a tablet has been erected to his memory in the Poet's Corner, inscribed, "*O rare Ben Jonson.*"

Christopher Marlowe, a dramatist, and worthily named Shakespeare's predecessor, established blank verse in plays. He wrote *Faustus, The Jew of Malta,* and *Edward II.* He was killed in a tavern brawl.

Edmund Spenser, a celebrated poet, wrote *Shepherd's Calendar* and *The Faerie Queene,* an allegorical poem, written in a stanza of nine lines, called "*Spenserian.*"

Richard Hooker, a learned divine, and eminent theological writer. His chief work is *Laws of Ecclesiastical Polity,* a defence of the English Church against the Puritans.

Roger Ascham, tutor to the children of Henry VIII, and Lady Jane Grey, was Latin Secretary to Mary and Elizabeth, and Professor of Greek at Cambridge. He was the author of the *School-master* and *Toxophilus, or The School of Archery.*

THE STUART PERIOD

JAMES I

Francis Bacon, Viscount St. Albans, was the son of Sir Nicholas Bacon, Lord Keeper to Elizabeth. He studied for the Bar, and in 1618 became **Lord Chancellor.** In 1621 he was **impeached** by the Commons for **receiving bribes;** no less than twenty-two instances were clearly proved against him. His only apology was " *that the presents he had received had never influenced the course of justice.*" He was **dismissed from office,** sentenced to pay a fine of £10,000, and to be imprisoned during the King's pleasure, but the King remitted his fine and released him, providing him with a pension of £1,800 a year. Bacon spent the remainder of his life in the study of philosophy. His own remark on his fall was this, " I was the justest judge that was in England these fifty years; but it was the justest sentence in Parliament that was these 200 years." His principal works are, *Essays, Novum Organum,* and *The Advancement of Learning.* He died in 1626.

George Villiers, Duke of Buckingham, became the favourite of James I after the disgrace of Carr, Earl of Somerset. He accompanied **Prince Charles to Spain,** where his insolence greatly offended the Spanish Court. From 1625 to 1628 he was the chief adviser of Charles I, and by his instrumentality **eight ships,** which had been prepared ostensibly to act against Spain, were lent to France to be **used against the Huguenots.** This caused great dissatisfaction, and the " *great delinquent,*" as Buckingham was called, was **impeached,** and only saved by the dissolution of Parliament. To regain his lost popularity he led an expedition of 100 ships **in aid of the Huguenots** at **La Rochelle,** but suffered an ignominious defeat at Rhé and returned home. While engaged in fitting out a second expedition, he was **assassinated** at Portsmouth by **John Felton** (1628).

Sir Edward Coke, Attorney-General under James I, who conducted the prosecution of Sir Walter Raleigh in 1603. He was appointed **Lord Chief Justice** in 1613, but removed from this office some years later on account of his opposition to James' tyranny. In the reign of Charles I he entered the House of Commons, and in 1628 played an important part in the drawing up of the **Petition of Right.**

Sir Walter Raleigh was a famous sailor, discoverer, and author. In 1584 he established the **colony of Virginia,** in North America, so called in honour of the Virgin Queen Elizabeth and, although the settlement was not at first successful, it afterwards flourished. On the accession of James I he was accused of complicity in the **Main Treason** to set Arabella Stuart on the throne. He was condemned, and remained in **prison thirteen years,** during which time he wrote his *History of the World.* In 1615 James I, being in want of money, released Raleigh, and gave him a fleet of thirteen ships to go in search of a **gold mine in Guiana,** which Raleigh said had been discovered by Captain Keymis in 1596. He was strictly enjoined not to fight the Spaniards, but this was almost impossible, as the Spaniards already possessed that country. When Raleigh reached the mouth of the Orinoco, he sent an expedition under Captain Keymis up the river to discover the mine. The Spaniards, however, had been informed that the English were coming, and attacked the expedition, which in turn took and burnt the Spanish village of St. Thomas, where Raleigh's son was killed. Himself disheartened, and his crew mutinous, he sailed home, where the vengeance of the Spanish Ambassador, Gondomar, awaited him, and the sentence of death, which had been passed fifteen years before, was now carried out and he was executed.

CHARLES I

Thomas Wentworth, Earl of Strafford, was one of the leading members of the opposition to the Crown in the beginning of the reign of Charles I. After Buckingham's death he deserted the popular cause and went over to the King, partly from ambitious motives and partly from a desire not to go too far on the side of democracy. He then became the King's chief adviser, and having been made President of the Council of the North, ruled most tyrannically. In 1633 he was appointed Lord-Deputy of Ireland, where his government, although in some respects beneficial to that country, was little better than a reign of terror. His scheme of Thorough made the King's power absolute. " *The King,*" he wrote to Laud, " *is as absolute here as any prince in the world can be.*" When the Long Parliament assembled, Charles sent for Strafford to come to London, promising that " *not a hair of his head should be touched.*" On his return, Pym, followed by 300 of the Commons, who had never forgiven him for his apostasy, impeached him at the bar of the House of Lords, with locked doors, on the charge of illegal and tyrannical government. The impeachment, however, fell through, and a Bill of Attainder was brought in against him. This passed both Houses. The King gave the royal assent only with great reluctance, after his advisers had recommended it as a duty to please the Parliament and after Strafford had released him from promises of protection. Strafford was executed, and the King's ablest supporter was thus removed.

John Pym, " *King Pym,*" as the Royalists called him, was born in Somersetshire, of good birth and fortune, and became the chief leader of the Parliamentary party in the reign of Charles I. He was " *of great experience in Parliamentary affairs,*" took part in the impeachment of Buckingham, assisted Wentworth in drawing up the Petition of Right, and brought in the Grand Remonstrance. He was also the prime mover in the impeachment of Strafford and Laud. When Charles returned from Scotland in 1641 he was most loyally received by the citizens of London. This encouraged him to make an attack upon the House of Commons by seizing the Five Members, his most daring opponents, of whom Pym was one. Accordingly, he went down to the House with a band of armed men, but timely notice of what he intended to do had been sent to Pym, and when Charles arrived " *all the birds had flown.*" The citizens of London refused to give up the culprits, and a week afterwards they were conducted back to the House in triumph by a strong military escort. It was clear that war was inevitable, and both parties began to make preparations for the struggle. In 1643 Parliament, acting on Pym's advice, made an agreement with the Scots, and signed the Solemn League and Covenant, so as to secure their assistance for the war. Pym died the same year, and was buried in Westminster Abbey. By order of the Convention Parliament (1660) his body was removed to St. Margaret's Church.

Sir John Eliot was one of the Parliamentary leaders in the reign of Charles I. He played an important part in the **impeachment of Buckingham,** for which he was imprisoned, but afterwards released. In 1629 he brought in his famous **resolutions** against religious changes and illegal taxation, sometimes called the "*Short Remonstrance.*" The Speaker, Sir John Finch, refused to put the question, as the King had ordered him to adjourn the House, whereupon a **scene of disorder ensued.** The doors were locked, and the Speaker was forcibly held in his seat by Hollis and Valentine, while the "resolutions" were read amidst the acclamations of the Commons. Eight days after the King dissolved Parliament with a speech which characterized his opponents as "vipers," and a proclamation was issued intimating his intention of governing without Parliaments. Eliot was sent to the Tower. As he refused to beg pardon of the King, he was kept in confinement for three and a half years, when he fell very ill and entreated the King to release him till he should regain his health, but the King refused, and not long after Eliot died.

William Laud, the son of a well-to-do clothier, was born at Reading and educated at Oxford. Under the patronage of James I he obtained high preferment. Charles I made him **Archbishop of Canterbury** and his chief adviser in Church matters. Laud was much in favour of **forms and ceremonies,** which the Puritans thought Romish, and Laud himself they imagined to be little less than a Papist in disguise. By the aid of the Star Chamber he punished all those Puritans who would not conform to his views; hundreds of ministers were deprived of their livings; Leighton, Prynne, Bastwick, and Burton, for writing pamphlets against his government and against the Bishops, were fined, mutilated, and imprisoned. His attempts **to introduce into Scotland a Prayer Book** modelled on that used in England met with the fiercest opposition, and led to the drawing up of the **National Covenant** and the invasion of England by the Scots, known as the **Bishop's War.** On the meeting of the Long Parliament, Laud, the "*great incendiary,*" as the Scots called him, was **impeached** and imprisoned, and in 1644 was voted guilty of "*endeavouring to subvert the laws and overthrow the Protestant religion.*" He was beheaded the next year.

John Hampden was a gentleman of Buckinghamshire and a cousin of Cromwell, who in 1637 refused to pay his share of the **tax of ship-money,** which amounted to 20s. The question was tried before twelve judges, seven of whom gave judgment in favour of the Crown and five in favour of Hampden. "*Which judgment,*" says Clarendon, "*proved of more advantage and credit to the gentleman condemned than to the King's service.*" He sat in the Long Parliament for the County of Buckingham, and was **one of the Five Members** whom Charles I attempted to arrest. When the Civil War broke out he took a colonel's commission in the Parliamentary army, and, while endeavouring to check a marauding force under Prince Rupert at **Chalgrove Field,** he was mortally wounded, and retired to Thame, where he died.

Lucius Carey, Lord Falkland, was at first in favour of the popular cause, but, after the debate on the Grand Remonstrance, he went over to the side of the King and became one of his chief advisers. His virtues and abilities gained him the name of the "*Glory of the Royalists.*" Weary of the struggle, and conscious of the calamities impending over the nation, at the **First Battle** of **Newbury** he insisted on being placed in the front rank, and was mortally wounded in the first charge. His last words were " *Peace, peace.*"

Sir Thomas Fairfax was a zealous Presbyterian who took the side of the Parliament in the Civil War. He held an important military command in the Parliamentary army, was defeated by the Duke of Newcastle at Atherton Moor, but gained the Battle of **Marston Moor**. When Essex and Manchester gave up their commissions owing to the Self-denying Ordinance, Fairfax was appointed **commander-in-chief**, and won the Battle of **Naseby**. In 1650 he refused to march against the Scots, and Cromwell was sent in his place. He played an important part with Monk in the **restoration** of Charles II.

Earl of Essex was the son of the Earl of Essex, the favourite of Elizabeth. He opposed the policy of Charles I, and on the breaking out of the Civil War was made **commander-in-chief of the Parliamentary forces**, and fought the Battles of **Edgehill** and **First Newbury**. Being hemmed in by the royal forces in Cornwall, he left his army to its fate, and escaped by sea to Plymouth. He, like Manchester, was, in Cromwell's plain words, " afraid to conquer," and so, on the passing of the Self-denying Ordinance, was **deprived of his command.** He died the following year.

James Graham, Marquis of Montrose, a distinguished Royalist leader, defeated the Covenanters at **Tippermuir** and **Kilsyth.** He was, however, totally routed by Leslie at **Philiphaugh,** and fled to Flanders. In 1650 the " *Great Marquis,*" as he was called, returned to Scotland, failed in an attempted Royalist rising, was captured by the Covenanters, and hanged at Edinburgh. To Charles II's disgrace, he disowned the efforts made by Montrose in his favour.

David Leslie was a celebrated Scottish general who defeated Montrose at **Philiphaugh,** and when Charles I, after the Battle of Naseby, surrendered himself to the Scottish army at Newark, Leslie handed him over to the Parliamentary Commissioners on receiving the sum of £400,000, the amount of arrears of pay due to the Scots. He was subsequently defeated by Cromwell at **Dunbar** (1650).

Sir John Finch, the Speaker in Charles I's Third Parliament, advised the extension of ship-money to inland counties.

Dr. Alexander Leighton, a Scottish divine, was the author of a book called *Sion's Plea against Prelacy,* full of the strongest language against the Bishops and against the Queen; the former he denounced as " *men of blood,*" the latter as a " *Canaanite and idolatress.*" At Laud's instigation he was brought before the Star Chamber, fined £10,000, whipped, pilloried, deprived of his ears, branded, and imprisoned for eleven years, at the expiration of which time he was released by the Long Parliament.

Prynne, a lawyer, who in 1632 published a work entitled *Histrio-Mastix* (scourge for stage-players), against stage plays and players, interludes, dancing, and other festivities. As some of these amusements were patronized by the Court, the Star Chamber condemned the book as a seditious libel, and the author was heavily fined, deprived of his ears, and sentenced to perpetual imprisonment in Jersey.

Thomas Hobbes, tutor to Charles II, was educated at Oxford. He was author of a celebrated treatise on political philosophy called the *Leviathan,* which was censured by Parliament as upholding absolute monarchy.

THE COMMONWEALTH AND PROTECTORATE

Sir Harry Vane was a member of the Short and Long Parliaments, and took part in the prosecution of Strafford. He was an active soldier on the Parliamentary side in the Civil War, and **presided over the Admiralty** during the Commonwealth, but opposed Cromwell's power in the Parliament summoned under the Instrument of Government, and was for a time imprisoned in Carisbrook Castle. After Richard Cromwell's abdication he was appointed one of the Committee of Safety. At the Restoration he was excepted from the Act of General Pardon and Oblivion, found guilty of treason, and executed.

Robert Blake, a distinguished English Admiral in the time of the Commonwealth. In the **First Dutch War** (1652–1653) he was defeated off the Naze by Van Tromp, who, after the victory, cruised in the Channel with a broom at his mast-head, signifying that he had swept the English from the seas. In 1653 Blake **defeated the Dutch** in three successive battles off Portland, the North Foreland, and the Texel, and completed the ruin of the naval power of Holland. In 1657 he captured the Spanish Plate Fleet **off Cadiz,** and inflicted a crushing defeat on the Spaniards at **Santa Cruz,** but died the same year, while his ship was entering Plymouth harbour.

George Monk at first supported the cause of Charles I, but, on being taken prisoner by the Parliamentary army at Nantwich, 1644, was released on condition that he should serve under the Commonwealth. He was appointed **Governor of Scotland** by Cromwell, on whose death he determined to restore the monarchy. He marched to London and **summoned a Convention,** which invited Charles II to return. For his services he was created **Duke of Albemarle,** and given command of the fleet.

Henry Ireton was a Parliamentary general who married Cromwell's daughter. He completed the subjugation of Ireland in 1649. At the Restoration his body, together with that of Cromwell, was dragged from its tomb in Westminster Abbey and hanged at Tyburn.

John Milton (1608–1674), the greatest epic poet of modern ages, was educated at St. Paul's School and at Cambridge. Before his twenty-fifth year he wrote *Comus, Lycidas, L'Allegro,* and *Il Penseroso.* In 1649 he was appointed Latin Secretary to Cromwell, and became a political writer. His best prose work is said to be *Areopagitica,* a plea for the liberty of the Press. After the Restoration he became poor and neglected; then it was that he wrote his grandest poems, *Paradise Lost, Paradise Regained,* and *Samson Agonistes.*

CHARLES II

Edward Hyde, Earl of Clarendon, was a well-known Royalist in the reign of Charles I, and the faithful **companion of Charles II** in his exile. On the Restoration he was created **Earl of Clarendon,** and became the **King's chief adviser.** Under his administration severe laws, including the Corporation Act, Act of Uniformity, the Conventicle Act, and the Five Mile Act, were passed against the Nonconformists. In 1667 he was **impeached** for the disastrous management of the Second Dutch war, and banished. While in exile he wrote his famous *History of the Great Rebellion.*

Sir Thomas Osborne, afterwards Lord Danby, became the King's chief adviser on the breaking up of the " Cabal " in 1673. He was impeached by the Commons for his participation in the secret treaties between Charles II and Louis, and committed to the Tower.

Anthony Ashley Cooper, Earl of Shaftesbury, was a member of the Convention Parliament of 1659, and was appointed one of the Commissioners who was sent to Breda to recall Charles II. At the Restoration he held several important offices, and became a member of the famous **Cabal Ministry.** In 1672 he was made **Lord Chancellor,** but deprived of his office the following year through the influence of the Duke of York, and became the leader of the Opposition. For a short time he was **President of the Council of Thirty,** and while in this office he passed the **Habeas Corpus Act,** called in those days " *Lord Shaftesbury's Act.*" Taking advantage of the excitement caused by the " Popish Plot " against the Roman Catholics, he tried to pass the Exclusion Bill, but failed. He was **accused of High Treason,** and, although acquitted, fled to Holland, where he died in 1683.

Algernon Sidney, was an opponent of the arbitrary rule of Charles I. In the reign of Charles II, he, with Russell, Shaftesbury, and Monmouth, held frequent meetings to consider measures for resisting the Government policy. Among the subordinates of their party were some old soldiers of Cromwell's army, who formed a plot to kill the King, as he passed from Newmarket to London, near a lonely farm-house called the **Rye House** in Hertfordshire. The plot was betrayed by Rumbold, an old republican officer, and the owner of the Rye House. Although Sidney **knew nothing whatever of the plot,** he was found guilty and executed. He died rejoicing " *that he suffered in the good old cause.*"

Lord William Russell was one of the chief leaders of the Whig Party in the reign of Charles II. He was tried for supposed implication in the **Rye House Plot,** and condemned to death on very insufficient evidence, Charles remarking, " *If I do not take his life, he will soon take mine.*" He was executed in 1683.

Titus Oates, a minister of low character, had been discharged from a naval chaplaincy for misconduct. He was the fabricator of the famous **Popish Plot,** which bears his name. For his supposed services in divulging this plot he was liberally rewarded and lodged at Whitehall. In the reign of James II he was convicted of perjury, treated with great severity, and imprisoned, but William III liberated him and gave him a pension.

Sir Edmundbury Godfrey was the magistrate before whom Oates made his depositions. Some days after Godfrey was found murdered on Primrose Hill, thrust through with his own sword. His mysterious murder increased the popular excitement caused **by the Popish Plot,** and strengthened the belief in Oates' statement.

John Dryden (1631–1700), one of the greatest of English poets. His chief works are: *Absalom and Achitophel,* a political satire on Monmouth and

Shaftesbury; *Annus Mirabilis*, commemorating the events in the year 1666; *Hind and Panther*, written in defence of the Roman Catholic Faith; *Translation of the Æneid*; and the Ode entitled *Alexander's Feast*. He also wrote many plays.

Samuel Butler, son of a Worcestershire farmer, wrote *Hudibras*, a mock-heroic poem, to caricature the Puritans.

John Bunyan in early life was a tinker, then a soldier, and afterwards a Non-conformist minister. He was imprisoned twelve years in Bedford gaol for breach of the Conventicle Act. His chief works are two allegories, *Pilgrim's Progress* and *The Holy War*.

Richard Baxter, a Presbyterian divine; his chief works are *The Saint's Everlasting Rest* and *A Call to the Unconverted*.

JAMES II

Duke of Monmouth was an illegitimate son of Charles II. He suppressed the rebellion of the **Covenanters** in 1679, and afterwards **joined the Shaftesbury Party** in trying to pass the Exclusion Bill. He was pardoned for his share in the **Rye House Plot,** but banished to Holland. On the accession of James II, he invaded England in the hope of gaining the Crown, but was defeated at **Sedgemoor,** and two days after captured hiding in a ditch in peasant's clothes. He was taken to London and there executed. Sedgemoor was the last battle fought in England.

Judge Jeffreys, a notoriously cruel and unjust judge, who, through the influence of James, Duke of York, became **Lord Chief Justice.** He was sent by James II to punish the adherents of Monmouth in what is known as the **Bloody Assize,** after which he was made Lord Chancellor. At the Revolution he was seized by the mob while attempting to leave England, but rescued and conveyed to the Tower, where he died.

Sir Christopher Wren, a famous architect, built **St. Paul's Cathedral** and many other fine buildings.

WILLIAM III

Graham of Claverhouse, Viscount Dundee, was the bitter enemy of the Covenanters in the reign of Charles II, and a devoted adherent of the Stuart family. He assisted Monmouth in quelling the rebellion of the Covenanters in 1679, and, when William III came to the throne he raised the standard of rebellion against him, and defeated the royal forces at **Killiecrankie,** but was himself mortally wounded in the action.

Lord Somers, an eminent Whig minister, became Lord Chancellor in 1697. At his earnest entreaties William III gave up his intention of quitting England, when, in 1698, after the Peace of Ryswick, a Bill was passed reducing the army and demanding the dismissal of his favourite Dutch guards.

Lord Russell defeated the French fleet sent to invade England in the cause of James II at the Battle of **La Hogue,** 1692.

John Locke, a philosopher, wrote *An Essay on the Human Understanding.* His theories of government had great influence not only in England but also in France and America. In 1696 he assisted Montague, Somers, and Sir Isaac Newton in issuing the **new coinage.**

Burnet, Bishop of Salisbury, was one of the most intimate friends of William III. He wrote a *History of his own Times.*

Daniel Defoe, a prolific writer, wrote *Robinson Crusoe, Journal of the Plague Year, Moll Flanders,* and many political works.

ANNE

John Churchill, Duke of Marlborough, one of England's greatest generals, was the son of a Devonshire gentleman. He served in the French army during the reign of Charles II, and was afterwards taken into the service of **James, Duke of York,** who created him Lord Churchill. He defeated Monmouth at **Sedgemoor,** but deserted James II for William. Like almost all the great statesmen of his time, he intrigued to **bring back the exiled King James II,** and was dismissed from office by William, but afterwards restored to his favour. On his death-bed William is said to have recommended Marlborough to Anne as the fittest person " *to lead the armies and direct the councils.*" He was made **commander-in-chief of the Allies** in the War of the Spanish Succession, and completely crushed the military power of France at the Battles of Blenheim (1704), Ramillies (1706), Oudenarde (1708), and Malplaquet (1709), and swept the French out of the Netherlands. The fall of the Whig Ministry, and the unpopularity of this great " Whig " War of the Spanish Succession, brought about Marlborough's dismissal. He was accused of having **misused public money,** and deprived of his command. Under George I he recovered his former honours and died in 1722.

Earl of Peterborough, the " *Mad Earl,*" as he was called, was a distinguished general in the reign of Anne. During the War of the Spanish Succession he won many victories **in Spain** for the Archduke Charles, and in 1705 captured **Barcelona.**

Sir George Rooke, an English admiral, captured **Gibraltar** in 1704.

Sir Cloudesley Shovel rose from the post of cabin boy to that of Admiral. He took part in the capture of Gibraltar and of Barcelona. He was ship-wrecked and drowned off the Scilly Islands, 1707.

Lord Godolphin, a celebrated Whig statesman, at the beginning of the reign of Anne was Lord High Treasurer, then the highest minister of the Crown. He, with Marlborough, held the chief power in the ministry during the War of the Spanish Succession.

Robert Harley, Earl of Oxford, a very able Tory statesman, with the assistance of his cousin, Mrs. Masham, succeeded in turning the Queen against Marlborough, and procuring his dismissal. Harley then became the Queen's chief minister, and in 1713 concluded the " *shameful Treaty of Utrecht* " with the French. For his share in negotiating this treaty he was impeached in the reign of George I and imprisoned, but after two years he was released, and retired into private life.

Henry St. John, Viscount Bolingbroke, was a Tory statesman who assisted Harley in negotiating the Treaty of Utrecht. On the accession of George I he was impeached by the Whigs, but fled to France, where he joined the Pretender. Afterwards he returned, and became the leader of the opposition against Walpole.

Alexander Pope, a celebrated poet, wrote *Essay on Criticism, The Rape of the Lock, Translation of Homer, The Dunciad, Essay on Man,* and other works. He died in 1744.

Jonathan Swift, the greatest prose writer of his period, a master of satire, was private secretary to Sir William Temple, and afterwards became Dean of St. Patrick's. His chief works are *Gulliver's Travels, Tale of a Tub, Drapier's Letters, The Battle of the Books, The Conduct of the Allies,* and *Journal to Stella.* He died insane in 1745.

Joseph Addison, prose-writer and poet, famous for his contributions to the *Tatler* and *Spectator.* He wrote *Cato,* a tragedy. He died in 1719.

Sir Isaac Newton, Professor at Cambridge, and President of the Royal Society for twenty-five years. He discovered the *Law of Gravitation.* His chief work is his *Principia,* a Latin treatise on Natural Philosophy. He was appointed **Master of the Mint,** and died in 1727.

THE HOUSE OF HANOVER

GEORGE I

Sir Robert Walpole, a great financier, held high office under the Whig Government in the early part of Anne's reign. In the reign of George I he rose to the position of **Prime Minister,** and was the first to whom this title is usually given. For 21 years (1721–1742) he held the reins of Government, and after the failure of the South Sea Scheme, he came to the rescue and **restored public credit.** He maintained his political influence mainly **through bribery,** and was violently opposed in Parliament by the **Patriots.** In 1733 he brought in his **Excise Bill,** which was rejected by the Commons. His policy was **peace,** and when war was declared against Spain the bells rang loudly for joy. " *They are ringing the bells now,*" said he, " *but they will be wringing their hands soon.*" Owing to the failure of the war, Walpole was compelled to resign, and was raised to the peerage as the **Earl of Orford.**

James Francis Edward, the " *Old Pretender,*" was the son of James II by Mary of Modena. By the Treaty of Utrecht he was expelled from France, and in 1715 made an attempt in Scotland to gain the English throne, but failed, and in company with the Earl of Mar re-embarked for France, and died at Rome in 1765.

Earl of Mar was the leader of the rebellion of 1715 in favour of the Old Pretender. He was defeated at **Sheriffmuir** by the Duke of Argyle, and although the Pretender landed in Scotland shortly after, the rebellion failed, and he was compelled to withdraw to **France.**

GEORGE II

William Pitt, Earl of Chatham, the " *Great Commoner,*" entered Parliament in 1734 and became the great opponent of Sir Robert Walpole and his policy. As **Secretary of State** he successfully directed the Government during the Seven Years' War (1756–1763). He **advocated the claims of the American Colonists,** " *maintaining that taxation and representation in Parliament ought to go hand in hand.*" His death in 1778 put an end to all hopes of peace.

Admiral John Byng, son of Admiral Byng, failed in 1757 to relieve **Minorca,** which had been attacked by the French. He was court-martialled and shot, " *pour encourager les autres.*"

Robert Clive went out to India as a **Clerk in the East India Company.** On the outbreak of the Seven Years' War, he entered the army and won rapid promotion. In 1751 he **captured Arcot,** and in 1757, after the tragedy of the Black Hole, he defeated Surajah Dowlah at **Plassey.** This victory led to the British supremacy in Bengal. On his return to England, a motion was made in the House, condemning the methods he had used for acquiring his wealth, and this had such an effect on his mind that he committed suicide (1774).

General Wolfe, a distinguished English general, was appointed by Pitt to the command of the expedition against **Quebec.** He defeated Montcalm on the Heights of Abraham, but fell in the moment of victory. All **Canada** passed into the hands of the English.

William, Duke of Cumberland, was the second son of George II. He was defeated by the French at **Fontenoy** (1745), and recalled to suppress the rebellion in favour of the Young Pretender. In 1746 he gained the victory of **Culloden.**

Charles Edward Stuart, the " *Young Pretender,*" was the son of the Old Pretender. He landed in Scotland in 1745 and proclaimed his father King as James VIII at Perth. He defeated the royal forces under Sir John Cope at **Preston Pans** (1745), and advanced into England as far as Derby. Losing heart, he retreated northwards, and although he **overthrew the royal troops** under Hawley at **Falkirk,** he was completely routed by the Duke of Cumberland at **Culloden.** After many exciting adventures he escaped to France, but was compelled to leave that country by the Treaty of Aix-la-Chapelle. He retired to Rome, where he died.

James Thomson, a poet, was the author of *The Seasons* and *The Castle of Indolence.*

Samuel Richardson, a novelist, wrote *Pamela, Clarissa Harlowe,* and *Sir Charles Grandison.*

Thomas Gray, a very learned poet, wrote *Elegy in a Country Churchyard, The Bard,* and *Ode to Eton College.*

GEORGE III

Thomas Pelham, Duke of Newcastle, was **Secretary of State** under Walpole's Ministry in 1724, and on the death of his brother Henry Pelham, in 1754, became **Whig Prime Minister.** In 1757 he was again Prime Minister with **Pitt as Secretary of State,** but resigned office in 1762, " because he was never consulted in matters of policy or of patronage." It was said of him that " *nothing in his public-life became him like the leaving of it.*"

Lord Bute was **Prime Minister** from 1762 to 1763. He exercised unbounded influence over George III, and in 1763 brought about the **Treaty of Paris.** It was against the Government of Lord Bute that **Wilkes** directed his violent attacks in the famous *North Briton.* He was very unpopular and ultimately was compelled to resign.

George Grenville became **Prime Minister** on the resignation of Lord Bute in 1763. During his ministry **Wilkes was prosecuted** for libel. Grenville passed the **American Stamp Act** in 1765, notwithstanding the protests of six of the Colonies. He resigned his office in 1766. " *He was a man of routine and not a statesman.*"

Marquis of Rockingham succeeded Grenville as **Prime Minister.** In 1766 he repealed the obnoxious American Stamp Act, and passed an Act declaring **general warrants to be illegal.** The following year he resigned. In 1782 he was again Prime Minister, and during his ministry he **repealed Poyning's Law** and other oppressive Acts, thereby making the **Irish Parliament independent.**

Duke of Grafton became **Whig Prime Minister** on the resignation of the Marquis of Rockingham (1766). During his ministry **Charles Townshend** passed his famous **American Revenue Act,** imposing import duties on tea, glass, painters' colours, and paper, which caused great irritation on the part of the Colonists. Many of the **Junius letters** were addressed to him.

Lord North was Tory Prime Minister from 1770 to 1782. He repealed all the American import duties except that on tea, passed the **Royal Marriage Act** in 1772, and in the following year an Act for the **Regulation of India,** under which Warren Hastings became the first Governor-General. During his ministry **Sir George Savile** passed his **Roman Catholic Relief Bill.** " Lord North was a man of great administrative ability, an excellent debater, but wholly under the influence of the King."

William Pitt (" *the younger* "), one of England's greatest statesmen, was the second son of the Earl of Chatham. In 1783 he became **Prime Minister** when only twenty-five years of age. He remained eighteen years in office. During his ministry he passed his famous **India Bill,** ably conducted the administration of Government during the troublesome **times of the French Revolution,** restored **order in Ireland** after the great rebellion of 1798, and in 1800 passed a bill for the **Union of Great Britain and Ireland.** He was again Prime Minister from 1804 to 1806, when he died in office. The news of the defeat of the Austrians and Russians by Napoleon at **Austerlitz** is said to have killed him. " He was the first Prime Minister since the beginning of the reign who had *possessed the entire confidence* of the King and the nation."

Lord Grenville, third son of George Grenville, became **Premier** on the death of Pitt. With the assistance of Fox he made an attempt to form a ministry of *the ablest men of all parties,* called for this reason **the Ministry of All the Talents.** In 1807 he passed an Act for the **Abolition of the Slave Trade,** and resigned the same year.

Charles James Fox, an eminent statesman and third son of Lord Holland, was the **great rival** of the **younger Pitt,** and the leader of Whig opposition during his long administration. He was opposed to the American War of Independence, and approved of Parliamentary Reform and Catholic Emancipation. Like many others of his time, he expressed sympathy with the French Revolution, and this cost him the friendship of Burke. His **India Bill** passed the Commons, but was rejected by the Lords at the instigation of George III. He was **Foreign Secretary** in the ministry of " All the Talents," died in 1806, and was buried in Westminster Abbey.

Arthur Wellesley, Duke of Wellington, was born near Trim, Ireland, and first gained distinction at the storming of **Seringapatam.** He afterwards defeated the Mahrattas at **Assaye,** for which he was knighted. The campaigns of the **Peninsular War** were successfully conducted by him, and at **Waterloo** he defeated Napoleon himself, for which victory he was rewarded with the estate of Strathfieldsaye, and an annual pension of £4,000. Subsequently he became **Premier** and passed the **Roman Catholic Relief Bill** in 1829, but his opposition to the Reform Bill of 1832 made him unpopular for a time. He died in 1852 and was buried in St. Paul's Cathedral.

Sir John Moore, a distinguished general, was born at Glasgow, and served in Egypt under Abercrombie. He evolved a training system for light infantry. In 1809 he commanded the British army in the Peninsular War, but was killed at **Corunna.**

Horatio Nelson, England's greatest naval hero, was born at Burnham Thorpe Rectory (Norfolk), became a midshipman at the age of twelve, and served in an Arctic expedition. He distinguished himself at **St. Vincent** in 1797 and defeated the French at the **Battle of the Nile,** which won for him a peerage and a pension. In 1801 he successfully bombarded **Copenhagen,** and finally crushed the French naval power at **Trafalgar,** where he was killed by a musket ball on the deck of his own ship, the *Victory.* Before the battle commenced he hoisted the famous signal, " *This day England expects every man to do his duty.*" He was buried in St. Paul's Cathedral.

Sir Ralph Abercrombie had command of the British army in Egypt, and was mortally wounded in the Battle of **Alexandria** in 1801.

Sir Sidney Smith, a distinguished general, defended **Acre** against Napoleon in 1799, and thus compelled him to give up his scheme on Eastern conquest. Napoleon always said of him, " *That man made me miss my destiny.*"

George Washington, a famous American general, was the founder and first President of the United States. He first served in the war against the French in 1754, and took **Pittsburgh.** On the outbreak of the American War of Independence he was made **commander-in-chief** of the American army. He reorganized the colonial troops and brought the war to successful issue. In 1789 Washington was elected **First President,** and died in 1799. He was " *first in war, first in peace, and first in the hearts of his countrymen.*"

Warren Hastings went out to India as a writer in the East India Company's service, and ultimately succeeded Lord Clive in the administration of the Indian Empire. He became the **first Governor-General** under Lord North's Regulation Act. On his return to England, he was **impeached by the Commons,** under the leadership of Burke and Sheridan, for rapacity and oppression. After a trial which lasted seven years he was acquitted, 1795.

Edmund Burke was a distinguished statesman, orator, and writer. He was in favour of using conciliatory measures towards the American Colonists, and took part in the impeachment of Warren Hastings. His chief works are *An Essay on the Sublime and Beautiful* and *Reflections on the Revolution in France.* He laid down the theories of English conservatism.

Richard Brinsley Sheridan, a dramatic author and orator, took part in the impeachment of Warren Hastings. His chief plays are *The Rivals* and *The School for Scandal*.

Charles Townshend (1725–1767), a statesman who was a zealous supporter of Grenville's American Stamp Act. When **Chancellor of the Exchequer** in the Grafton Ministry, he *passed an Act for taxing tea* and five other articles imported into America. This did much to bring about the American War of Independence.

Lord Liverpool (1770–1828), a Tory statesman, held the post of **Foreign Secretary** in the Addington Ministry in 1801, and on the death of Perceval became **Prime Minister.** In 1820 he brought in a bill of " pains and penalties " against Queen Caroline, but the bill was abandoned.

Lord Brougham (1779–1868), a distinguished lawyer and statesman, was educated at Edinburgh. He ably defended Queen Caroline at her trial and vehemently denounced the formation of the Holy Alliance. He assisted greatly in carrying the Great Reform Bill of 1832 through the House of Lords. In reforming the laws and advancing public education and science, he was most zealous during the whole of his life.

Henry Grattan (1750–1820), an eminent Irish statesman and orator, was the leader of the movement in Ireland in favour of Sir George Savile's Roman Catholic Relief Bill of 1778. His opinion was that " *the Irish Protestant could never be free till the Irish Catholic had ceased to be a slave*." In 1782 he secured for Ireland legislative independence by passing what was called the " Declaration of Right," and the Irish Parliament in gratitude voted him a reward of £50,000. He opposed the bill for the Union of England and Ireland, and devoted the remainder of his life and energies to the cause of Roman Catholic Emancipation.

Lord Fitzwilliam (1748–1833) was a member of Pitt's Ministry, and in 1795 was sent to Ireland to introduce reforms. Ireland was at this time in a most disturbed state, owing to the existence of three great parties: (1) the **Roman Catholics,** forming the greater bulk of the nation, who wanted emancipation from political disabilities; (2) the **Protestants** or Orangemen anxious for Parliamentary Reform; (3) the **Revolutionists** or **United Irishmen** eager to overthrow the Government and establish a republic under the protection of France. Fitzwilliam dismissed the worst of the officials, John Beresford, called from his unbounded influence, " King of Ireland." Beresford, however, represented to King George III that Fitzwilliam was favouring Roman Catholic Emancipation, and so Fitzwilliam was recalled. This was followed by an outburst of popular indignation, and was one of the causes of the Irish Rebellion of 1798.

William Cobbett (1762–1835) was a political and miscellaneous writer and popular agitator, whose writings and speeches exercised a powerful influence over the working classes in the reign of George III. Born at Farnham, Surrey, he was in turn ploughman, clerk, soldier, pamphleteer, and journalist. He became the editor of a newspaper, the *Weekly Political Register*, in which he constantly attacked the Government, maintaining that all the existing evils could be cured by Parliamentary Reform. He also advocated universal suffrage and annual Parliaments. His work was the beginning of the great agitation which ended in the passing of the Reform Bill of 1832. He was fined and imprisoned several times for libelling the Government, and sat as a Member for Oldham in the Reform Parliament of 1833.

John Wilkes (1729–1797), was an alderman of London, notorious for the violence of his political conduct. He was elected Member of Parliament for Aylesbury, and started a paper called the *North Briton*, in opposition to Lord Bute's paper, the *Briton*. In " No. 45 " of his paper he published an offensive libel against the King and the Government. A general warrant was issued by Grenville, the Prime Minister, against the author, printers, and publishers of the paper, and Wilkes and forty-eight others were arrested and sent to the Tower. He was, however, shortly afterwards released by the order of **Pratt**, the Chief Justice, *on the ground that no one could arrest a Member of Parliament for libel.* Wilkes was regarded as the champion of liberty; pictures and busts of him were sold everywhere, and the popular cry was " Wilkes and Liberty." He was again prosecuted for printing an obscene poem, but escaped to France and was outlawed. In 1769 he returned and was elected for Middlesex, but not allowed to take his seat. Subsequently he was elected three times in succession, but the Commons declared the election void. In 1774, however, *on re-election he took his seat without any further opposition.*

General Burgoyne (1730–1792), an English general, took part in the American War of Independence. After the English had defeated Washington at **Brandywine,** to make their victory complete it was determined that General Burgoyne should march from Canada down the valley of the Hudson and form a junction with Clinton from New York. On his way he was completely hemmed in by an overwhelming force of the enemy, and failing to break through their lines, he retreated to **Saratoga,** where a **Convention was signed,** *by which the English laid down their arms and were marched off as prisoners to Massachusetts.* This disaster was the turning-point of the war in favour of the colonists.

Lord Cornwallis (1738–1805), a distinguished English general, took a prominent but unsuccessful part in the close of the American War of Independence. Having defeated the colonists at **Guildford,** he formed the plan of marching northwards and joining Clinton, just as Burgoyne had endeavoured to do in 1777. At **Yorktown,** on Chesapeake Bay, however, he was surrounded by a force of the enemy three times as large as his own, and was compelled to capitulate. In 1786 he succeeded Warren Hastings as **Governor-General of India,** and under his administration Tippoo Sahib was reduced to obedience. In 1798 he became **Viceroy of Ireland,** and during the terrible scenes of the Irish Rebellion of 1798, the " Irish Reign of Terror," he did much by his wise and judicious rule to reduce the country to comparative tranquillity. He was a second time appointed Governor-General of India, but died soon after his arrival in that country.

Lord Rodney (1718–1792), a gallant admiral, distinguished himself in 1759 by destroying the stores prepared at Havre for the invasion of England, and in 1780 completely defeated the Spanish fleet off **Cape St. Vincent.** In 1782 England was at her lowest ebb, but Rodney's brilliant and decisive victory over the French fleet under Count de Grasse, in the West Indies, known as the **Battle of St. Lucia or Dominica,** " revived the expiring conviction in Europe that England was still Queen of the seas." A barony and a pension of £2,000 were bestowed on him for his services.

General Elliot (1718–1790), a distinguished soldier, was renowned as the **defender of Gibraltar**, during the terrible siege of 1779–1782.

John Howard (1726–1790), a philanthropist, travelled throughout Europe visiting prisons, and advocated a more humane treatment of criminals. He died at **Kherson** of a fever contracted while visiting a prison in that town.

POETS

Oliver Goldsmith (1728–1774), poet and prose writer, was born near Longford in Ireland. His chief poems are *The Traveller* and *The Deserted Village*, and his principal prose work is the charming tale, *The Vicar of Wakefield.* He was also the author of two well-known comedies, *The Good-Natured Man* and *She Stoops to Conquer.*

William Cowper (1731–1800), poet, wrote *The Task* and several minor poems, including *John Gilpin.*

Robert Burns (1759–1796), Scotland's great " National Poet," was an Ayrshire farmer. He was the author of the famous poem *Tam o' Shanter*, and upwards of 200 patriotic and popular songs.

Percy Bysshe Shelley (1792–1822), a great lyric poet, whose chief works are *Queen Mab, Alastor,* and *Prometheus Unbound.* He was drowned at Spezzia in Italy.

John Keats (1796–1820) was born in London, and apprenticed to a surgeon, but devoted his time and attention to poetry. He was a great Romantic poet. His works include *Endymion, Hyperion,* and many *Odes.*

Lord Byron (1788–1824), born in London and educated at Harrow, was a poet of the Romantic School, whose work had great influence in English and European literature. His poems include *Childe Harold, The Giaour, Don Juan,* and *Manfred.* He died of a fever at **Missolonghi** while assisting the Greeks in their struggle for independence.

Thomas Moore (1779–1852), the " National Poet of Ireland," was the author of *Lalla Rookh,* the Irish Melodies, and many lyric poems.

Thomas Campbell (1777–1844), a poet, born at Glasgow, wrote the *Pleasures of Hope* and several popular ballads and lyrics.

Samuel Taylor Coleridge (1772–1834), a native of Devonshire, was one of the " Lake Poets," and a friend of Wordsworth's. He was a poet of originality and genius, and wrote *The Ancient Mariner, Christabel,* and several prose works.

Sir Walter Scott (1771–1832), a Scottish barrister, but especially distinguished as a novelist and poet, was born at Edinburgh. His chief poems are *Lay of the Last Minstrel, Marmion,* and the *Lady of the Lake,* but his fame chiefly rests on his *Waverley Novels.*

William Wordsworth (1770–1850), born at Cockermouth, and one of England's greatest poets. He was the founder of the " Lake School of Poets," and became Poet Laureate after Southey. His chief works are *The Prelude, The Excursion,* and *Lyrical Ballads.*

H

Robert Southey (1774–1843), one of the " Lake Poets," was born at Bristol, and educated at Westminster School and Oxford. In 1813 he was made Poet Laureate. He was the author of the poems, *Joan of Arc, Thalaba, Curse of Kehama*, and others, and wrote several prose works, the most popular of which is his *Life of Nelson*.

PROSE WRITERS

David Hume (1711–1776), an eminent historian and philosopher, was born at Edinburgh. He was the author of a *History of England*, a *Treatise on Human Nature*, and some *Essays*.

Sir William Blackstone (1723–1780) was an eminent lawyer and judge, and the author of *Commentaries on the Laws of England*.

Samuel Johnson (1709–1784), a native of Lichfield, is best known as the compiler of the *English Dictionary* which bears his name. Among his other works are: two poems, *London* and *Vanity of Human Wishes*; *Irene*, a tragedy; and his *Lives of the English Poets*.

Adam Smith (1723–1790), a Scotsman, was Professor of Logic in Glasgow University. His chief work is *The Wealth of Nations*, a classic work on political economy.

Edward Gibbon (1737–1794), a celebrated historian, was born in Surrey. His most famous work is *The Decline and Fall of the Roman Empire*.

William Paley (1743–1805) was a distinguished divine, and author of the *Evidences of Christianity* and *Natural Theology*.

ARTISTS, ETC.

Thomas Gainsborough (1727–1788), born in Suffolk, was a famous landscape and portrait painter. **Sir Joshua Reynolds** (1723–1792), a native of Devonshire, became President of the Royal Academy and the greatest of English portrait painters. **Benjamin West** (1738–1820), a famous historical painter, was born in America, and also became President of the Royal Academy. **John Flaxman** (1755–1826), born at York, was one of the most celebrated of English sculptors. Some of his finest works are *Illustrations of Homer and Dante*.

George Frederick Handel (1684–1759), an illustrious musical composer, was born at Halle, Hanover. His greatest works are his Oratorios, including *The Messiah, Israel in Egypt, Samson*, and *Judas Maccabeus.* He was buried in Westminster Abbey.

David Garrick (1716–1779) was the most celebrated actor of his day.

INVENTORS, DISCOVERERS, ETC.

James Brindley (1716–1772), born in Derbyshire, a distinguished engineer, was employed by the Duke of Bridgewater to construct a canal from *Worsley to Manchester*. He afterwards constructed the *Grand Trunk Canal*, and was the founder of the English canal system.

Sir Richard Arkwright (1732–1792), born at Preston, was originally a hairdresser. His mechanical genius showed itself in his invention of the " spinning frame " for cotton mills, and he set up the first cotton mill in England at Matlock.

Josiah Wedgwood (1739–1795), the great English potter, was born at Burslem. He greatly improved the manufacture of porcelain, and invented a beautiful ware called the " *Queen's Ware*."

James Watt (1736–1819), a Scotsman, and celebrated civil engineer, who, in consideration of the great improvements he made in the steam engine, almost deserves the title of its inventor.

John Rennie (1761–1821), a famous civil engineer, built *London Bridge*, *Southwark Bridge*, the *East and West India Docks* in London, the *Plymouth Breakwater*, and many canals.

John Smeaton (1724–1792) was an eminent civil engineer, whose greatest work was *Eddystone Lighthouse*.

Thomas Telford (1757–1831) was a celebrated civil engineer, born in Eskdale. Numerous bridges, roads, and canals were constructed under his direction, among which may be mentioned the *Suspension Bridge over the Menai Strait* and the *Caledonian Canal*.

Dr. Edward Jenner (1749–1823), born in Gloucestershire, discovered the method of *vaccination* for preventing small-pox.

Captain James Cook (1728–1779), a celebrated navigator, sailed twice round the world. On his third voyage he was killed by the natives of the Sandwich Islands.

GEORGE IV and WILLIAM IV

STATESMEN

George Canning (1770–1827), a brilliant and distinguished statesman, held office of **Foreign Secretary** in the Duke of Portland's Ministry, 1807. He threw all the blame of the failure of the great Walcheren expedition in 1809 on Lord Castlereagh, the Secretary for War, when both the ministers resigned office and afterwards fought a duel. He was again **Foreign Secretary** under Lord Liverpool in 1822, and was opposed to the Holy Alliance. He was a staunch supporter of the Roman Catholic Emancipation Bill, and the Repeal of the Corn Laws, but was opposed to Parliamentary Reform. He acknowledged the independence of the Spanish Colonies in America, and sympathized with the Greeks in their attempt to gain national independence. He succeeded Lord Liverpool as **Prime Minister,** but died shortly after.

William Huskisson (1770–1830), one of the first English statesmen who advocated the principles of free trade. As **President of the Board of Trade,** under Lord Liverpool, he passed the Reciprocity Duties Act, and encouraged trade and manufactures by reducing the duties on raw silk and cotton. He was **accidentally killed** at the opening of the first railway in England, that between Liverpool and Manchester.

Sir Robert Peel (1788–1850), the most distinguished statesman of his age, was educated at Harrow and Oxford. In 1821 he proposed and carried a bill for the resumption of cash payments by the Bank of England, and in 1828 became **Home Secretary** in the Duke of Wellington's Ministry. In this capacity he passed several bills for the reform of the criminal laws. He at first opposed the Roman Catholic Emancipation Act, but ultimately gave way, and in 1829 the Bill was carried. In the same year he organized his **system of police** in London. He was **Prime Minister** for the first time in 1834, but resigned the same year. In 1841 he was again Prime

Minister, and during his ministry passed a bill for the **Repeal of the Corn Laws.** This lost him the favour of his party, and he was forced to resign.

Lord Grey (1764–1845), a distinguished statesman, was educated at Eton and Cambridge. At an early age he entered Parliament as a zealous Whig, and in 1830 became **Prime Minister.** He was largely responsible for the **Great Reform Bill of 1832** and the **Act for the Emancipation of Slaves.**

Daniel O'Connell (1775–1847), the " Liberator," was an eloquent Irish lawyer, and the leader of the Catholic Association in support of Catholic Emancipation. Having been elected Member of Parliament for Clare, he was disqualified because he was a Roman Catholic, but on the passing of the Roman Catholic Emancipation Act he was allowed to take his seat. He then began the agitation for the Repeal of the Union, which reached its height in 1843. On the failure of the great " Repeal " meeting at Clontarf, he was arrested on a charge of conspiracy and sedition, tried, fined, and imprisoned. The Lords, however, reversed his sentence and he was released. He died at Genoa, while on his way to Rome to ask the Pope's blessing.

THE ARTS AND SCIENCES

Jane Austen (1775–1817) was one of the greatest of English novelists, whose work shows great delicacy, intuition, and analysis of character. Her novels include *Pride and Prejudice, Persuasion, Emma, Mansfield Park,* and *Sense and Sensibility.*

Sir Humphry Davy (1778–1829), a native of Cornwall, was the son of a woodcarver, and was apprenticed to a surgeon. He made many discoveries in chemistry and electricity, and invented the *Safety Lamp.*

George Stephenson (1781–1848), the founder of English railways, was born near Newcastle, and began life as a coal-pit engine-boy. In 1816 he constructed a locomotive engine capable of drawing wagons on a railway, and was afterwards employed as the engineer of the railway between Liverpool and Manchester. In a competition for the best locomotive, four inventors, including Stephenson, sent in their engines, but Stephenson's, called the " Rocket," far outrivalled all the others. He took the lead in railway engineering, and lived to see the railway system established in England.

Sir William Herschel (1738–1822), born in Hanover, a distinguished astronomer, greatly improved the telescope, and discovered the planet *Uranus.*

Samuel Crompton (1753–1827), the inventor of the spinning-frame, known as the " Mule," so called because it combined the leading features of Arkwright's and Hargreaves's invention.

Mrs. Siddons (1755–1831) was the most celebrated English tragic actress of her time. **Edmund Kean** (1787–1833) was an eminent tragedian.

VICTORIA

STATESMEN

Lord Melbourne (1779–1848), a Liberal statesman, held the office of **Prime Minister** on the accession of Queen Victoria. He violently opposed the Repeal of the Corn Laws. Under his administration the **Municipal Reform**

Act and the **Marriage Act** were passed, and the **New Postage Scheme** was adopted.

Lord Palmerston (1784–1865) was educated at Harrow and Cambridge. In 1809 he became **Secretary for War,** and held that office for nearly twenty years under various ministries. He was **Foreign Secretary** in Lord Grey's administration in 1830, and again under Lord John Russell in 1846. In this capacity he won his world-wide reputation. Having expressed his approval of the *coup d'état* of 1851, he resigned office at Lord John Russell's request, but on the resignation of Lord Aberdeen in 1855, he became **Prime Minister,** and carrying on the policy of alliance with France in the **Crimean War,** *brought that conflict to a successful issue.* In 1858 he was defeated on the " Conspiracy to Murder " Bill and resigned, but was again Prime Minister the next year and continued in office till he died. He upheld and followed the political principles of Canning, on whose death he was regarded as the ablest of that statesman's disciples. His policy was that of a mediator between the Whigs and Tories; " *the Whigs accepted him as their leader, the Tories trusted him for his conservatism.*" He was essentially a *European* rather than an *English* statesman, and cared little for the great social movements in England of his own time.

Lord John Russell (1792–1878), a distinguished Liberal statesman, was educated at Westminster School. He was a strong advocate of the Repeal of the Test and Corporation Acts, the Roman Catholic Emancipation Bill, and the Repeal of the Corn Laws. In 1832 he introduced his famous **Parliamentary Reform Bill,** which passed amidst the greatest national excitement. In 1846 he became **Prime Minister,** and in 1850 passed a bill giving a representative government to four of the Australian colonies. He was again Prime Minister in 1865, but resigned on the defeat of Gladstone's Reform Bill of 1866.

Lord Derby (Edward Smith Stanley) (1779–1869), a famous Tory statesman, was educated at Eton and Christ Church, Oxford. He strenuously opposed the Liverpool and Manchester Railway Bill. Under Lord Grey he was appointed Chief Secretary for Ireland, but his administration in that country was very unpopular. He vigorously advocated the **Emancipation of Slaves** Act, but opposed Sir Robert Peel in his Free Trade policy, and became the acknowledged leader of the Protectionists, including Lord Bentinck, Disraeli, and others. He was **three times Prime Minister,** in 1852, 1858, and 1866, and during his last ministry the **Second Great Reform Bill** of 1867 was passed.

Lord Beaconsfield (Benjamin Disraeli) (1805–1881), a great Conservative statesman, entered Parliament in 1837, and became the chief leader and theorist of the " Young England Party " against Sir Robert Peel's Ministry. He joined the Protectionists and vehemently opposed the Repeal of the Corn Laws. In 1867 he brought in and carried his famous **Reform Bill;** purchased the **Khedive's Shares in the Suez Canal** (1875); and in 1876 passed the **Additional Titles Bill.** He was one of the British plenipotentiaries at the **Berlin Congress.** His social and political ideas were expressed in several novels, including *Coningsby, Sybil,* and *Tancred.*

Richard Cobden (1804–1865), the " Apostle of Free Trade," was one of the chief promoters of the **Anti-Corn-Law League.** Sir Robert Peel ascribed the credit of passing the Repeal of the Corn Laws *to the eloquence of Cobden*. In 1860 Cobden successfully negotiated a treaty, based on Free Trade principles, with France.

John Bright (1811–1890), a distinguished politician, and one of the most eloquent speakers of his time, was the son of a cotton-spinner at Rochdale. He became a leading member of the Anti-Corn-Law League, and entered Parliament in 1843, devoting all his energies towards the **Repeal of the Corn Laws**. As a member of the Peace Society he energetically denounced the policy which led to the Crimean War. In 1869 he was appointed **President of the Board of Trade.** He was opposed to Gladstone's policy on the Egyptian question in 1882, and also to his Home Rule policy.

William Ewart Gladstone, one of the greatest statesmen of his time, was born in 1809, and educated at Eton and Christ Church, Oxford. He entered Parliament in 1832 as Member for Newark. He was Chancellor of the Exchequer in Lord Aberdeen's Ministry (1852), and also in Lord Palmerston's Ministry (1855). In 1868 he became **Prime Minister** and passed his bill for the **Disestablishment of the Protestant Church of Ireland,** his **First Irish Land Act,** and a bill abolishing **Purchase in the Army.** He again became Prime Minister in 1880 and succeeded in passing his Second Irish Bill and his famous **Great Reform Bill** (1884). He was Prime Minister a third time in 1886, and brought forward his Home Rule Bill for Ireland, which was, however, defeated, and he resigned. In 1892 he was Prime Minister for a fourth time, and brought forward his Second Home Rule Bill, which shared the same fate as its predecessor. Gladstone retired from active Parliamentary life in 1894 and died in 1898.

Lord Salisbury (1830–1903), educated at Eton and Christ Church, Oxford, became a Fellow of All Souls College, and entered Parliament in 1853. He was one of the British representatives at the Berlin Congress in 1878, and on the resignation of Lord Rosebery in 1895 became **Prime Minister.**

Lord Rosebery (1847–1929). In Gladstone's third and fourth Ministries he was **Foreign Secretary,** and when in 1894 the great Liberal Minister resigned, Lord Rosebery became **Prime Minister.** His views on the Armenian Question differed from those of Gladstone, and in 1896 he resigned the leadership of the Liberal Party. He wrote several historical biographies, and helped raise the standard of English horseracing.

Joseph Chamberlain (1836–1914), at the age of 16 entered business in Birmingham. In 1873 he was elected Mayor of Birmingham, and carried out many reforms. In 1876 he became **M.P. for Birmingham,** and became **President of the Board of Trade** in 1880 in Gladstone's Cabinet, but being opposed to the Home Rule Policy, he resigned office in 1886. In 1895 he became **Colonial Secretary** in the New Unionist Government. He was a great exponent of Imperialism. In 1902 he brought the Boer War to a successful issue, and the following year introduced his **New Tariff Reform,** but resigned office the same year. In 1906 he was seized by an illness which compelled him to give up public life.

Roberts of Kandahar, Earl (1832–1914), was born in India and joined the Bengal Artillery at the age of 19. He went through the **Indian Mutiny** and was present at the siege and **capture of Delhi, the Relief of Lucknow,** and the **Battle of Cawnpore.** He also took part in the **Abyssinian Expedition** of 1867 and the **Afghan War** of 1879. In 1900 he was made commander-in-chief in the **Boer War,** and in 1902 finally subjugated the Boers. The same year he was raised to the peerage, and the House of Commons granted him £100,000 for his services.

Kitchener of Khartoum, Viscount (1850–1916), was commander-in-chief of the British forces in India (1902–1909). Subsequently he remodelled the Egyptian army and overthrew the Khalifa's army at **Omdurman.** For his services he was raised to the peerage and received a grant of £30,000. After Lord Roberts returned to England, Kitchener was made commander of the forces in South Africa, and brought the Boer War to a close. He received the thanks of Parliament, a viscounty, and a further grant of £50,000. He reorganized the Indian army, and on leaving India in 1909 was created Field-Marshal. He became War Minister on the outbreak of the First World War, and created the vast new armies needed. He was drowned on a voyage to Russia.

POETS

Alfred Tennyson (1810–1892), the most popular poet of his time, and the chief representative of Victorian literature, was born in Lincolnshire. His works include *In Memoriam, The Princess, Maud, Idylls of the King*, and *Enoch Arden.*

Matthew Arnold (1822–1888) was educated at Winchester, Rugby, and Balliol. After serving as private secretary to Lord Lansdowne, he became an inspector of schools in 1850. Some of his best-known poems are *The Scholar Gipsy, Dover Beach, Sohrab and Rustum*, and *The Forsaken Merman.* He was also a literary and social critic of considerable power and influence.

Robert Browning (1812–1889) was born in London, and educated at home. His chief works include *Paracelsus, The Ring and the Book, Pippa Passes*, and *Dramatis Personae.*

Elizabeth Barrett Browning (1806–1861), wife of Robert and daughter of a wealthy West Indian, was born in Durham in 1806. Her chief works include *Cowper's Grave, Sonnets from the Portuguese*, and *Aurora Leigh.*

Gerard Manley Hopkins (1844–1889), a Roman Catholic priest, is now considered one of the outstanding poets of the nineteenth century. His best-known poem is *The Wreck of the Deutschland.*

Dante Gabriel Rossetti (1828–1882) also a painter; **Algernon Charles Swinburne** (1837–1909); **Francis Thompson** (1859–1907).

PROSE WRITERS

Lord Macaulay (1800–1859), a great historical writer, wrote a *History of England*, several *Essays*, and *The Lays of Ancient Rome.*

Henry Hallam (1777–1859) wrote the *Middle Ages* and *Constitutional History of England*, for many years a standard work.

Lord Lytton (1805–1872), statesman, novelist, and dramatist, wrote *Rienzi, Last of the Barons*, and many other novels; also a celebrated play called *The Lady of Lyons.*

Thomas Carlyle (1795–1881), born in Dumfries-shire, was a famous essayist and historian, author of *History of the French Revolution, Frederick the Great*, and many other works.

William Makepeace Thackeray (1811–1863), a novelist of realism and psychological insight. His chief works include *Vanity Fair, Henry Esmond*, and *The Newcomes*.

Charlotte Brontë (1816–1855), novelist; the chief force of her work is Romanticism of individual passion. Her chief novels are *Jane Eyre, Shirley*, and *Villette*.

Charles Dickens (1812–1870), one of the greatest of English novelists, excelled in narratives of lower and middle-class life, rich in characterization. His many works include *Pickwick Papers, David Copperfield, A Tale of Two Cities, Nicholas Nickleby*, and *Great Expectations*.

George Eliot (Miss Evans) (1819–1880), novelist; her chief works are *Adam Bede, Mill on the Floss, Silas Marner, Middlemarch*, and *Daniel Deronda*.

John Ruskin (1819–1900), a famous prose writer. His chief works are *Modern Painters* and *The Stones of Venice*.

Charles Darwin (1803–1884), the great exponent of the doctrine of Evolution. His most famous work is *The Origin of Species by Means of Natural Selection*.

Robert Louis Stevenson (1850–1894) was born in Edinburgh, and educated at private schools and Edinburgh University. He read for the Bar, but abandoned this in favour of literature and journalism. He suffered from ill-health, and was obliged to travel. He was a very prolific writer, producing tales of adventure, e.g., *Treasure Island*, short stories, sketches, essays, and verse.

Charles Kingsley (1819–1875) achieved fame as a social novelist with works such as *Alton Locke* and *Yeast*. He also wrote *Westward Ho!* and *The Water Babies*.

Charles Reade (1814–1884); **John Henry Newman** (1801–1890); **George Meredith** (1828–1909) also a poet; **Oscar Fingall O'Flahertie Wills Wilde** (1854–1900) dramatist and poet; **William Morris** (1834–1896); **Lewis Carroll** (1832–1898); **Samuel Butler** (1835–1902).

ARTISTS

John Constable (1776–1837), landscape painter; **Sir David Wilkie** (1785–1841), a painter, was born in Fifeshire; his best-known pictures are scenes from Scottish peasant life. **Sir Francis Chantrey** (1781–1841), a distinguished sculptor, was a native of Derbyshire. **Joseph W. Turner** (1775–1851) was the greatest landscape painter of the English School. **Sir Frederick Leighton** (1830–1896) and **Sir J. Everett Millais** (1829–1896) were Presidents of the Royal Academy. **William Blake** (1757–1827), poet and mystical painter. **Sir Edward Burne-Jones** (1833–1898). **William Morris** (1834–1896). **Aubrey Beardsley** (1872–1898); **M. Birket Foster** (1825–1899); **W. Holman-Hunt** (1827–1896); **D. G. Rossetti** (1828–1882); **G. F. Watts** (1817–1904).

INVENTORS, ETC.

Sir Rowland Hill (1795–1879) was the originator of the " penny post " system.

W. Fothergill Cooke (1806–1879), a retired Indian officer, and **Charles Wheatstone** (1802–1875), Professor of King's College, London, were the joint inventors of the *Electric Telegraph* (1845). The first submarine telegraph was laid down in 1851 from Dover to Calais, and the gigantic enterprise of laying a cable across the Atlantic was successfully accomplished in 1866.

Isambard K. Brunel (1806–1859) was one of the greatest engineers of his day. He laid down the Great Western Railway, and was the strenuous supporter of what is called the " Broad-Gauge " Railway, which, however, has been superseded by the " Narrow Gauge." To him is owed the introduction and adoption of the screw as a propelling power in the place of the paddle-wheel. He also designed the *Great Eastern* steamship.

Michael Faraday (1791–1867), born at Newington, Surrey, a distinguished chemist and natural philosopher, made many discoveries in physics and electricity.

David Livingstone (1817–1873), a famous explorer in Africa, discovered the *Victoria Falls* on the Zambezi and Lake Nyasa.

Lord Kelvin (1824–1907) worked out problems as to the strength, action, and effects of electric currents. His work led to the production of submarine cables and was instrumental in the receiving and recording of wireless messages.

Thomas Alva Edison (1847–1931), an American inventor, made numerous discoveries in wireless telegraphy.

Lord Lister (1827–1912) discovered the antiseptic system of treatment in surgery.

Sir Henry Irving (1838–1905) was the foremost English actor of his time, and the first to be knighted.

Guglielmo Marconi (1874–1937), Italian inventor of wireless telegraphy, set up wireless communication systems in England and abroad. In 1901 he first transmitted a radio message from England to Newfoundland.

Sir William Crookes (1832–1919), physicist and chemist, investigated radium electrons.

Alexander Graham Bell (1847–1922), a Scotsman, went to Canada in 1870. There he invented the telephone.

EDWARD VII and GEORGE V

STATESMEN

Arthur James, first Earl Balfour (1848–1930), was educated at Eton and Trinity College, Cambridge. He entered Parliament in 1874. He held various offices, and 1892–1895 **led the Opposition** in the Lower House. He succeeded Lord Salisbury as **Prime Minister** in 1902, but resigned in 1905 over the question of Protection. In 1915 he became **First Lord of the Admiralty** in the Coalition Ministry of Lloyd George. He acted as **one of the British Delegates at the Peace Conference in 1918** and was appointed **British Representative on the Council of the League of Nations.**

Sir Henry Campbell-Bannerman (1836–1908), a distinguished Liberal statesman, was educated at Glasgow University and Trinity College, Cambridge.
He entered Parliament in 1868 and became an ardent supporter of Gladstone, whom he succeeded as **leader of the Liberal Party** in 1895. He
adopted a policy of **Peace, Retrenchment, and Reform.** He opposed the
South African War, and stood for the principle of Free Trade. He became
Prime Minister in 1905, when he accorded self-government to South Africa
and set up the Union. Of his three reform bills, only the one concerning
Trades Disputes was accepted.

Herbert Henry, first Earl of Oxford and Asquith (1852–1928), was educated
at the City of London School and Oxford. In 1876 he was called to
the Bar. He entered Parliament as a Liberal in 1886, and took silk in
1890. In 1892 he became **Home Secretary** with a seat in the Cabinet.
His principal measure, a **Factory Bill,** was carried subsequently by a
Conservative Government. In 1905 Asquith became **Chancellor of the
Exchequer,** when he was responsible for the **Old Age Pensions Act.**
He became **Prime Minister** in 1907 and remained at the head of Government during the crisis of the struggle with the House of Lords, the
passing of **the Parliament Bill,** the Irish troubles, and the first half of
the First World War. In 1915 he reconstructed his ministry on a Coalition basis, admitting several leading Unionists. Towards the end of
1916 a difference arose between him and his chief colleague, Lloyd
George, and he retired. In 1920 he was returned for Paisley as **leader
of the Independent Liberal Party,** and in 1925 he was **raised to the
peerage.**

David, first Earl Lloyd-George of Dwyfor (1863–1945), was educated at a
National School. By private study he was able to qualify as a solicitor.
He took a forward part in the advanced Liberal and National Movement. He entered Parliament in 1890, as a Liberal. In 1905 he was
appointed **President of the Board of Trade,** and in 1908 he became
Chancellor of the Exchequer. He **supplemented the Old Age Pensions
Act** by a more sweeping measure and brought in a **National Insurance
Bill.** This was followed by a series of budgets largely directed against
classes and privileges. During the First World War Lloyd-George came
to the fore. In 1915 he was made **First Minister of Munitions,** and on
the death of Earl Kitchener he went to the War Office. In 1916 he
became **Prime Minister of the Coalition Government,** and at the close
of the war acted as **principal British delegate at the Paris Peace Conference** and was largely responsible for the Treaty signed at Versailles
in 1918. The " coupon election " of 1918 returned Lloyd-George to
power with a coalition of his supporters with the Conservatives. This
broke down in 1922, and after disputing Liberal leadership with
Asquith, Lloyd-George became leader in 1925; but the Liberal Party was
declining. From 1931 to 1935 Lloyd-George led an Independent Liberal
Party.

A. Bonar Law (1858–1923) was born in New Brunswick. He entered
Parliament as a Unionist in 1900, and in 1902 became **Parliamentary
Secretary to the Board of Trade.** Bonar Law supported **Imperial Preference and Protection.** In 1911 he became **Leader of the Opposition,**
and in 1915 took office in the Coalition Government as **Secretary of
State for the Colonies.** In 1916 he became **Chancellor of the Exchequer**
and member of the War Cabinet. On the defeat of the Coalition Govern-

ment in 1922, Bonar Law became **Prime Minister,** with a large majority, pledged to moderate reforms and no immediate measures for Protection. Ill-health forced him to retire in 1923, and he died at the end of the year.

Stanley Baldwin, first Earl Baldwin of Bewdley (1867–1947), was educated at Harrow and Trinity, Cambridge. He entered Parliament as a Unionist in 1908. From 1917 to 1921 he held office as **Financial Secretary to the Treasury,** and in 1921 became **President of the Board of Trade.** In the revolt against the Coalition Government of 1922 Baldwin was one of the principal supporters of Bonar Law. In 1922 he became **Chancellor of the Exchequer.** On the retirement of Bonar Law, Baldwin became **Prime Minister,** faced with great problems at home and abroad. He remained Premier until 1929, save for the short periods of Labour Government. In 1935 he succeeded MacDonald as head of the National Government. Baldwin's terms of office as Premier covered the General Strike of 1926, the Abdication crisis of 1936, and the period of " appeasement " until his retirement in 1937.

James Ramsay MacDonald (1866–1937) was educated at a Board School in Scotland. He took to journalism, and in 1894 joined the **Independent Labour Party** recently founded by Keir Hardie. He entered Parliament in 1906 and became Chairman of the Parliamentary Labour Party. He opposed England's participation in the First World War, and his pacifism cost him his Parliamentary seat in 1918. He became an M.P. again in 1922. He was first Labour Premier in 1924, and in 1929 again led the Labour Government. The Labour Party split in the 1931 financial crisis, and MacDonald and his followers were expelled from the Party, MacDonald forming a National Government with Conservative support. He retired from office in 1935.

Sir Joseph Austen Chamberlain (1863–1937), son of Joseph Chamberlain, was educated at Rugby and Cambridge. He entered Parliament as Unionist in 1892, and held various offices before and during the First World War. He was Chancellor of the Exchequer 1919–1921 and Foreign Secretary 1924–1929. He signed the Locarno Treaty and the Kellogg Pact. In 1926 he received the Nobel Peace Prize.

MEN OF LETTERS

Sir James Matthew Barrie (1860–1937) was a Scots novelist and playwright. Barrie had great success with such plays as *Quality Street* (1901) and *The Admirable Crichton* (1902), but he is best remembered, especially by children, for his delightful *Peter Pan* (1904).

Arnold Bennett (1867–1931) was one of the most popular novelists of the first part of the century, particularly famous for fiction set against the background of the " Five Towns "—that is, the pottery towns of Staffordshire.

Robert Bridges (1844–1930) qualified as a doctor, but abandoned medicine in 1882 to devote himself entirely to poetry. Was named Poet Laureate in 1913. Bridges produced the first edition of the poems of his friend G. M. Hopkins in 1918. His own best-known work is a long philosophical poem called *The Testament of Beauty* (1929).

Rupert Brooke (1887–1915) was one of the most promising of the young poets killed in the First World War. He was educated at Rugby and King's, Cambridge. With others he was concerned in the publication of *Georgian*

Poetry, 1911–1912, and of *New Numbers*, 1914. In 1913 he travelled in America, Samoa, and Tahiti. His first volume, *Poems*, appeared in 1911, and the second, *1914 and Other Poems*, in 1915 after his death.

Sir Arthur Conan Doyle (1850–1930). His best-known books are his Sherlock Holmes detective stories, and historical novels, e.g. *Micah Clarke* and *The White Company*.

Joseph Conrad (1856–1924), Polish by birth, was a novelist of considerable power. His first publication was *Almayer's Folly*, 1895. Other works are *An Outcast of the Islands*, *Nostromo*, *Typhoon*, *Lord Jim*, *The Nigger of the Narcissus*, *Chance*, *Victory*, *The Secret Agent*, and *Under Western Eyes*.

Thomas Stearnes Eliot (1888–1965). Poet, dramatist, and critic. Born in St. Louis in the United States, educated at Harvard. Settled in London after further studies at Oxford and in Paris. In 1927 he became a naturalized British citizen. His first important poem, *The Waste Land*, was published in 1922; his first full-length poetic drama, *Murder in the Cathedral* (about Thomas à Becket) in 1935. His other well-known poems include *Ash Wednesday* (1930) and *Four Quartets* (1943). Eliot is also one of this century's outstanding critics: the best of his literary and social criticism is collected in *Selected Essays*. He was awarded the Nobel Prize for Literature in 1948.

Edward Morgan Forster (1879–1970) is best known for his novels *A Room with a View*, *Howards End*, and *A Passage to India*.

John Galsworthy (1867–1933) was a novelist and dramatist. His best-known work is *The Forsyte Saga*, a series of books dealing with the fortunes of an English family. Among his plays are *The Silver Box*, *Strife*, and *Justice*.

Robert Graves (born 1895) has been writing poetry since 1914. The fruit of his lifetime's work is gathered in *Collected Poems 1959*. The best known of his prose works is *Goodbye to All That*, a book telling of his experiences during the First World War and afterwards: it is one of the finest autobiographies in the language.

Thomas Hardy (1840–1928). The essence of his writing is pessimism. Among his chief novels are *Far from the Madding Crowd*, *The Mayor of Casterbridge*, *Tess of the D'Urbervilles*, *Jude the Obscure*, and *The Return of the Native*. Some of the best-known of his poems are *The Dynasts*—an epic drama of the Napoleonic Wars, *Wessex Poems*, and *Poems of the Past and Present*. He received the Order of Merit in 1910.

Alfred Edward Housman (1859–1936) was a scholar and lyric poet. He graduated at Oxford and worked for ten years in the Patent Office before being appointed professor of Latin first at University College, London, and then at Cambridge. Housman's poetry, contained in the volumes *A Shropshire Lad* (1896) and *Last Poems* (1922), has proved continuously popular.

Henry James (1843–1916). Novelist and short-story writer, brother of the distinguished American philosopher and psychologist William James. Born in New York, educated in America and Europe. He came to live permanently in Europe in 1875, first for twenty years in London, and then at Rye, Sussex. He was naturalized a British citizen in 1915. Among James's novels may be mentioned *Roderick Hudson*, *The Portrait of a Lady*, *Washington Square*, *The Europeans*, *The Bostonians*, and *The Ambassadors*. As well as these and over a hundred short stories (the best known is perhaps *The Turn of the Screw*), he wrote plays, books on travel, and a series of fine critical prefaces for the later editions of his works.

James Joyce (1882–1941). Novelist, born in Dublin. He left Ireland in 1902 and spent most of the rest of his life abroad, earning a living by teaching languages in France, Italy, and Switzerland. Joyce is chiefly remembered for his two highly original novels *Ulysses* (1922) and *Finnegan's Wake* (1939). Other well-known books by him are *Dubliners* and *Portrait of the Artist as a Young Man*.

Rudyard Kipling (1865–1936) was awarded the Nobel Prize for Literature in 1907. The theme of the British Empire is a constant feature of his writing. His novels include *The Light that Failed, Stalky & Co., The Jungle Books, Just So Stories*, and *Rewards and Fairies*. His poems include *Departmental Ditties* and *Barrack Room Ballads*; books on travel, and historical works such as *France at War* and *A School History of England*.

David Herbert Lawrence (1885–1930) was one of the most powerful and original of English novelists. He was born in Eastwood, Nottinghamshire, the son of a miner, had a brief career as a teacher, and than spent the rest of his life travelling abroad and writing. His chief novels are *Sons and Lovers, The Rainbow*, and *Women in Love*. His other works include the novels *Aaron's Rod, Kangaroo, The Plumed Serpent, Lady Chatterley's Lover*, travel books, essays, and a body of fine poetry.

John Masefield O.M. (1876–1967). Poet, novelist, dramatist and essayist. His verse includes long narrative poems and poems of the sea. Among his novels are *Odtaa, The Bird of Dawning*, and *The Country Scene*. In 1930 he became Poet Laureate.

Sean O'Casey (1884–1964) was an Irish playwright. His best-known plays are *Juno and the Paycock* and *The Plough and the Stars*.

George Orwell (1903–50) is chiefly remembered as a political thinker. Born in India. His writings are mainly concerned with the poor and the loss of individual liberty. Two of his most famous books are *Animal Farm* and *Nineteen Eighty-Four*.

Wilfred Owen (1893–1918), killed while fighting in 1918, left some moving poetry, particularly poems dealing, like *Strange Meetings*, with the brotherhood of man as discovered even by enemies on the battlefield. *Insensibility* and *Exposure* are two more of his well-known poems. He is considered by many people the finest of the young poets of the First World War.

Siegfried Sassoon (1886–1967) was one of the most eloquent of the younger writers who expressed the horrors and wasteful destruction of the First World War. Two of his most popular books are *Memoirs of a Foxhunting Man* and *Memoirs of an Infantry Officer*. His *Collected Poems* appeared in 1947.

George Bernard Shaw (1856–1951), critic and playwright, was born in Dublin. His chief characteristic was a fearless intellectual criticism, and his plays are vehicles for his ideas. Among his many works are *Arms and the Man, Caesar and Cleopatra, Man and Superman, Pygmalion, Back to Methuselah*, and *Saint Joan*.

John Millington Synge (1871–1909) was an Irish dramatist and a considerable force in the creation of a flourishing Irish theatre. The best known of his remarkable plays are *The Shadow of the Glen, Riders to the Sea, The Well of the Saints, The Playboy of the Western World*, and *The Tinker's Wedding*, all written in the space of four years, 1903–7.

Edgar Wallace (1875–1932), as a boy worked as a newspaper seller and later became a journalist in Britain and South Africa. His experiences in Africa provided the background for the series of " Sanders " books, notably *Sanders of the River*. He also wrote many detective and racing stories (*The Four Just Men*, *The Squeaker*, *The Ringer*, etc.). Wallace wrote successful plays as well.

Herbert George Wells (1868–1946) was a novelist of vast output, writing on scientific and sociological themes. The former is represented by *Time Machine*, *The Invisible Man*, *The War of the Worlds*, etc., and the latter by *Kipps*, *Tono-Bungay*, *The History of Mr. Polly*, etc. He also wrote works of history, including *The Outline of History*.

Virginia Woolf (1882–1941) was a novelist and essayist. The best-known of her books are *Jacob's Room*, *Mrs. Dalloway*, *To the Lighthouse*, *Orlando*, *The Waves*, and *The Years*.

William Butler Yeats (1865–1939). Irish poet and dramatist. Born in Dublin. Studied painting for a time, but soon found his real calling as a playwright, lyric poet, and spokesman for Irish nationalism. Some of the best of his poetry is included in the volumes *The Green Helmet* (1912), *Responsibilities* (1914), and *The Wild Swans at Coole* (1917). He was the greatest force in the establishment of a flourishing Irish literary movement and the founding of a national drama at the Abbey Theatre in Dublin. His own plays include *The Countess Cathleen* (1892), *The Land of Heart's Desire* (1894), and *Deirdre* (1907). His finest prose works are collected in *Autobiographies* and *Essays*. Yeats was awarded the Nobel Prize for Literature in 1923.

Other prominent literary figures of the period include: **Richard Aldington** (1892–1962), **Edmund Blunden** (1896–1974), **Elizabeth Bowen** (1899–1973), **G. K. Chesterton** (1874–1936), **Ivy Compton-Burnett** (1892–1969), **Compton Mackenzie** (1883–1972), **W. H. Davies** (1871–1940), **W. W. Gibson** (1878–1962), **L. P. Hartley** (1895–1972), **Aldous Huxley** (1894–1963), **Rose Macaulay** (1889–1959), **Walter de la Mare** (1873–1956), **Katherine Mansfield** (1888–1923), **W. Somerset Maugham** (1874–1956), **George Moore** (1852–1933), **Gilbert Murray** (1886–1957), **J. B. Priestley** (born 1894), **Sir A. Quiller-Couch** (1863–1944), **Lytton Strachey** (1880–1932), **Edward Thomas** (1878–1917), **Hugh Walpole** (1884–1941), **Mary Webb** (1883–1928).

ARTISTS

Sir L. Alma-Tadema (1836–1912), **Sir M. Beerbohm** (1872–1956), **H. B. Brabazon** (1821–1906), **Frank Brangwyn** (1867–1956), **Walter Crane** (1845–1915), **W. P. Frith** (1819–1909), **Roger Fry** (1866–1934), **Harold Gilman** (1878–1919), **Eric Gill** (1882–1940), **Sir H. von Herkomer** (1849–1914), **J. D. Innes** (1887–1914), **Charles Keene** (1887–1914), **Sir John Lavery** (1856–1941), **Phil May** (1864–1903), **Ambrose McEvoy** (1878–1927), **Sir A. Munnings** (1878–1959), **Sir W. Nicholson** (1872–1949), **Sir W. Q. Orehardson** (1835–1910), **Sir W. Orpen** (1878–1931), **James Pryde** (1869–1941), **Charles Ricketts** (1866–1931), **Sir W. Rothenstein** (1872–1945), **Charles Shannon** (1863–1937), **Walter Sickert** (1860–1942), **P. W. Steer** (1860–1942).

SCIENTISTS'

E. D. Adrian (born 1889) researches in physiology. **Sir E. Appleton** (1892–1965) researches into propagation of radio waves. **John L. Baird** (1888–1946) invented system of television broadcasting. **Sir W. Bragg** (1890–1971) application of X-rays to crystal structure. **Sir W. Crookes** (1832–1919), researches on conduction of electricity through gases. **Sir J. Dewar** (1842–1923), study of gases, invented the vacuum flask. **Sir A. Eddington** (1882–1944), researches in astrophysics and writer of popular scientific works.

Sir R. A. Fisher (born 1890), studies in genetics. **Sir Ambrose Fleming** (1849–1945), researches in radio and invented thermionic valve. **Sir J. G. Frazer** (1854–1941), study of man, wrote *The Golden Bough*. **W. Friese-Green** (1855–1921), pioneer in photography, invented cinematograph. **Sir F. G. Hopkins** (1861–1947), discovered vitamins. **Sir James Jeans** (1877–1946), astronomer and writer of popular scientific works. **Sir W. Ramsey** (1872–1916), study of radioactive elements and inert gases. **Sir R. Ross** (1857–1932), discovered the cause of malaria. **Lord Rutherford** (1871–1937), study of radioactive elements and structure of the atom. **Bertrand Russell** (1872–1970) philosophy and foundations of mathematics. **Sir G. Elliot Smith** (1871–1937), studies in anatomy and archaeology. **F. Soddy** (1877–1956), study of radioactive elements and isotopes. **Sir J. J. Thomson** (1856–1940), researches into nature of the electron.

GEORGE VI AND ELIZABETH II

STATESMEN

Arthur Neville Chamberlain (1869–1940) was the youngest son of Joseph Chamberlain. He took a prominent part in Birmingham municipal affairs, and in 1918 entered Parliament as a Conservative. He was rapidly promoted in the Baldwin Ministry and prompted most of its domestic measures. He became Premier in 1937, and in 1938 came into conflict with his Foreign Minister, Anthony Eden (who resigned), over policy towards Italy. Chamberlain believed that appeasement of the dictators in Europe would prevent war. He made personal visits to Hitler, and at Munich signed an agreement which in effect left Czechoslovakia helpless, and in return obtained a treaty of friendship with Germany. Hitler's invasion of Czechoslovakia finally disillusioned Chamberlain. After the outbreak of the Second World War his apparent complacency over Britain's position, and especially the failure of Norway, roused public opinion against him. He resigned the Premiership on May 10, 1940, and took a post in the Churchill Government. Ill-health compelled his retirement, and he died in October.

Aneurin Bevan (1897–1960), the son of a Welsh coal-miner, left school at the age of thirteen. Later he continued his education at the Central Labour College, after which he became prominent in the political life of South Wales and the national Labour Party. He was Minister of Health 1945–1951, and Minister of Labour and National Service, 1951.

Ernest Bevin (1881–1951). Born of a working-class family Ernest Bevin became a prominent trade-unionist, and was made general secretary of the Transport and General Workers Union, being known as " the Dockers' K.C." He became a Labour M.P. in 1940, and in the Churchill Coalition Government was appointed Minister of Labour with responsibility for mobilizing the national manpower. In the Labour Government of 1945 he became Foreign Secretary, and soon became prominent in world affairs for his recognition of the dangers of Russian Communist expansion. In 1946 he gave the lead in the establishment of Western Federal Germany, and was also chiefly responsible for the idea of West European unity which took shape in the Brussels Treaty of 1948.

Clement Richard Attlee, first Earl Attlee (1883–1967), was educated at Haileybury and Oxford. He worked in the East End of London, and in 1922 became Labour M.P. for Stepney, succeeding Lansbury as leader of the Labour Party in 1935. During the Second World War he held office in the Churchill

Government. In 1945 Attlee became Prime Minister of the first Labour Government to hold power with an effective majority. He continued the Premiership in 1950, and from 1951 to 1955 was Leader of the Opposition after the Conservatives came to power. In 1955 he was granted a peerage and became the first Earl Attlee.

Sir Winston Leonard Spencer Churchill, K.G., O.M. (1874–1965), eldest son of Lord Randolph Churchill, was educated at Harrow, entered the Army in 1895, and saw active service in India, Egypt, and South Africa. He became a Conservative M.P. in 1900, but later turned to the Liberal Party. He was made Home Secretary in 1910, and was First Lord of the Admiralty in the early years of the First World War. He later held various offices until 1922. Returning to the Conservative Party, Churchill re-entered Parliament in 1924, and was Chancellor of the Exchequer in the Baldwin Ministry. From 1929 to 1939 he was out of office; his warnings of the growing menace of Germany went unheeded. In 1939 he again became First Lord of the Admiralty.

In May 1940 Winston Churchill succeeded Chamberlain as Prime Minister, and formed a Coalition Government. The sense that in a time of extreme peril Great Britain had found a national leader was confirmed during six years of war. His qualities as statesman and strategist were matched by his strength of personality, and gave him an unsurpassed place in British history. With Franklin Roosevelt and Joseph Stalin, Churchill took his full share also in the world-wide strategy of the Allies, and in the decisions which brought ultimate victory and which also did so much to shape the course of world events as the war drew to its close.

After the General Election of 1945 Churchill was leader of the Conservative Opposition, and in 1951 became Prime Minister of the Conservative Government. He resigned as Prime Minister in 1955, being succeeded by Sir Anthony Eden. He remained in the House of Commons as a private member.

Besides being an orator of first rank, Churchill had great qualities as an historical writer, as shown in his biography of the Duke of Marlborough, and above all, in his unique *Memoirs of the Second World War*. He also wrote *A History of the English Speaking Peoples*.

Sir Anthony Eden, K.G., **first Earl of Avon** (born 1897), served in the First World War. He entered Parliament in 1923, and in 1935 became Minister for League of Nations Affairs, taking a chief part in attempts to obtain a policy of collective action against Italian aggression in Abyssinia. He replaced Sir Samuel Hoare as Foreign Secretary and carried out the policy of non-intervention with regard to the Spanish Civil War. He resigned in 1938 in conflict with Chamberlain over policy towards Italy. From 1940 to 1945 he was again Foreign Secretary, and took office once more in the Conservative Government of 1951 until 1955. In April 1955 he succeeded Sir Winston Churchill as Prime Minister. He was responsible for Britain's intervention in Egypt in 1956. He resigned from office in 1957, and also from the House of Commons. In 1961 he was made a peer with the title of Earl of Avon.

Harold Macmillan (born 1894), was educated at Eton and Oxford, and served in the Grenadier Guards during the First World War, being wounded three times. He then served for a short period as A.D.C. to the Governor-General of Canada. He entered the House of Commons in 1924 as Member for Stockton-on-Tees. He was Parliamentary Secretary to the Ministry of Supply from 1940 to 1942, and was then sent to the Middle East to represent the Government as Minister in North-West Africa until 1945. When the Conservatives returned to power in 1951 he became Minister of Housing and

Local Government, and by 1953 had greatly increased the number of new houses being built. After short periods of office as Minister of Defence and Foreign Secretary, he became Chancellor of the Exchequer in 1955, and in 1956 was responsible for the introduction of Premium Bonds, which aroused a good deal of controversy. On the resignation of Sir Anthony Eden in 1957 the succession to the premiership was contested between R. A. Butler and Macmillan, and eventually the Queen was advised to send for the latter. He made a personal visit to Moscow in 1959, which was thought to bring some amelioration of the East–West tension. At the General Election of 1959 the Government was returned to power with a substantially increased majority. He resigned the Premiership in 1963.

Hugh Gaitskell (1906–1963), was educated at Winchester and New College, Oxford. For a time he was Reader in Political Economy at London University, being elected an M.P. in 1945. He became Minister of State for Economic Affairs in 1950, and Chancellor of the Exchequer in the same year. He was elected to the leadership of the Labour Party in 1955, a position he held until his death on January 18, 1963.

Edward Heath (born 1916), was educated at Chatham House School, Ramsgate. Balliol College, Oxford where he took PPE and won an organ scholarship. Served in the Royal Artillery in N. W. Europe in the war, where he won the MBE and was mentioned in dispatches. He came out of the army with the rank of Lieutenant–Colonel. He stood for, and won, the seat of Bexley in 1950 and has been the member for Bexley ever since. Political Career: in 1951, appointed Assistant Whip; 1952, Joint Deputy Chief Whip; 1953, Deputy Chief Whip; 1955, Chief Whip; 1959–60, Minister of Labour; 1960–63, Lord Privy-Seal and spokesman on foreign affairs. In October 1963, he was appointed Secretary of State for Industry, Trade and Regional Development; 1964, Shadow Cabinet, was responsible for economic affairs; 1965, Leader of the Conservative party. On 18 June, 1970, he became Prime Minister.

Jeremy Thorpe (born 1929), was educated at Eton and Trinity, Oxford. He became the M.P. for North Devon in 1959, having unsuccessfully contested it in 1955. He became the Leader of the Liberal Party in 1967.

Harold Wilson (born 1916), graduated from Jesus College, Oxford; became Lecturer in Economics at New College, Oxford. He held a number of government posts before becoming President of the Board of Trade, 1947–1951. He has been M.P. for the Huyton Division of Lancashire since 1950 and became the Leader of the Labour Party in 1963. In 1964, he led the Labour Party back to power and was re-elected in 1966. Since 1970, he has been the Leader of the Opposition in the House of Commons.

Sir Alexander Douglas Home (born 1903), was educated at Eton and Christ Church, Oxford. Among the offices he had held are: Secretary of State for Commonwealth Relations, 1955–1960; Lord President of the Council, 1957–1960; Secretary of State for Foreign Affairs, 1960–1963. In 1963 Sir Alec, who was then fourteenth Earl of Home and a member of the House of Lords, renounced his peerage in order to become Leader of the Conservative Party and Prime Minister of England.

MEN OF LETTERS
H. E. Bates (1905–1974), **Anthony Powell** (born 1905), **Graham Greene** (born 1904), **Evelyn Waugh** (1903-1966), **W. H. Auden** (1907–1973), **Stephen Spender**

(born 1909), **C. Day Lewis** (1904–1972), **Alun Lewis** (1915–1944), **Sidney Keyes** (1922–1943), **Dylan Thomas** (1914–1953), **J. R. R. Tolkien** (1892–1973), **Louis MacNiece** (1907–1963), **Roy Fuller** (born 1912), **Lawrence Durrel** (born 1912), **Kathleen Raine** (born 1908), **Elizabeth Jennings** (born 1926).

ARTISTS

Kenneth Armitage (born 1916), **Francis Bacon** (born 1910), **David Bomberg** (1890–1957), **Reg Butler** (born 1913), **Lynn Chadwick** (born 1914), **Hubert Dalwood** (born 1924), **Sir Frank Dobson** (1888–1963), **R. O. Dunlop** (1894–1973), **Sir Jacob Epstein** (1880–1959), **Mark Gertler** (1892–1939), **Duncan Grant** (born 1885), **Barbara Hepworth** (born 1903), **Ivon Hitchens** (born 1893), **Augustus John** (1878–1961), **Dame Laura Knight** (1874–1970), **Wyndham Lewis** (1884–1957), **L. S. Lowry** (born 1887), **B. Meadows** (born 1915), **F. E. McWilliam** (born 1909), **Henry Moore** (born 1898), **John Nash** (born 1893), **Paul Nash** (1889–1946), **C. R. W. Nevinson** (1889–1946), **Ben Nicholson** (born 1894), **Victor Pasmore** (born 1908), **John Piper** (born 1903), **Ceri Richards** (born 1903), **William Scott** (born 1913), **Sir Matthew Smith** (1879–1959), **Sir Stanley Spencer** (1891–1959), **Graham Sutherland** (born 1903), **Leon Underwood** (born 1890), **Christopher Wood** (1901–1930), **Jack B. Yeats** (1871–1957.)

SCIENTISTS

J. D. Bernal (1901–1971), researched in crystallography and social applications of science. **P. M. S. Blackett** (born 1897), researches in cunlear physics. **Sir J. Chadwick** (born 1891), researches in nuclear physics. **Sir J. D. Cockroft** (1897–1967), researched in nuclear physics. **F. H. Crick** (born 1916), studies into nature of living matter. **Sir Alexander Fleming** (1881–1955), discovered penicillin and founded science of antibiotics. **J. B. S. Haldane** (1892–1964), researched in biology, especially genetics. **Lancelot Hogben** (born 1895), studies in biology and writer of popular scientific works. **F. Hoyle** (born 1915), astrophysics, especially origin and structure of universe. **Sir Julian Huxley** (born 1887), biologist and writer of popular scientific works. **Sir B. Lovell** (born 1913), researches in radioastronomy, Director of Jodrell Bank. **Sir W. G. Penney** (born 1919), researches in nuclear physics. **G. Ryle** (born 1900), studies in astrophysics. **Sir G. P. Thomson** (1892–1965), researches in nuclear physics.